The *Blackwell Great Minds* series gives readers a strong sense of the fundamental views of the great western thinkers and captures the relevance of these figures to the way we think and live today.

blackwell great minds

edited by Steven Nadler

1 **Kant** by Allen W. Wood
2 **Augustine** by Gareth B. Matthews
3 **Descartes** by André Gombay
4 **Sartre** by Katherine J. Morris
5 **Charles Darwin** by Michael Ruse
6 **Schopenhauer** by Robert Wicks
7 **Camus** by David Sherman

Forthcoming
Aristotle by Jennifer Whiting
Nietzsche by Richard Schacht
Plato by Paul Woodruff
Spinoza by Don Garrett
Wittgenstein by Hans Sluga
Heidegger by Taylor Carman
Maimonides by Tamar Rudavsky
Berkeley by Margaret Atherton
Leibniz by Christa Mercer
Shakespeare by David Bevington
Hume by Stephen Buckle
Kierkegaard by M. Jamie Ferreira
Mill by Wendy Donner and Richard Fumerton
Socrates by George H. Rudebusch
Hobbes by Edwin Curley
Locke by Samuel Rickless

blackwell great minds

camus

David Sherman

⟨W⟩WILEY-BLACKWELL

A John Wiley & Sons, Ltd., Publication

Blackwell Publishing was acquired by John Wiley & Sons in February 2007. Blackwell's publishing program has been merged with Wiley's global Scientific, Technical, and Medical business to form Wiley-Blackwell.

Registered Office
John Wiley & Sons Ltd, The Atrium, Southern Gate, Chichester, West Sussex, PO19 8SQ, United Kingdom

Editorial Offices
350 Main Street, Malden, MA 02148-5020, USA
9600 Garsington Road, Oxford, OX4 2DQ, UK
The Atrium, Southern Gate, Chichester, West Sussex, PO19 8SQ, UK

For details of our global editorial offices, for customer services, and for information about how to apply for permission to reuse the copyright material in this book please see our website at www.wiley.com/wiley-blackwell.

Library of Congress Cataloging-in-Publication Data

Sherman, David, 1958–
    Camus / David Sherman.
        p. cm. — (Blackwell great minds ; 7)
    Includes bibliographical references and index.
    ISBN 978-1-4051-5930-2 (hardcover : alk. paper) — ISBN 978-1-4051-5931-9 (pbk. : alk. paper) 1. Camus, Albert, 1913–1960. I. Title.
    B2430.C354S54 2009
    194—dc22

                                                                    2008018540

A catalogue record for this book is available from the British Library.

Set in 9.5/12pt Trump Medieval by Graphicraft Limited, Hong Kong
Printed in Singapore by Utopia Press Pte Ltd

1   2009

In Memory of my Teacher and Friend,
Robert C. Solomon

contents

acknowledgments

Much of this book was produced in Austin, Texas, where I had the opportunity to work by virtue of the kindness of Dean Jerry Fetz, who granted me a well-timed sabbatical in the fall of 2006. To him, as well as my colleagues in the philosophy department at the University of Montana, I owe a debt of gratitude.

I would like to express my appreciation to our dear friends, Nesha and Russ Haldeman, who open both their hearts and their home to Nancy and me every time that we return to Austin. So, too, good friends such as Don Becker, Sherry Blum, Janet Cooper, and Delbert Henderson help to make Austin a very nice place to be. I would also like to express my appreciation to my in-laws, Martha Bollier, Bill Bollier, and Jane Krause, as well as their families, who make our excursions to South Texas enjoyable ones.

Most of all, however, I would like to express my affection and gratitude to Kathy Higgins and Bob Solomon. Their warmth and support have helped to sustain me for many years, and our many get-togethers in the fall of 2006 are now especially treasured, as Bob passed away shortly thereafter. Aside from the fact that Bob was a wonderful philosopher, whose work in European philosophy did much to illuminate and whose work on the philosophy of emotions was nothing short of groundbreaking, he was a wonderful teacher and friend, and I am surely not alone when I say that I miss him very much. Bob, for more reasons than I can say here, this one's for you.

Finally, I would like to express my love and gratitude to Nancy, my "without which not."

abbreviations

The abbreviations used in citations refer to the following works:

CTOP Caligula and Three Other Plays, trans. Stuart Gilbert (New York: Vintage Books, 1958)

EK Exile and the Kingdom, trans. Justin O'Brien (New York: Vintage Books, 1991)

F The Fall, trans. Justin O'Brien (New York: Vintage Books, 1991)

FM The First Man, trans. David Hapgood (New York: Vintage Books, 1996)

HD A Happy Death, trans. Richard Howard (New York: Vintage Books, 1995)

LCE Lyrical and Critical Essays, trans. Ellen Conroy Kennedy (New York: Vintage Books, 1970)

MS The Myth of Sisyphus and Other Essays, trans. Justin O'Brien (New York: Vintage Books, 1991)

P The Plague, trans. Stuart Gilbert (New York: Vintage Books, 1991)

R The Rebel, trans. Anthony Bower (New York: Vintage Books, 1991)

RRD Resistance, Rebellion, and Death, trans. Justin O'Brien (New York: Vintage Books, 1995)

S The Stranger, trans. Matthew Ward (New York: Vintage Books, 1989)

introduction:
situating camus

I am not a philosopher, because I don't believe in reason enough to believe in a system. What interests me is knowing how we must behave, and more precisely, how to behave when one does not believe in God or reason.

I am not an existentialist, although of course critics are obliged to make categories. I got my first philosophical impressions from the Greeks, not from nineteenth-century Germany, whose philosophy is the basis for today's French existentialism.

I'm not sure I'm an intellectual, and as for the rest, I support the left wing in spite of myself and in spite of itself.

Albert Camus[1]

With these disclaimers, Albert Camus disavows virtually every conventional characterization of him. If Camus was not the "philosopher of the Absurd," one of the fundamental pillars of post-War French existentialism, and, more generally, an intellectual who was in many ways the moral conscience of his generation, what was he? What's more, after rejecting these characterizations, which seem to be plainly applicable, how could he then characterize himself as a supporter of the left wing, especially given his attacks on Soviet communism and the Algerian national liberation movement, not to mention his estrangement from the left-wing French intellectual establishment. Still, albeit with certain qualifications, Camus was all of these things. He was a philosopher of sorts, although surely not in the professional sense; he was an existentialist, once we get clear on what we mean, and he meant, by this expression; he was, without any qualification whatsoever, an intellectual, and, indeed, precisely the sort of intellectual that is tragically all but disappearing in the world today; and, finally, he was a left-winger, whose unrepentant anti-totalitarian views are now generally recognized to be part and parcel of any left-wing position that is worth its salt.

Although Camus was trained in philosophy, his finest works were, without a doubt, his novels. Crucially, however, according to Camus, there are no hard and fast distinctions between philosophy and good literature. In one of his two philosophical works, *The Myth of Sisyphus* (the other is *The Rebel*), Camus declares that "the great novelists are philosophical novelists" (MS, p. 101), and, in a review of Jean-Paul Sartre's philosophical novel *Nausea*, he offers a basis for distinguishing amongst philosophical novels: "A novel is never anything but a philosophy expressed in images. And in a good novel the philosophy has disappeared into the images. But the philosophy need only spill over into the characters and action for it to stick out like a sore thumb, the plot to lose its authenticity, and the novel its life" (LCE, p. 199). Conversely, for Camus, just as philosophy disappears into the images of a good novel, which are themselves expressions of some aspect of our experience and, ultimately, our concrete form of life, in a good philosophy the images of the novel disappear into the concepts. Strikingly, then, if Camus's statement of the novel's relation to philosophy is inverted, the resulting statement of philosophy's relation to the concrete images that constitute the novel is one that he would similarly endorse: "A philosophy is never anything but a novel (a concrete expression of our life experiences) expressed in concepts. And in a good philosophy the novel (the concrete expression of our life experiences) has disappeared into the concepts." So far so good. But if in a lifeless novel the philosophy spills over into the characters and action, in a lifeless philosophy the novel's (i.e., *life's*) characters and action are driven from (rather than incorporated into) the concepts: "But the novel (the concrete expression of our life experiences) need only be driven out by the philosophy for the concepts to lose their authenticity, and the philosophy its life." This is why Camus approves of Aristotle's *Ethics*, which, "in one of its aspects, is but a long and reasoned personal confession. Abstract thought at last returns to its prop of flesh" (MS, pp. 100–101).

What this suggests is that Camus was working at the margins of philosophy, attempting to rehabilitate the interests of flesh-and-blood human beings, which had been all but driven from philosophy by virtue of its overweening proclivity for systematic reason. Such an endeavor falls squarely within a highly respectable line of philosophical inquiry, and, indeed, it may well be the impulse that motivates what is best in philosophy. Friedrich Nietzsche, Camus's philosophical hero, did not "believe in reason enough to believe in a system," but very few philosophers would maintain that he was not a philosopher of the first rank. (Unfortunately, however, there are more than a few philosophers who would maintain that he did have a "system," which says more about these philosophers and the philosophical temperament of our times than it does about Nietzsche.) So, too, the more recent French poststructuralist movement, which owed more to its existentialist predecessors than it ever cared to acknowledge, also put systematic reason in its cross hairs, and it frequently used terms such as "margins," "borders," boundaries," and "interstices," to signal its desire to open philosophy to reason's "other." Still, Camus's claim that he was not a philosopher does contain more than a grain of truth. In any attempt to offer a "philosophy of the concrete," either the philosophy or the concrete is going to suffer, depending on the approach, and there is no question but that Camus's philosophical concerns were best captured in literary form. In this way, he differs from Nietzsche and the poststructuralists, whose experiments with form remained more or less within philosophy's confines, and is more akin to the philosophical novelist Fyodor Dostoyevsky, who, like Camus, also penned a number of highly significant philosophical essays. Moreover, to put it simply, some of Camus's philosophical arguments were not especially good, as some philosophers have been only too willing to point out. Still, as I shall argue throughout, Camus's basic concerns were, first, to describe a conflicted modern sensibility whose quandaries are not amenable to a rational resolution, and, second, to determine how to use the impoverished reason with which we are left to produce outcomes that are most in accord with his unwavering humanism. His basic concern was not to make airtight analytical arguments, although this can by no means excuse his more egregious arguments. Thus, while I am obliged to point out some of the worst mistakes in Camus's arguments, I shall not dwell on them but instead shall attempt to penetrate to the philosophical intuitions that motivated them.

Given that "the Absurd," the notion with which Camus is most often associated, was first devised by the father of existentialism, Søren Kierkegaard, and that Camus is almost universally taken to be at the heart of the French existentialist movement, his persistent claim that he was not an existentialist is rather strange. Still, while Camus's disclaimer is not ultimately persuasive, it can be made comprehensible. In a 1945 interview, Camus states that *The Myth of Sisyphus* "was directed against the so-called existentialist philosophers" (LCE, p. 345), and, in a qualified sense, it was. At the time, however, Camus viewed existential philosophy as more or less synonymous with its religious variant, which he consistently rejected because it involves some form of a "leap of faith." Thus, while he directly attacks religious existentialists like Kierkegaard, Karl Jaspers, and Leo Chestov, he only refers to Martin Heidegger's *Being and Time* in passing and does not refer to Sartre's *Being and Nothingness* at all. Neither of these works, which are indisputably among the most important in existential philosophy, is religious. It is, ostensibly, for this reason that Camus later shifts his position on existentialism, rejecting the label for reasons similar to the reasons that he denies being a philosopher. Heidegger and Sartre, albeit in different ways, are concerned with "ontology," the systematization or classification of Being (i.e., the basic structures of existence), and, as we have seen, Camus opposes systematizing thought. Lastly, from a personal standpoint, Camus had good reason to repudiate the term. It was Sartre who had popularized existentialism, and to be characterized as an existentialist was, inevitably, to be sucked into Sartre's orbit, which Camus fought against. Indeed, even Sartre tended to struggle against the term "existentialism," arguing that any "ism" invariably pigeonholes a thinker, neatly packaging him up to be sold in the market like a bar of soap.

Nevertheless, when properly qualified, the statement that Camus was an existentialist is correct. Like Heidegger and Sartre, Camus was influenced by Edmund Husserl, whose philosophical methodology, "phenomenology," aims to get back "to the things themselves," by which he means things as we directly experience them. Now, in *The Myth of Sisyphus*, as we shall see, Camus attacks Husserl for aiming to get to the "extra-temporal essences" of the objects of experience, but this attack is one with which both Heidegger and Sartre agree. Trained in the sciences, Husserl was an epistemologist (one who is concerned with getting to the ultimate grounds of our knowledge), while Heidegger, Sartre, and Camus were all existentialists, philosophers who are concerned not with the ultimate grounds of our knowledge but with the ultimate grounds of our ways of being in the world. In this sense, they were all existential phenomenologists. However, unlike Heidegger and Sartre, who furnish what they both call a phenomenological ontology, Camus remains firmly planted on the grounds of the concrete experience itself, refusing to systematize it. He is, in other words, an existential phenomenologist shorn of the sorts of theoretical apparatuses toward which Heidegger and Sartre are drawn. It is for this reason, the desire to remain firmly bound to the concrete experience, that some of Camus's best philosophy is found in his literary works, while the philosophical works as such can occasionally get bogged down. For Camus, when philosophical reason gets airborne, it falsifies the sorts of experiences that inspire it, but this skittishness with respect to philosophical reason in no way undermines the fundamentally "existential" nature of his concerns.

Camus's attacks on Soviet communism and the Algerian national liberation movement do not invalidate his claim that he was a leftist, but they do reflect how the complexities of historical and personal contingencies affect the positions that the individual adopts and how these positions are then characterized. Particularly after Nikita Khrushchev's revelations about life under Stalin, Soviet communism came to be seen as little more than "state capitalism," a system that in many ways mirrored the rigidified class structures of the western capitalist nations (although it cannot be denied that, on the whole, it had fewer civil liberties and a more elaborate social safety net). As a result, the very notion of what constitutes a leftist changed, and, in any event, it surely came to be the case that one did not have to refrain from attacking the Soviet Union to establish one's leftist bona fides. Indeed, leftist opponents of western capitalism, such as the philosophers of the Frankfurt School, had been doing so for some time. Camus's position on the Algerian national liberation movement is a somewhat tougher one to square with his purported leftism, but it must be emphasized that Camus never refrained from attacking the ugly injustices of French colonial rule, even if he ultimately believed that Algeria should remain linked to France. As a *pied-noir* (a French Algerian) it would have been difficult for him to have taken a position that would have resulted in his family's expulsion from Algeria, the only country that they knew, and the federal scheme that he advocated was based on democratic principles. In any case, even if one disagrees with Camus's particular position on the Algerian War, his leftist commitments, which included a staunch commitment to the working classes that trended toward anarcho-syndicalism, cannot be denied, even though they were not tidily expressed in his politics.

What Camus was, in the final analysis, was one of the leading intellectuals of his time, a great existential novelist who refused to cede what he took to be the moral high ground in highly polarized political times. By virtue of this position, he was unable to find the grounds on which he could satisfy the demands of any political constituency, and thus he was attacked by virtually every political constituency. According to Theodor Adorno, the Frankfurt School philosopher who (along with Herbert Marcuse and Max Horkheimer) also refused to side with either Soviet-style communism or American-style capitalism, "wrong life cannot be lived rightly,"[2] a truth that is surely manifested in the particulars of Camus's own conflicted life (public and private). And yet, as Adorno also contends (and there is no contradiction here), a free man is one who refuses to bow to the coercive structure of bad alternatives but rather criticizes the situations produced by these coercive structures with the aim of changing them,[3] and this was certainly Camus's own view. Indeed, by bearing witness to the violence of his times rather than giving up the ground of his humanist commitments, Camus has served as a model for many thinkers who refuse to falsify their moral experience in the name of something "higher." No less rigorous a philosopher than Bernard Williams makes just this point in his last work, *Truth and Truthfulness*. After declaring that one can have confidence in an intellectual "only if one can respect the writer's dealing with everyday truths," Williams defends Camus against Sartre and, more generally, the French left, which held him in contempt for what they saw as his "fatuous humanism, subjective moralism, and incompetence in philosophy": "Camus may have been less a professional philosopher than Sartre, but it is far from clear that he was a worse one. What is certainly true is that he was a more honest man, and his authority as an intellectual lay in that fact."[4]

In what follows, I shall consider Camus's works from the perspective of this "intellectual honesty," which manifests itself in his refusal to falsify Williams' "everyday truths," or what we might more accurately call the "truths" of individual experience. This refusal can be understood on (at least) two levels. At the first level, generally speaking, the phenomenological portraits in the literary works reflect the existential temptations of an overwhelmed modern consciousness, while the philosophical-political works reflect the efforts of a morally committed consciousness to come to grips with a modern world that seems unable to make good the moral imperative. To be more precise: Camus's literary works contain an array of characters who represent particular responses to "the modern predicament," which, at its philosophical root, is the experience of "the Absurd," and what he skillfully does is use these characters to work through the underlying logic of these existential responses, or what, following Hegel, we can call "forms of consciousness." Whether we are dealing with Meursault of *The Stranger*, who seeks to innocently throw himself back into "life" and ends up on trial for his life, or Clamence of *The Fall*, who scornfully aims to put himself on the throne of unimpeachable judgment and ends up as a compulsive, lifeless game player, we see the unfolding logic of two modern temptations at their purified extremes. Thus, it is not that these characters are themselves champions for the truth but, rather, that they truthfully reflect, albeit in purified form, everyday existential temptations, and Camus uses them to tease out the implications of these temptations. Alternatively, if the experience of "the Absurd" is at the root of our nihilistic individual and collective ways of being, Camus's philosophical-political works reflect his attempt to draw more life-affirming implications from "the Absurd" rather than succumb to its more superficial logic. "The realization that life is absurd cannot be an end, but only a beginning," Camus contends, and what we must ponder are "the consequences and rules for action that can be drawn from it" (LCE, pp. 201–2). Although, as Camus points out, "the Absurd" can appear to countenance seducers and conquerors, what it truly demands is creation, and, ultimately, self-creation, with which the repetition-compulsions of both serial seduction and conquest, not to mention the vicissitudes of totalitarian politics, are wholly inconsistent. Indeed, for Camus, the underlying condition of self-creation is a non-negotiable moral imperative, albeit one that does not neatly dovetail with conventional bourgeois morality, certain aspects of which are part and parcel of the nihilistic response to the Absurd that Camus sets himself against.

Whether from a literary or philosophical-political perspective, Camus's works convey an existential sensibility that continues to resonate for "we postmoderns," but it resonates in ways that are not so easily captured by philosophical discourse, which leads to the second level on which we might understand Camus's refusal to falsify the "truths" of individual experience. Thus, while many recent French postmodern philosophers have argued some variation of the claim that to recapture the sensuous, particular, concrete, individual experience, we must refrain from doing (conceptual) violence to the "otherness" of the objects of our experience, their theoretical (not to mention systematic) approaches lose both the object and the experience in the process. Phrases such as *différance* (Derrida) and *différend* (Lyotard), not to mention (ontological) disquisitions on the relation between repetition and difference (Deleuze), do not get us any closer to either the concrete objects of experience, or (therefore) the desired experience itself. Camus, in contrast, starts from the perspective of the sensuous, particular, concrete, individual experience (i.e., from the phenomenological perspective), teases out its implications, and refuses to surrender it for the sake of philosophical rigor or political expediency. His thought, in other words, starts from the experiential excess that is beyond philosophy's boundaries, and it is for this reason that, shortly before his death, Camus declared that the most neglected part of his work had been "the obscure part, what is blind and instinctive in me. French critics are mainly interested in ideas."[5] Still, without more, this leaves us with a deep problem: what is blind and instinctive in us is precisely what must be whipped into shape by the "higher" demands of morality, which generally require us to abstract from the sensuous, particular, concrete, individual experience. In other words, how could Camus have been an advocate of both "the lived experience" and "the moral imperative," which seem to conflict. The preliminary answer, which will be teased out during the course of the book (and especially in the "philosophical-political" chapters), is that there is a complicated relation between lived experience and the moral imperative, and that it was Camus's important insight to recognize the bilateral (or, as some philosophers would put it, "dialectical") nature of the relation. In other words, Camus recognized that syllogistic moral reasoning, stripped of the concrete lived experience, could be employed to justify a political violence at least as horrifying as a lived experience that does not advance to the level of moral reasoning.

These two levels correspond, at least crudely, to what ethicists call normative ethics and meta-ethics, respectively. Generally speaking, normative ethics deals with questions concerning the principles and rules by which we should live (i.e., the determination of goodness and badness with respect to principles and rules, which, in turn, determines the rightness and wrongness of our actions) and meta-ethics deals with the overall standing of the moral enterprise itself (i.e., its basic nature, its viability, and, ultimately, whether it can even be justified). This approach seems right to me because one cannot help but be struck by the ethical force of Camus's works, whether literary or philosophical-political, and it is for this reason (rather than the *mere* fact that he was a great novelist) that he is a part of the Blackwell Great Minds series. As was already emphasized, however, Camus was not even a professional philosopher, much less a systematizer, and even those of his commitments that raise crucial philosophical issues do so from the margins of the philosophical enterprise. If Camus is tentatively searching for the grounds and content of a phenomenological ethics, then a systematic ethical exposition should not be expected, and, indeed, one shall not be forthcoming. To systematize Camus's commitments in the name of making him consistent, and, therefore, a "respectable" philosopher, would not only be to misrepresent his thought, but, even worse, to butcher what is most important in it. If the impulse to systematize Camus's theoretical commitments is to be resisted, so, too, is the impulse to psychologize them (as certain critics are inclined to do, especially within the framework of the Sartre-Camus quarrel). It may well be the case that "all philosophy is personal," as Nietzsche famously contended, but to simply fob off the philosophy without analyzing how it stands, even if only with respect to how it coheres with the life that engenders it, is to do unwarranted violence to thought itself.

Because I am primarily concerned with Camus's ideas, I shall structure this book along conceptual, rather than chronological, lines (although, for the most part, the conceptual and the chronological go hand-in-hand). Accordingly, after an introductory chapter on Camus's life, I shall primarily consider *The Myth of Sisyphus* in chapter 2 (The Absurd). Although *The Myth of Sisyphus* was published shortly after *The Stranger*, its exposition of the Absurd sets the philosophical stage for virtually all that follows. In chapter 3 (Life), I shall consider the two other works that constitute what Camus called his "cycle" on the Absurd, *The Stranger* and *Caligula*, and in chapter 4 (Scorn), I shall again deviate from the order in which Camus's works were published (but this time more drastically) by considering *The Fall*. This progression is justified on the following grounds: toward the end of *The Myth of Sisyphus*, Camus offers two ways of dealing with the Absurd – one can either fully throw oneself back into "life" or surmount it by scorn – and by directly following Camus's philosophical exposition of the Absurd with his paradigmatic examples of these two gambits, I can better depict the concept of it. In chapter 5 (Solidarity), I shall consider *The Plague*, which, Camus asserts, represents the movement in his thought from solitary revolt to solidarity. Although Camus begins his move to the political here, by examining solidarity in the framework of a natural metaphor that basically represents an absolute evil (like Nazism), he avoids complex political issues. In this sense, *The Plague*, although considered part of Camus's second "cycle" on revolt, actually reflects a collective response to the problem of the Absurd. In chapter 6 (Rebellion), I shall consider what might crudely be called Camus's ethical and political philosophies by considering *The Rebel* (and, to a lesser extent, two plays, *State of Siege* and *The Just*), which examines the moral basis for political engagement and the failures of teleologically driven political doctrines. In chapter 7 (*Realpolitik*), I shall consider Camus's relationship to *realpolitik* as it is manifested in the public break with Sartre over *The Rebel* and his positions on the Cold War and the Algerian War. Finally, in chapter 8 (Exile and Rebirth), I shall consider *Exile and the Kingdom*, a collection of short stories that explores the quandaries of the modern consciousness as it is thrown back on to itself by the profane world, and *The First Man*, an autobiographical novel that Camus hoped would constitute an artistic rebirth of sorts but was not completed at the time of his death.

notes

1   Olivier Todd, *Albert Camus: A Life*, trans. Benjamin Ivry (New York: Alfred A. Knopf, 1997), pp. 408, 379, and 408, respectively.
2   Theodor W. Adorno, *Minima Moralia*, trans. E. F. N. Jephcott (New York: Verso, 1974), p. 39.
3   Theodor W. Adorno, *Negative Dialectics*, trans. E. B. Ashton (New York: Continuum, 1992), p. 226.
4   Bernard Williams, *Truth and Truthfulness* (Princeton: Princeton University, 2002), pp. 11–12.
5   Todd, *Albert Camus*, p. x.

camus's life

One of Camus's most fascinating protagonists, Jean-Baptiste Clamence, the self-styled "judge-penitent" of *The Fall*, proclaims that "charm is a way of getting the answer yes without having asked any clear question" (F, p. 56). Camus himself possessed such charm. A handsome man, who might be described as a better-looking version of Humphrey Bogart, Camus looked and lived the part of "the existentialist," and in many respects he was the very embodiment of the cultural reputation that the intellectual came to have in France following World War II. Unlike most great thinkers, whose personal lives can be easily relegated to a long (or, perhaps, not so long) footnote, Camus lived a fascinating, complicated, and, ultimately, conflicted life. As with all highly accomplished human beings, Camus not only had an interesting mixture of qualities, but the strengths and weaknesses that constituted these qualities were often intertwined. Rightly depicted shortly after his death as "the present heir of that long line of French moralists whose works perhaps constitute what is most original in French letters,"[1] he could be insufferably self-righteous. Rightly depicted as a sensualist trying to redeem the moment of happiness in a world all too devoid of it, he was a womanizer who could cause unhappiness in those around him, not the least of whom was his wife. And, rightly depicted as someone who was both personally and politically committed, he could be aloof and indifferent. On the whole, however, Camus was an admirable and decent man who, more often than not, evidenced warmth, humor, and a concern for the plight of his fellow human beings, especially the least fortunate. What he undoubtedly was not was the *bon homme* (literally the "good guy," meant pejoratively in the narrow sense of the conventionally "moral man"), who is considered "nice" only by virtue of an utter lack of interesting qualities that might threaten others.

Camus was born on November 7, 1913, in Mondovi, Algeria, which, at the time, was a French colony. Camus's family were *pieds-noirs*, a term signifying that, although Algerian born, they were of French descent. His father, Lucien, a cellarman for a wine company, was drafted by the French army in 1914 and killed later that year in the Battle of the Marne, one of the bloodiest of World War I. His mother, Catherine Sintès, a cleaning woman of Spanish descent, was illiterate and partly deaf. Camus grew up in a small three-bedroom apartment in Belcourt, which he shared not only with his mother and older brother, Lucien, but also with his mute uncle, Etienne, and his maternal grandmother, Madame Sintès, who, by all accounts, ran the household in a despotic fashion. Although a poor, working-class town made up of *pieds-noirs*, others of European descent (mostly Spanish and Italian), and, of course, Arabs, Belcourt was not without its charms, not the least of which was its hot, sun-drenched climate and its close proximity to the beach, which facilitated in Camus a lifelong love of soccer and swimming. As he would later write in "Return to Tipasa," by virtue of having grown up in this world instead of the cold, damp, greyness of northern Europe, he had come to appreciate that "within me there lay an invincible summer" (LCE, p. 169). In no small part, Camus will self-consciously bring this "Mediterranean sensibility" to bear in his work.

As a student Camus excelled in his studies, and, early on, was particularly influenced by Louis Germain, who recognized Camus's potential. Under Germain's tutelage, Camus earned a full scholarship at a relatively prestigious high school located in nearby Algiers and, therefore, was able to continue with an education that his family could not otherwise have afforded. In 1930, while still in high school, he was diagnosed with tuberculosis, a disease that would plague him for the rest of his life, and he was forced to leave school for the better part of a year. To avoid infecting his brother, with whom he had to share a bed, Camus began to live at the home of his aunt and uncle, Antoinette and Gustave Acault. As owners of a butcher shop, the Acaults were comparatively well off, and Gustave was an intellectual of sorts, engaging his nephew in long conversations about literature and politics. The Acaults showed Camus that life contained possibilities that transcended the hardscrabble existence that he had known, which had produced in him a fatalistic indifference that he never completely left behind. On returning to high school, Camus was deeply influenced by his philosophy teacher, Jean Grenier, who, with the publication of his book *Islands*, was a rising star in literary circles, and his celebrated friend André Malraux, whose influential book *Man's Fate* had greatly impressed Camus. At this time, Camus was already beginning to evidence the philosophical commitments that he would largely retain for the rest of his life. Unlike many French thinkers, who were taking their philosophical cues from Husserl, Heidegger, and, to a lesser extent, Karl Jaspers, Camus's interests tended not toward German philosophy but rather toward the ancient Greeks. The one notable exception to Camus's general indifference toward German philosophy was Nietzsche, who, initially trained as a philologist, had himself been enamored of the ancient Greeks, and,

in particular, their aesthetics, to which Camus himself was also powerfully attracted.

In 1932, Camus met Simone Hié, who was addicted to morphine,
and in 1934, one year after he enrolled at the University of Algiers to do
graduate work in philosophy, he married her. While matriculating at
the University of Algiers, whose philosophy department now included
Grenier, Camus not only worked odd jobs but also found the time to par-
ticipate in political and literary activities. Although he viewed Communist doctrine as little more than a secular religion, Camus joined the
Communist Party because it was committed to improving the living
conditions of the working classes and redressing the political oppression
of the indigenous Arabs. As a burgeoning intellectual, Camus's tasks ran
mostly along cultural lines, as he gave lectures and ran a popular theater
for the Party, the Théâtre du Travail. Around this time, Camus also began
working on his first book, which, composed of five short essays, would
deal with the experiences of his childhood. Alternatively translated as
The Wrong Side and the Right Side and *Betwixt and Between*, the book
would be published two years later. In 1936, Camus completed his work
at the University of Algiers by successfully defending his dissertation,
"Christian Metaphysics and Neoplatonism: Plotinus and St Augustine,"
and, later that year, he separated from his wife, who was rapidly deteri-
orating because of her morphine addiction. The following year, he broke
with the Communist Party, founded his own independent theater company, Théâtre de l'Equipe, and began working on a short novel, *A Happy
Death*, which he chose not to publish. Revolving around a character
named Mersault, who kills a wealthy invalid to acquire the money he
thinks that he needs to live more fully, *A Happy Death* is, in many
respects, a dry run for Camus's now classic novel *The Stranger*.

Although Camus was ambivalent about the Communist Party throughout his association with it, his politics were decisively leftist, marked by
an unwavering support for the working classes and an equally unwavering opposition to heavy-handed colonialism and, most of all, fascism.
He had previously been somewhat involved with an anti-fascist assemblage called the Amsterdam-Pleyel movement, and, in the fall of 1938,
with fascism firmly rooted in Spain and Germany (and threatening to
spread elsewhere), he went to work as an editor and journalist for the
Alger Républicain, a new newspaper both sympathetic to the working
classes and dedicated to fighting fascism. Camus was hired by the paper's
charismatic editor Pascal Pia, with whom he established a close relationship, and was initially charged with reporting on matters of local government. Distinguishing between working class *pieds-noirs* and the rich
colons, who set the rules of colonial administration, Camus attacked
corrupt colonial practices as they manifested themselves in the judicial
and economic realms. He would wryly recount the politicized nature of

the local criminal trials and, in what was arguably his best series of articles, examined the plight of the nearby Kabylians, whose abject poverty was viewed with serene indifference by the colonial authorities. As war between France and Germany became all but inevitable, Camus turned his attention toward the international political scene, with respect to which he clung to a pacifist line. With the advent of war in late 1939, however, the *Alger Républicain* was all but doomed, as its positions continually ran afoul of the strictures of the military censors, and the paper was banned in early 1940. Pia was able to secure editorial positions for both himself and Camus at the relatively apolitical *Paris-Soir*, and Camus left for Paris, but not before publishing his second collection of essays under the book title *Nuptials* and proposing to Francine Faure, whom he would marry later that year.

During 1940, while all of Europe was plunged into war and France fell to the Germans, who occupied the country and established the collaborationist Vichy government of Marshal Pétain, Camus (while working for *Paris-Soir*) all but finished what he would refer to as his "first cycle," which was comprised of "three absurd works": *The Stranger* (a novel), *The Myth of Sisyphus* (a philosophical essay), and *Caligula* (a play). Toward the end of the year, Francine met Camus in Lyons, where they married. Shortly thereafter, he was laid off by *Paris-Soir*, and, with no real job prospects, the couple left for Oran, where the Faure family resided. (Located in Algeria, Oran would be the site of Camus's novel *The Plague*). After a period of unemployment, Camus accepted teaching positions at local schools, and it is during this time period, the spring of 1941, that he learned that *The Stranger* would be published by the French publishing house Gallimard. In the spring of 1942, right around the time that *The Stranger* was published, Camus underwent another severe bout of tuberculosis, and, on the advice of his doctor, he and Francine set off for the mountains of southern France later that summer so that Camus could convalesce in the mountain air, which was supposed to be beneficial for tubercular patients. Francine returned to Algeria in September, intending to head back to France later that fall, but in early November the Allies took control of Algeria, and Camus was effectively trapped in France.

For roughly the next year, during which Camus continued to live by himself in southern France's Haute-Loire region, *The Myth of Sisyphus* was published, and he worked in earnest on what would be his next major "cycle," which would deal with revolt. This cycle, just like the first one on the Absurd, would be comprised of a novel, philosophical essay, and play, and during this year Camus worked hard on the novel and the play, *The Plague* and *The Misunderstanding*. In the fall of 1943, Camus moved to Paris, which he had been visiting with increased frequency over the previous months, and he took a position as a manuscript reader at Gallimard. As the author of *The Stranger* and *The Myth of Sisyphus*, Camus's reputation was starting to take off, and his presence in Paris (indeed, at Gallimard no less) just helped to intensify this phenomenon. During this period of time, Camus met Malraux, who had not only been an early inspiration to Camus but had also favorably reviewed *The Stranger* for Gallimard when the publishing house was deciding whether it should be published. It is also during this period of time that he met Sartre and Simone de Beauvoir, which produced what is arguably the most highly publicized intellectual friendship-cum-confrontation of the twentieth century. In many ways, Sartre and Camus were polar opposites: Sartre, the son of an upper-middle-class Parisian family, had gone to the best schools, while Camus, the son of working-class *pieds-noirs*, had gone to provincial schools; Sartre was a short, ugly, bespectacled man, while Camus was tall and handsome; Sartre was a first-rate philosopher, powerfully influenced by German philosophy, and a somewhat lesser novelist, while Camus was a first-rate novelist and a somewhat lesser philosopher, influenced more by the ancient Greeks than by the Germans (with the notable exception of Nietzsche). Nevertheless, for a relatively short period of time, Camus and Sartre became close friends, haunting the Parisian café scene, where they would drink and look to pick up women.

In late 1943, Camus joined the French Resistance and became active in the underground Resistance paper *Combat*, which he served as both an editor and a writer (pseudonymously, of course). By early 1944, the handwriting was already on the wall for the occupying Nazi regime, and Camus's articles, reflecting this state of affairs, are marked no less by a concern with post-occupation political realities than with the realities of the Nazi occupation. The motto affixed to each edition of *Combat* under Camus was, accordingly, "from resistance to revolution." For Camus, however, what this meant was a democratic, working-class "revolution" from below, one that was beholden to the sorts of classical moral principles generally rejected by the Communist Party, which was also angling for power in the post-War era. During the waning months of the Nazi occupation, Camus met the beautiful actress Maria Casarès, whom he cast in the upcoming performance of *The Misunderstanding*, and with whom he began an affair. Casarès, who was of Spanish descent like Camus's mother, would, with varying degrees of involvement, play a role in Camus's life until his death.

In August 1944, Paris was liberated, and *Combat*, which would now be placed under the direction of Pia, was able to begin publishing out in the open. Shortly after the liberation, Camus began to publish a series of essays or so called "letters" in *Combat* grouped under the title *Letters to a German Friend*, in which he seeks to make sense of what has occurred and voices what he takes to be the moral imperatives for post-War Europe.

During this period of time, Camus and Casarès break off their affair, as Francine meets Camus in Paris, gets pregnant shortly thereafter, and gives birth to twins (Catherine and Jean) the following year. In the meantime, beyond the mechanics of putting out a paper, Camus is struggling with a variety of knotty policy questions at *Combat*, two of which stand out. The first question, how France should deal with those who had collaborated with the Germans during the occupation, put him in a difficult position. Camus had always been opposed to capital punishment, but justice seemed to require that the most egregious collaborators, who were directly or indirectly responsible for the deaths of many members of the Resistance, should themselves be put to death. Camus, who was taking a strong stand on the need for retributive justice after the war, supported the use of the death penalty. As the post-War trials made clear, however, there were many ambiguous cases, and the practicalities of meting out justice to collaborators proved to be far more nettlesome than the abstract concept of doing so. With this issue at stake, Camus became embroiled in an ongoing debate with Françoise Mauriac, a staunchly Catholic artist, who had himself been involved in the Resistance but was arguing for mercy rather than justice. As time passed, and individuals of dubious guilt came to be charged, Camus moved closer to Mauriac's position. The second question, which dealt with the contours of the Post-War French political reality, was even more intransigent. Increasingly, the options seemed to be narrowing to two, either supporting the conservative war hero Charles de Gaulle (favored, for example, by Malraux) or supporting the French Communist Party (a position toward which Sartre was moving, although hesitantly). Camus's ideal, as was reflected by his continuing support for the Socialist Party, was some variant of democratic socialism, but this was not a viable political option, and Camus was beginning to feel boxed in.

The 1945–6 time frame already contains within it, in encapsulated form, the seeds of what will become full-blown preoccupations for Camus, preoccupations that will torment him for the rest of his life. In 1945, Camus spent a few months in Algeria, where Arab hostility toward French colonial rule was rapidly growing. After a demonstration in which some Europeans were killed, the French authorities machine-gunned thousands of Arabs from the air, an incident that Camus later reported on in *Combat*. Camus's articles on this incident reflect his more general ambivalence concerning French colonial rule, for while unequivocally condemning the French response, the Algerian-born Camus could not bring himself to acknowledge that such things were the inevitable result of colonial rule, much less to support Algerian independence. Camus was also becoming increasingly ambivalent toward his friends. In 1946, he was spending a good deal of time not only with Sartre but also with the philosopher Maurice Merleau-Ponty, a friend of Sartre's, and Arthur Koestler, a well-known novelist and journalist. At the time, Merleau-Ponty still supported the Soviet regime (although he would later come to reject it on various grounds, the more theoretical among them reflected in *Adventures of the Dialectic*), while Koestler had become a staunch anti-communist, having already published *Darkness at Noon*, a novel that highlighted how the Soviet Revolution had increasingly come to devour its own. The four would argue over drinks, and while Camus did not especially like the belligerent Koestler, it was Koestler's view of the Soviet Union for which Camus had the most sympathy. At a party, Camus lambasted Merleau-Ponty for his critical review of Koestler's new book, *The Yogi and the Commissar*, and Camus stormed out, breaking with Merleau-Ponty. This incident foreshadows his subsequent break with Sartre and de Beauvoir, and, indeed, much of the French intellectual left. Crucially, although Camus would have no truck with Soviet communism, he was not a fan of American capitalism either. In a trip to the United States earlier that year (at the invitation of Alfred Knopf, his American publisher), he was put off by its crass commercialism, and, with the exception of New York's Chinatown, its general lack of community, but he did find Americans to be friendly and was entertained by the New York night scene (as well as an American college student, Patricia Blake, with whom he had a brief affair).

By early 1947, *Combat* was largely spent, as both political and personal tensions within the paper grew, which, in turn, undermined the coherence of the paper's editorial positions. Pia, who was friendly with Malraux and appeared to be moving toward the Gaullist position, left the paper, breaking his friendship with Camus in the process, and a few months afterward Camus left the paper as well. (Camus continued to support himself as a reader at Gallimard, a position that he would hold for the rest of his life, and played a role in facilitating the careers of some younger writers.) Later that year, *The Plague* was published, and the book, which became more popular than *The Stranger* (perhaps because it was less morally ambiguous), brought Camus even greater fame. Camus followed up his publication of *The Plague* with *State of Siege* in 1948, but the play received mixed reviews at best. Shortly thereafter, Camus rekindled his romance with Casarès by virtue of a chance encounter in the street, and the affair became for him a second marriage of sorts, although it did not preclude him from pursuing a fair number of more fleeting affairs. So, too, he met the poet René Char, who had been a revered participant in the French Resistance, and the two became fast friends. Toward the end of the year, a time during which the Cold War was firmly establishing itself, Camus engaged in a number of fleeting political activities. Along with Sartre, as well as a host of others, he spoke at the Revolutionary Democratic Union, and around this time he also helped to co-found the Group for International Liaisons in the Revolutionary

Union Movement, which was committed to criticizing both the United States and Soviet Union in the name of the working class. In 1949, Camus produced his play *The Just*, which received strong reviews, and spent roughly three months lecturing throughout South America, but the year ended badly for him, as he suffered another severe bout of tuberculosis.

While continuing to carry a relatively heavy workload at Gallimard, Camus poured himself into *The Rebel* at the start of the 1950s, and the book was published in the fall of 1951. Although *The Rebel* extols neither the United States nor western-style capitalism, by virtue of its attack on the Soviet Union and communism, more generally, it received mixed reviews from right-wing commentators, and thus had the effect of painting Camus into a corner. Camus had no sympathy for the right, which did not particularly like him either, but the scattered support that the book received in its quarters exacerbated the hostility with which it was received by the French left, and it had the effect of politically isolating Camus. This process culminated in mid-1952, when the book was reviewed by *Les Temps Modernes*, which was under Sartre's editorship. The review itself was written by Francis Jeanson, who had previously published a well-respected book on Sartre's philosophy, but Camus took the criticisms to be Sartre's. Refusing to respond to Jeanson, Camus fired over his head at Sartre, who, in turn, nastily responded, thus bringing their friendship to an end. To make matters worse, the fight was not confined to the intellectual community but was sensationalized by the general press, and the wide-ranging consensus (even amongst Camus's friends) was that Sartre had gotten the better of the exchange. In response, Camus basically retreated from the political arena, although he did take part in a protest against Spain's admission to Unesco in late 1952.

Camus's withdrawal from public life over the next year or so was also attributable to the fact that Francine had plunged into a severe depression, which necessitated an extended period of hospitalization, during which she was given electroshock therapy on multiple occasions. Feeling guilty about the part that he had played in her illness by virtue of his highly publicized affair with Casarès, as well as his more general domestic failures, Camus himself also fell into a depression (albeit one that was much less severe than Francine's). Nevertheless, during this period of time, he was able to work on a collection of essays that (like *The Wrong Side and the Right Side* and *Nuptials*) harkened back to his life in Algeria, and in 1954 these essays were published under the book title *Summer*. These nostalgic essays, as events would soon make abundantly clear, bore very little resemblance to the realities that were in the process of overtaking Camus's Algeria.

In November 1954, the Algerian revolution began, and Camus was again fundamentally torn. He fully recognized the injustices of French colonial rule, as well as the deeply ingrained prejudices of the *pied-noir* community from which he hailed, but he could not bring himself to support Algerian independence, much less the violent means that the FLN (Front for National Liberation) was using to secure it. Camus was largely sympathetic to the policies of the French government, which, under Pierre Mendès-France, intended to significantly improve the plight of the Arabs under colonial rule, but the Mendès-France government fell in early 1955 and the third way that Camus favored fell with it. Shortly thereafter, Camus joined the newspaper *L'Express*, which was committed to Mendès-France's policies, and, for the better part of the following year, contributed articles dealing with the crisis. In early 1956, Camus traveled to Algeria, where he proposed a truce to the parties, but his efforts were singularly unsuccessful. On the one hand, the Arabs to whom Camus spoke were overwhelmingly unsympathetic, for they believed that he was naïve with respect to the political realities of Algeria, which included the use of torture by the French forces. On the other hand, many of the *pieds-noirs* to whom Camus spoke were hostile, for they saw him as a traitor, and at one meeting some of them clamored for his death. Camus's own hopes for Algeria revolved around a federal scheme within which the various groups would freely associate, but, the merits of this position aside, it was not politically viable.

Recognizing that his own positions could not find any meaningful expression, given the prevailing political climate, Camus refrained from taking public political stances on his return to France. On a variety of occasions, however, he quietly intervened on behalf of the victims of French repression, which was becoming increasingly arbitrary and severe in response to the Arab revolt, and he did come out publicly on behalf of the Hungarians, whose own revolution against Soviet domination had been brutally put down by the Soviet army. For the most part, however, Camus threw himself into the theater, mostly adapting and directing the production of foreign plays (such as William Faulkner's *Requiem for a Nun*). In the spring of 1956, Camus's classic novel *The Fall* was published, and, in 1957, a collection of essays assembled under the title *Exile and the Kingdom* was published. So, too, in 1957, Camus published an essay titled "Reflections on the Guillotine," in which he lays out his opposition to the death penalty. In this essay, Camus tells a story about his father, about whom he otherwise knew very little. A supporter of the death penalty, Camus's father attended the execution of a man who had been convicted of an especially heinous crime. After viewing the execution, he returned home, went to lie down, and then began to vomit. Camus's father never discussed the incident, but from that point forward he opposed capital punishment.

In late 1957, Camus was awarded the Nobel Prize for Literature. He believed that he had been selected for political reasons (he was neither a Gaullist like Malraux nor a Communist like a number of other writers who had been in the running), and, in any event, that he was too young for such an award, which is generally given in the twilight of one's career. Still, although Camus felt burdened by his selection, he accepted the award (unlike Sartre, who refused it when selected in 1964). Camus attended the induction ceremonies with Francine, from whom he had been separated for roughly a year, his children, a few close friends, and the Gallimard family. In his acceptance speech, he declared that rather than serve "those who make history" the writer should serve "those who are subject to it,"[2] but what came to be most remembered about his appearance was his impromptu response to an Arab nationalist who had extemporaneously confronted him. When the Arab reproached Camus for not supporting the FLN, he responded that if confronted with a choice between defending justice and defending his mother he would defend his mother. Camus's off-the-cuff reply was neither vapid nor the manifestation of a deeply ingrained colonial attitude, as many critics took it to be. More charitably, he should be interpreted as saying that any concept of justice that could justify a terrorist act killing his mother is no concept of justice or, alternatively, that he was being put in the untenable position of having to choose between justice and his mother (and, indeed, what exactly would we think of someone who sacrificed his own mother for even a lofty concept of justice).

At the beginning of 1958, Camus suffered from another severe bout with tuberculosis, which caused him no small amount of despair, but the symptoms gradually subsided and he was able to resume working. He threw himself back into the theater, producing an adaption of *The Possessed*, a novel by Dostoyevsky. The play, which opened in early 1959, received mixed reviews. In the meantime, Camus bought a home in Lourmarin, a town located in the Provence region of southern France. By moving to Lourmarin, he hoped to benefit both his lungs and his temperament, neither of which was faring particularly well in Paris. During 1959, Camus worked diligently on an autobiographical novel, *The First Man*, which was to be dedicated to his mother: "To you, who can never read this book." On January 3, 1960, Camus set off for Paris with the family of Michel Gallimard, but on the following day, January 4, the car spun out of control and slammed into a tree. Camus, who was in the passenger seat, was killed instantly.

notes

1 Jean-Paul Sartre, "Albert Camus," in *Situations*, trans. Benita Eisler (New York: Fawcett Publications, 1965), p. 79.
2 Albert Camus, "Nobel Prize Address," reproduced in David Sprintzen, *Camus: A Critical Examination* (Philadelphia: Temple University Press, 1988), p. vii.

further reading

Lottman, Herbert, *Albert Camus: A Biography* (New York: Doubleday & Company, 1979).

McCarthy, Patrick, *Camus* (New York: Random House, 1982).

Todd, Olivier, *Albert Camus: A Life*, trans. Benjamin Ivry (New York: Alfred A. Knopf, 1997).

the absurd

HAMM: We're not beginning to . . . to . . . mean something?

CLOV: Mean something! You and I, mean something! (*Brief laugh.*) Ah that's a good one!

HAMM: I wonder. (*Pause.*) Imagine if a rational being came back to earth, wouldn't he be liable to get ideas into his head if he observed us long enough.

(*Voice of rational being.*) Ah, good, now I see what it is, yes, now I understand what they're at!

(*Clov starts, drops the telescope and begins to scratch his belly with both hands. Normal voice.*)

And without going so far as that, we ourselves . . . (*with emotion*) . . . we ourselves . . . at certain moments . . . (*Vehemently.*) To think perhaps it won't all have been for nothing!

Samuel Beckett, *Endgame*[1]

The Absurd is both an experience and a concept. As an exceedingly rough first approximation, we might say that it is a concept born of an experience, a deep, visceral experience that life, with its joys and its sorrows, with its loves and its hates, with its spectacular acts of magnanimity and its despicable acts of pettiness, with its grand victories and crushing defeats – in other words, life itself – finally adds up to absolutely nothing. As this first approximation suggests, the Absurd is a phenomenon that is universal instead of particular in scope. The particulars that constitute our existences might be boring, painful, or deeply unjust, but these particulars, in and of themselves, are not absurd, nor, indeed, is their aggregation. (For the moment, it should be pointed out that although these particulars, individually or collectively, are not absurd, this does not preclude the possibility that they might be responsible for engendering both the experience and the concept *of* the Absurd). The Absurd, rather, is a sort of universal acid bath that dissolves the importance of these sorts of distinctions from a "higher" perspective (the perspective of Hamm's otherworldly "rational being," for example, in the excerpt with which this chapter opens). This is one of the reasons that Beckett's *Endgame* is particularly representative for our present aims:

with the exception of a few odd props, the world of Hamm and Clov is stripped of all the particulars that might distract from the essence of the experience (and, of course, the meaning of this "being stripped" can itself be interpreted in numerous ways). Furthermore, as this bit of dialogue from Beckett's *Endgame* suggests, the Absurd is essentially tied up with (but not only with) questions of meaning and justification, and, as such, it is grist for the philosophical mill (although, on closer examination, the rather sneaking suspicion might arise that this mill is responsible for producing its own grist).

Although Camus was not the first to articulate either the experience or the concept of the Absurd, he was, perhaps, the first to articulate the particular sense that it has for us. Of course, the world has drastically changed since the early 1940s, but the sociohistorical circumstances within which Camus articulated the Absurd, the experience of the Great Depression and World War II, of massive pauperization and rationalized annihilation (in both the gassing of concentration camp prisoners and the bombing of civilian populations), are circumstances which "(post)modern man" has not yet moved beyond. The forms in which the malaise is expressed surely have changed, but the major breakdown in the enlightenment project's non-negotiables (capitalism, the democratic state, and, more generally, the reconciling power of reason itself) has left many with a sense of being adrift. Even during the 1950s and 1960s, when Keynes's economic theory and the liberal welfare state had society "humming along," even the so-called "winners" experienced a profound malaise: the deadened "corporate man," with his three-martini lunch and four pack a day habit, the long hours at work followed by a train ride to a sterile suburban home, and the frenzied consumption that exacerbated rather than filled the void, was the stuff of the more penetrating sociological and literary analyses. Then, of course, there was the subordination of women, African-Americans, and other minorities, not to mention "the Bomb," against which the human race was supposedly insulated by a perverse logic known as "mutually assured destruction" (MAD). Without offering a genealogy, suffice it to say that in our contemporary "postmodern" age both the experience and the concept of the Absurd remain. Capitalist globalization processes, embodied by the justifiably despised World Trade Organization, are rapidly making good Karl Marx's contention that "all that is solid melts into air, all that is holy is profaned, and man is at last compelled to face with sober senses his real conditions of life":[2] the acid bath of global capital and the experience of the Absurd are, to be sure, mutually reinforcing. And yet, we also live in an age in which religious fundamentalism, with its arrogant monopoly on all of the old absolutes, is resurgent. This weird convergence, far from belying the Absurd, is rather a manifestation of it. As Camus observed in *The Myth of Sisyphus*, the experience and the concept of the Absurd is marked by "antinomy," the contradiction between two sets of principles not amenable to reconciliation through reason. Indeed, to borrow an old Hegelian phrase, it may well be only now that the Absurd has genuinely come to be "adequate to its concept."

In this chapter, I shall closely consider *The Myth of Sisyphus*, which is arguably Camus's defining philosophical work. To lay the foundation for this analysis, however, there are two matters that must first be considered. To begin with, I must consider, albeit briefly, Camus's earliest published works, the lyrical essays that comprise *The Wrong Side and the Right Side* and *Nuptials*, for these works depict the point of departure, the experience of living before absurdity dawns. Then, I must briefly consider, from a historical perspective, the philosophical grounds of the Absurd to make sense of Camus's position, which, in certain ways, is only the self-conscious articulation of a long, gradual process.

Life Before the Fall

> These barbarians lounging on the beaches give me the foolish hope that, perhaps without knowing it, they are modeling the face of a culture where man's greatness will finally discover its true visage. These people, wholly engaged in the present, live with neither myths nor consolation.
>
> Albert Camus, "Summer in Algiers," *Nuptials*[3]

The lyrical essays that comprise Camus's two earliest books, *The Wrong Side and the Right Side* and *Nuptials*, are a celebration of his place in the natural world. The hot sun and sand, the cool water, which, in refreshing, leaves the body with a slightly salty taste, the panoramic Algerian landscape under a bright blue sky, and the youthful vigor to take full advantage of these things make the young Camus "proud of the human condition," and the rebukes of those who would say that this pride is misplaced do not in any way lessen his feeling (LCE, p. 69). This pride that Camus experiences is not a reflective pride, which by its nature is self-justifying, but rather an immediate pride, one that arises spontaneously and is in need of no self-justification. Indeed, it is marked by an utter lack of self-referentiality, for even to analyze the feeling (at least while undergoing it) would be to tear at the fabric of the delicate synthesis that it reflects.

The beatific nature of Camus's imagery notwithstanding, to be "wholly engaged in the present" raises a fundamental question concerning the very standing of the moral enterprise, as Camus's reference to "these barbarians" acknowledges. Morality, we are taught, necessitates a step back, a less than "wholly engaged" perspective from which to adjudge the propriety of the actions that we are contemplating. Indeed, while the two predominant enlightenment moralities, Millean utilitarianism and Kantian deontology, differ in fundamental respects – the former is concerned with consequences (maximizing happiness) and is neutral with respect to acts in the abstract while the latter is concerned with acts (doing one's duty) and is neutral with respect to their concrete consequences – what they share is this step back, and, more specifically, a reliance on a rational decision-making calculus to determine what to do. Camus denies that this modern *modus operandi* is a necessary condition of morality, however:

> In such abundance and profusion, life follows the curve of the great passions, sudden, demanding, generous. It is not meant to be built but to be burned up. So reflection or self-improvement are quite irrelevant . . . Not that these men lack principles. They have their code of morality, which is very well defined. You "don't let your mother down." You see to it that your wife is respected in the street. You show consideration to pregnant women. You don't attack an enemy two to one, because "that's dirty." If anyone fails to observe these elementary rules "He's not a man," and that's all there is to it. This seems to me just and strong . . . Shopkeeper morality is unknown. (LCE, pp. 86–87)

Camus's position here resonates with a tradition that has been revivified in philosophy over the past few decades, a tradition known as Aristotelian virtue ethics. Unlike Millean utilitarianism and Kantian deontology, which focus on consequences and acts, respectively, the focus of virtue ethics is on the agent, the actual full-blooded person, and it considers whether this person is of fine character overall rather than one who just refrains from doing the wrong thing but otherwise amounts to very little. (Mill himself recognized this problem, clearly evidenced in Bentham's version of utilitarianism, and thus he gives utilitarianism a twist toward Aristotle's virtue ethics, albeit with mixed results.) The person of fine character need not completely abstract from who he is to determine what to do but rather reasons from who he is to determine what to do. This reasoning also involves a step back of sorts, but there is no pretense that this form of practical reasoning is in any way "pure," or that it does not arise from this full-blooded person and, more generally, the society that formed him. This is why Camus states, as we previously saw, that Aristotle's "*Ethics* itself, in one of its aspects, is but a long and reasoned personal confession. Abstract thought at last returns to its prop of flesh" (MS, pp. 100–101).

It was Nietzsche who had first argued that all moral philosophies are merely a "personal confession" of its adherents, and it was Nietzsche who had first argued that Kantian deontology is a "shopkeeper morality." (What's more, given his depiction of "the last man" in *Thus Spake Zarathustra*, Nietzsche would have had no problem applying the term to

Millean utilitarianism either). More generally, as we shall observe, Camus will take more than a few of his cues from Nietzsche, whose naturalism also caused him to favor the ancient (pre-Socratic) Greeks. In the meantime, however, what should be noticed is that in Camus's youthful writings the Absurd does not yet rear its head. Indeed, even when he speaks of his Algerian experiences in the dualistic terms that are part and parcel of the disunity that constitutes the Absurd, he only does so for the purpose of emphasizing an underlying unity: "It was neither I nor the world that counted, but solely the harmony and silence that gave birth to the love between us" (LCE, p. 72). With the advent of the Absurd, the harmony will be gone, and the silence will be transfigured: no longer the reflection of an underlying harmony that is taken for granted, it is now the world that will be silent in the face of humanity's uncomprehending "why."

A Short Pre-History of the Absurd

> The eternal silence of these infinite spaces frightens me.
> Blaise Pascal, *Pensées*[4]

In one of his most poorly understood passages, Nietzsche, through the mouth of "the madman," informs a crowd of people that "God is dead." This revelation is not met with anger or disbelief, as one might expect, but instead with mockery and laughter, for the crowd possesses that sort of cynical pseudo-sophistication that is not unknown in our own times: after all, "everyone knows" that God is dead. What makes the madman mad, and what the crowd fails to understand, is not that God is dead or even, for that matter, that we are the ones who have killed him. Rather, what makes the madman mad, and what the crowd fails to understand, is how much of our lives, how much of our self-understanding, although seemingly unrelated, is inextricably intertwined with the concept of God, and, therefore, must die with Him. The lightning has already struck and it is only the madman who can "hear" the impending thunder, the sound of the earth crumbling below his feet: "What were we doing when we unchained this earth from its sun? Whither is it moving now? Whither are we moving? Away from all suns? Are we not plunging continually?"[5] As for the crowd, this monumental repercussion is not yet appreciated: "This tremendous event is still on its way, still wandering; it has not yet reached the ears of man . . . This deed is still more distant from them than the most distant – *and yet they have done it themselves.*"[6]

The Absurd is not only a product of the death (and, therefore, further back, the birth) of God, although, in modern times, it is this absence that constitutes its proximate cause. Formally (i.e., conceptually), the Absurd is the result of the space for God, the wholly disengaged rational, objective viewpoint that found expression at least as far back as Plato's theory of Forms (which is one of the reasons that Nietzsche refers to Christianity as "Platonism for the masses"), and it is this viewpoint that is referenced by Hamm's otherworldly "rational being" (in the excerpt from Beckett's *Endgame* that opened this chapter). When this space that we ourselves have created is hollowed out, as it is with the death of God (which, as Nietzsche asserts, is something that we have also done ourselves), or if its prevailing content ceases to function in such a way that it can provide meaning and justification for our lives, the absurd sensibility can arise. In modern times, as we will now see, Descartes opens up the theoretical possibility of the absurd sensibility, Hume and Kant then bring this possibility to fruition, Kierkegaard and Nietzsche philosophize as to its practical (or, if you prefer, existential) repercussions, and Camus, who writes in a time in which "this tremendous event" has finally been heard, offers "the description, in the pure state" of the "absurd sensitivity that can be found widespread in the age" (MS, p. 2).

By most accounts, what underlies the modern philosophical project (both historically and conceptually) is the so-called "philosophy of subjectivity," which, initiated by Descartes, turned philosophy inward by making subjectivity the foundation of indubitable knowledge. Descartes's emphasis on the well-distributed power of reason, "the natural light" in every person that obliges each of us to accept as true only that which we clearly recognize to be so, is a crucial moment in the slow movement away from a Church-based worldview to a (Godless) humanistic one. Thus, while nominally limited to narrow epistemological concerns, Descartes's dualism of rational mind and matter, the result of estranging consciousness from the world so as to ground its knowledge of it, is not just a decisive sociocultural phenomenon but also a portent of the Absurd. This was vaguely intuited by Descartes's contemporary, Pascal, who cried that "the eternal silence of these infinite spaces frightens me" (but, perhaps, did not himself do the Church any favors by arguing that, without proof, it is rational to believe in God's existence, given the relative costs of falsely believing and falsely disbelieving). Of course, the objective certainty that Descartes sought was gotten on the sly, as the rationality that he put into question by methodically doubting everything at the beginning of the *Meditations* was then used to prove the existence of God, who mediates the relation between mind and matter, and, therefore, allows Descartes's contemporaries to trust in their sense perceptions, as well as their (now less solidly grounded) Church-based worldview. Nevertheless, the damage was done.

After Hume delivered a devastating blow to the Cartesian project by showing that truths about the world ("matters of fact," one of which is the alleged existence of God) could not have the same sort of ironclad necessity as the truths of mathematics and logic ("relations of ideas"),

Kant upped the subjective ante with his recourse to transcendental idealism, which, he asserted, made good the truths of empirical realism. For Kant, in other words, there is a necessity with respect to our empirical truths (and, most of all, the truths of the natural sciences) because these truths are made good by the nature of our own minds, which provide the template for what can count as objective truths *for us*. How the world is "in itself," however, is beyond the bounds of our reason. Even with respect to objective matters, then, Kant thinks not only that subjectivity must be the starting point but also that there is a limit to reason, which he turns into a virtue by arguing that reason's limitations make room for faith. It is when Kant moves from theoretical to practical philosophy, however, that the specter of absurdity truly arises. Although the belief in such things as God, freedom, and the immortality of the soul have no place in Kant's theoretical philosophy, in his practical philosophy they are needed as regulative ideas, or, as he articulates it, "*postulates* of pure practical reason," for without them his moral philosophy, based on necessity, would collapse in the face of the world's contingence. This suggests not just that faith can begin only where theoretical reason ends but also that faith is the very condition of the possibility of pure practical reason. Still, although Kant's faith in God and practical reason are not rationally grounded, as his attacks on the sundry proofs for God's existence and his need for the postulates clearly attest, his ungrounded faith is of such a nature that it does not yet provoke the experience of absurdity.

With his articulation of the paradoxical concept of "subjective truth" and, specifically, its relation to religious faith, Kierkegaard is the first to explicitly broach the concept of the Absurd. In the *Concluding Unscientific Postscript*, he declares: "Instead of the objective uncertainty [of believing in God's existence], there is here a certainty, namely, that objectively it is absurd; and this absurdity, held fast in the passion of inwardness, is faith."[7] Although opposed to the basic doctrines of enlightenment reason, this concept of absurdity (crystallized, for Kierkegaard, in the paradox that Christianity's eternal truths have a historical becoming with God's Incarnation in the personage of Christ) is a product of it. Kierkegaard's distinctive form of Protestantism, with its emphasis on "the subjective inwardness" of a believer that passionately confronts God in a "vertical relation," is a result of the enlightenment promise that individual subjectivity has a right to its satisfaction, the (ultimately Cartesian) promise that both he and his nemesis Hegel seek to make good. Indeed, his rejoinder to Hegel's emphasis on a rationally structured ethical totality (i.e., a "horizontal relation" that subsumes everything within it, including the absolutely "other" that is God) must be viewed as an attempt to vindicate this right of subjectivity against Hegel's totalizing "System."

However, as Kierkegaard relates in *Fear and Trembling*, even believing in the absolutely "other" that is God, which makes clear to the believer his infinite nature, is only the last stage on the way to true faith. Still operating from the standpoint of the understanding, these believers (of whom Kierkegaard counts himself one) are only "knights of resignation" for whom the world's privations empty life of all hope, joy, and meaning. It is only by embracing the absurdity that is part and parcel of true faith that one becomes a "knight of faith" who can joyfully partake of life, since with meaning-conferring faith hope springs eternal: all things, including (indeed, perhaps, especially) those that are not amenable to reason, are possible. Despite the subjective bounty to be had by the individual of faith, then, Kierkegaard believes that he cannot rationally argue for Christianity but rather must "seduce" his reader into it. What's more, it is not even Kierkegaard qua Kierkegaard who is doing the seducing, for out of respect for the individual's right to self-determination he writes pseudonymously: by undermining the authority of the authorial position, Kierkegaard gives his reader the room to make an uncoerced choice of whether to subjectively embrace the objective absurdity that is the Christian faith.

Kierkegaard's crucial insight, however, is that absurdity is not confined to the paradoxes of religious faith. He is, perhaps, the first to see that all "existential" choices (i.e., fundamental orienting choices made by an individual about how he is to be in the world), which determine what counts as a subjective truth for that individual, are actually just a matter of faith. In setting forth his "existential dialectic," which is a deliberate refashioning of Hegel's historical dialectic along individual lines, Kierkegaard says, in essence, that every choice of oneself is ungrounded. Accordingly, in opposition to what he takes to be the ultimate convergence of thought and being in Hegel's dialectic, in which there seems to be a rational necessity with respect to the movement from one (collective) "form of consciousness" to another, Kierkegaard sees thought and being as divided. As a result, although Kierkegaard explicitly privileges the notion of being an "existing" individual, which is an individual for whom there is a higher-order commitment that coherently delineates the ultimate rules by which he lives, he can only implicitly privilege the "religious," as opposed to "ethical" or "aesthetic," sphere of existence. In other words, there can be no reason for choosing to live by the rules of any sphere of existence, for it is the completely ungrounded choice of a sphere of existence that brings anything that can count as a reason into existence in the first place. Even in an entirely secular sense, therefore, choosing to be an existing individual by choosing to live in conformity with the rules of one sphere of existence as opposed to another involves nothing more than a "leap of faith."

At this point, our "first approximation" of the Absurd (i.e., that it is "a concept born of an experience"), which was offered at the start of this chapter, must be revised. As this brief history of the birth of the concept of the Absurd implies, even if the concept of the Absurd is born of the modern experience, the modern experience, in turn, is born of self-concepts that are generated by the historical unfolding of philosophy. This means that the experience of the Absurd has its own conceptual preconditions. Nevertheless, to say, as a "second approximation," that the Absurd is "an experience born of a concept" would be no more correct than the "first approximation," for the historical unfolding of philosophy is born of the historical unfolding of human experience, of which philosophy is a part. What all of this means, then, is that the experience of the Absurd and the concept of the Absurd stand in a "dialectical" relation, a relation, in other words, in which the two terms mutually inform one another in an ongoing process in which neither assumes primacy. Indeed, as we shall see, since Camus, and, more generally, the existentialist moment, something akin to both the experience of the Absurd and the concept of the Absurd remain, although both terms have, in some sense, morphed.

Camus's Absurd Problematic

> After Buddha was dead, his shadow was still shown for centuries in a cave – a tremendous gruesome shadow. God is dead; but given the way of men, there may still be caves for thousands of years in which his shadow will be shown. And we – we still have to vanquish his shadow, too.
> Friedrich Nietzsche, *The Gay Science*[8]

To state the issue of the Absurd more technically, at its heart, whether considered experientially or conceptually, is the problem of groundlessness, contingence, and, ultimately, meaninglessness with respect to those fundamental aspects of "the human condition" that seem as if they should be open to rational justification. For Descartes and Hume, the demand for rational justification is limited to epistemological problems, problems concerned with distinguishing knowledge (truths that we attain in methodologically justifiable ways) from (mere) true belief (truths that we attain in methodologically unjustifiable ways). If not for God, who underwrites the veracity of our sense perceptions, Descartes would have been left with an unbridgeable chasm between his own consciousness and the world, and thus, epistemologically, would have collapsed into skepticism, the very thing against which he fought. Hume, an atheist, did collapse into skepticism, but it is a rather limited skepticism, one that does not bear on our worldly concerns (and, indeed, in certain respects his moral philosophy tended to be shockingly unskeptical). Famously confessing that his reasoned speculations would frequently result in "*philosophical* melancholy," Hume's natural inclinations would come to the rescue: he would dine, play backgammon, and otherwise have fun with his friends, at which point, he tells us, his philosophical ruminations would appear so "cold, strained, and ridiculous" that he could not bear the thought of returning to his study, preferring instead to throw his books into the fire. Why is *philosophical* reason so impotent for Hume?

One might say that despite his atheism, Hume continued to philosophize "in the shadow of God." For Descartes, truths about the world had to be "necessary" (in that they could not be otherwise), and it is God alone that makes such truths possible. Responding to his predecessors in the empiricist tradition, John Locke and Bishop George Berkeley, who continued to believe in God, Hume argued that God cannot be experienced, and, therefore, there is no basis for believing in his existence. Properly understood, however, Hume's avowed skepticism is the manifestation of the "God's eye view" without God, and if his philosophical reason is impotent it is because he continues to hold it up to this impossible standard. (Indeed, one might plausibly argue that if the resonances of the absent God are removed from the Humean equation, which, in some sense, was his aim in getting clear on such metaphysical concepts as freedom and causation, he was truly no skeptic at all). We might say, then, that for Hume "skepticism is sin without God," to which we must quickly add that it is the omnipresent "without God" that is the very condition of the "sin" that is Hume's skepticism. I put matters in this way because Camus, who is also an atheist, says in *The Myth of Sisyphus* that "the absurd is sin without God" (MS, p. 40), and while he simply meant to say that in the absence of God the Absurd is our "original" sin, the fact is that it is the omnipresent "without God" that is the very condition of the sin that is Camus's Absurd. As was the case with Hume, then, Camus's notion of the Absurd is the manifestation of "the God's eye view" without God, the retention of a standard that he continues to employ even as he denies the existence of the God to which it once referred. Yet, there is a crucial difference between Hume's epistemological groundlessness and Camus's existential groundlessness: skepticism could be left behind in the study, while the Absurd is ubiquitous, encompassing the very "natural" inclinations in which Hume once sought existential refuge. The problem of the Absurd, consequently, is not the particular epistemological problem of skepticism but rather the universal existential problem of nihilism, the thoroughgoing belief in nothing.

Unlike Hume, whose skepticism compelled him to call into question the existence of the external world, Camus commences his philosophical inquiries straightforwardly from Descartes's dualistic perspective: there is consciousness and there is the material world. Without Descartes's God, however, there can be no necessary knowledge, which leads Camus to say that his approach "acknowledges the feeling that *all* true knowledge is impossible" (MS, p. 12). But while Camus rejects all "true" knowledge, he does not reject reason itself, although he certainly seeks to limit its pretensions: "My reasoning wants to be faithful to the evidence that aroused it. That evidence is the absurd. It is that divorce between the mind that desires and the world that disappoints, my nostalgia for unity, this fragmented universe and the contradiction that binds them together" (MS, pp. 49–50). Accordingly, Camus's existential skepticism does not go all the way down. It is as if he follows Descartes's *Meditations* through the first two meditations, the radicalization of doubt (culminating in the "evil genius hypothesis" that methodically calls into question all of our sense perceptions) and the renowned *cogito ergo sum* ("I think, therefore I am") but then, for the most part, refuses to go further, as Descartes builds back toward the world through varied proofs of God's existence, all of which (as Kant will subsequently point out) go well beyond the actual limits of pure reason. As Camus puts it, "between the certainty I have of my existence and the content I try to give to that assurance, the gap will never be filled. Forever I shall be a stranger to myself" (MS, p. 19).

Although, to use an Hegelian term, Camus's "self-certainty" is limited to the *cogito*, and although, as I indicated earlier, epistemological skepticism is but a particular kind of skepticism while the Absurd is universal, Camus is not an epistemological skeptic in the classical sense. He does not rule out the sorts of mundane truths that can be gleaned from everyday experience, and, indeed, much like Descartes (who depends on God to guarantee them), he believes in immediate, self-evident truths. Thus, on the heels of his claim that there is no "true knowledge," Camus says that "solely appearances can be enumerated" (MS, p. 12). There is no contradiction here. As we shall observe in a later section, unlike early modern philosophers such as Descartes, Hume, and Kant, who come out of a philosophical paradigm in which the preeminent question is whether the representations in my head correspond with the objects "out there," Camus implicitly starts from the perspective of twentieth-century existential phenomenology, which discards this "inside-outside" epistemological paradigm altogether. Through the notion of "intentionality," the epistemological question had been reconstituted by Husserl (following his teacher Franz Brentano) and then, with Heidegger (who was motivated by "the question of the meaning of being"), basically supplanted by the existential question of whether there is more to the world than observable "phenomena," the stripped-down appearances of which we are aware.

The divorce between mind and world for Camus is, therefore, not a problem of knowing, strictly speaking, but rather a problem of meaning, and if "the meaning of life is the most urgent of questions" (MS, p. 4), it is only because of Camus's "nostalgia for unity," the lack of which motivates him to open *The Myth of Sisyphus* with the hyperbolic claim that "there is but one truly serious philosophical problem, and that is suicide" (MS, p. 3). Camus has rightly been taken to task for this opening, which can be attacked in a variety of ways. Why is suicide the only truly serious philosophical problem? It would seem that, for Camus, "the meaning of life" is the only truly serious philosophical problem, and the question of suicide simply follows from its failure to be properly addressed. But why commit suicide even if life has no meaning? "Life" itself might have no meaning but the constituents of our lives might have meaning for us, and, even if this is not the case, they might still make life worthwhile (or, indeed, joyful). What's more, although Camus admits that "there are many causes for a suicide," his implicit claim that these are merely proximate causes, all ultimately reducible to the recognition (if only instinctive) that the "habit" of living is of a "ridiculous character" since it is without "any profound reason," does not follow (MS, pp. 5–6). Even if the proximate cause of suicide is rarely the ultimate cause, it need not be the case that the ultimate cause is life's meaninglessness. Indeed, it is probably more often the case that a person commits suicide because he or she believes that life does have some meaning, a meaning to which they have not measured up. Without belaboring the point, Camus's opening gambit is not especially good, but the problem of the meaning of our lives (if not "*the* meaning of life") is, nevertheless, one that resonates for us, and thus it must be made sense of.

One Giant Leap Back, One Small Step Forward: the Problem of Meaning

> Perhaps the religious question without a religious answer amounts to antihumanism, since we cannot compensate for the lack of a cosmic meaning with a meaning derived from our own perspective.
> Thomas Nagel, *The View from Nowhere*[9]

The starting point for Camus, "the *feeling* of absurdity," is, as we have seen, the consequence of a Cartesian divorce between the universe (alternately depicted as "indifferent," "not reasonable," and "divested of illusions and lights") and consciousness, which "everything begins with" and "nothing is worth anything except through." For Camus, however, there is no Cartesian God to reconcile this "divorce between man and his life" (MS, pp. 6–13, *passim*). This is a rather odd position. On one hand, Nagel is surely right: "the religious question without a religious answer amounts to antihumanism," and, in certain respects, as we shall see, Camus's metaphysical view of moral and political matters manifests this. What's more, Camus's position here, as well as others like it (in what might loosely be characterized as the existentialist movement), opened the door to the French poststructuralist movement, which, despite its variations, was unified by its unrepentant antihumanism. (And, indeed, in particular cases, such as the later works of Jacques Derrida, this antihumanism increasingly came to manifest a patently religious problematic.) On the other hand, Camus's emphasis on consciousness as the source of all value is at the very heart of a particular kind of humanism, and this humanistic commitment, as we shall see, in no small part accounted for Camus's view of moral and political matters as well.

In any case, to this point, we have considered Camus's conception of the Absurd from the "shadow of God" perspective, but, at least conceptually, it is not just the breakdown of religion that culminates in "the God's eye view without God" perspective. There are also strictly secular philosophical considerations that push us toward "the God's eye view without God" perspective, which, in the secular context, might be more accurately described (following Nagel) as "the view from nowhere." These secular philosophical considerations, paradoxically enough, arise out of a deliberate move away from the "the God's eye view" perspective in its religious incarnation only to deliver us right back up to it in its secular ("view from nowhere") incarnation.

To make sense of this claim, we must first recall that the Church-based worldview was supplanted by enlightenment reason, the epitome of which was science, and that unlike religious dogma, which would twist (or repress) the facts to uphold the viability of its hypotheses, science discards hypotheses that cannot be borne out by the facts. By virtue of this experimental nature, the sciences made fans of even the most iconoclastic philosophers, one of whom was Nietzsche, who sung its praises in such "middle period" writings as *Human All Too Human*. Yet, science itself soon became the new dogma, as all human endeavors increasingly had to be justified from its unique perspective (and for some philosophers this continues to be the case). What, exactly, is science's unique perspective? The answer, quite simply, is its "objectivity." With respect to natural phenomena, the assumption of this perspective is fair enough, but when it is extended to existential matters, which are intrinsically "subjective" in nature, it is inappropriate. As Camus rightly asserts, "if through science I can seize phenomena and enumerate them, I cannot, for all that, apprehend the world" (MS, p. 20). The basic problem is that the further we step back from a situation, both in terms of space and time, the greater our supposed objectivity, and if we take this impulse to its logical conclusion, a perspective that is infinitely removed in space and time is the most "objective" of all. Yet, the assumption of this "objective" perspective, "the view from nowhere," obscures instead of clarifies the world (understood as our intersubjectively constituted "lifeworld") precisely because it steps outside of it, which is the underlying thrust of Camus's complaint.

Indeed, by stepping outside of our (life)world to better apprehend it, "the view from nowhere" essentially transplants the "inside-outside" schema from the old epistemological problematic on to the existential terrain, where it is no more open to a satisfactory resolution. By its very nature, "the view from nowhere" is necessarily "outside" of these intrinsically "inside" concerns, and from such a perspective they appear not only small but farcical.

Although Camus clearly recognizes the problem of scientism (the extension of science's objectifying processes beyond their proper object domain) he is prone to assume the perspective of its existential correlate, "the view from nowhere," as is exhibited in the second section of *The Myth of Sisyphus*, "Absurd Walls" (which directly follows from his discussion of suicide in the opening section, "Absurdity and Suicide"). The following (uncharacteristically misanthropic) description is particularly revealing:

> Men, too, secrete the inhuman. At certain moments of lucidity, the mechanical aspect of their gestures, their meaningless pantomime, makes silly everything that surrounds them. A man is talking on the telephone behind a glass partition; you cannot hear him, but you see his incomprehensible dumb show: you wonder why he is alive. (MS, pp. 14–15)

The glass partition that separates Camus (qua the detached observer) from the "inhuman" man on the phone (qua the engaged participant) is an "absurd wall" but not in the way that Camus would use this term. Camus is the one who has erected this absurd wall, and if he was on the other side of it, the situation might appear to him in a drastically different light. Imagine, for instance, that the man's "dumb show" was the result of having just learned that his child had been killed in an accident: under these circumstances, Camus's "lucidity" would not prompt him to "wonder why [the man] is alive," notwithstanding the fact that, from the "nowhere" perspective of the Absurd, there would, technically, be absolutely no reason to change his assessment. Of course, Camus is not on the other side of the glass partition, but the point is that it does not take a particularly well-developed imagination to picture a wide range of possibilities (only one of which is that, viewed from the "inside," there actually *is* something "inhuman" about the man). Such an imagination, indeed, is indispensable to the moral moment.

I suggested earlier that there are strictly secular philosophical considerations that push us toward "the God's eye view without God perspective" (which I have been calling "the view from nowhere" in the secular context) that are independent of the religious worldview (whose ongoing secular influence in the aftermath of God's "death" I have been calling "the shadow of God"). Camus alludes to these secular philosophical considerations when he says that "if I were a tree among trees, a cat among animals, this life would have a meaning, or rather this problem would not arise, for I should belong to the world" (MS, p. 51). It is by virtue of the distinctive nature of human consciousness, which is capable of self-consciousness and, ultimately, reason, that human beings objectify their world and, as a result of this process, risk estranging themselves from both their world and themselves. To step back and reflect on matters is to be human, and this capacity is certainly indispensable to a well-lived (not to mention moral) life. The problem of the Absurd, accordingly, is one that arises out of "the human condition," but whether it is inexorable is an entirely different matter. Ironically, in his lyrical essays, which were fleetingly discussed in the first section of this chapter, Camus himself not only speaks of a life without the Absurd, but of people who are one with their natural world and "wholly engaged in the present." Nevertheless, these essays, both youthful and without any philosophical pretensions, are better viewed as an idealization, a nostalgia (ontogenically and phylogenically rooted) for what never actually was.

Bracketing for the time being the exceedingly complex question of validly coordinating these two extremes, the unreflective immersion in the situations that constitute our lives and the reflective "step back" from them, what is clear is that neither extreme is existentially tenable in its own right (as we shall see in our analyses of *The Stranger* and *The Fall*, each of which offers a purified phenomenological portrait of one of these extremes), and both raise an insurmountable challenge to "the meaning of meaning." The problem of meaning is surely clear enough for the unreflective consciousness immersed in life: the problem, for the most part, is that meaning does not even arise. To use Socrates' terminology, this is "the unexamined life," and while Socrates might have been unduly didactic in asserting that such a life "is not worth living," we would be hard pressed to argue that such a life is the optimal one for human beings. Where the problem of meaning's meaning genuinely arises, however, is in the reflective step back. Few people would deny that stepping back to reflect on our engagements is indispensable to the well-lived life, but the problem is that even our vaunted reason, the initial recourse to which is necessary, runs into problems that are indigenous to it. Kant famously maintained that the veritable "rule of reason" is to trace the conditioned back to unconditioned sources in order to unify knowledge, given that reason inherently seeks out "first principles," but that such a move, which ultimately seeks to go behind experience, gives rise to what he called "transcendental illusion." Camus's notion of the Absurd itself derives from such an illusion (or, to be more precise, nostalgia for the promises of such an illusion), and his language (albeit unintentionally) tracks Kant rather closely:

The mind's first step is to distinguish what is true from what is false. However, as soon as thought reflects on itself, what it first discovers is a contradiction. . . . To understand is, above all, to unify . . . [and] if thought discovered in the shimmering mirrors of phenomena eternal relations capable of summing them up in a single principle, then would be seen an intellectual joy of which the myth of the blessed would be but a ridiculous imitation. That nostalgia for unity, that appetite for the absolute, illustrates the essential impulse of the human drama. (MS, p. 17)

It is only nominally, then, that Camus refuses to submit to this appetite for the absolute, which manifests what he calls "philosophical suicide," for his recourse to the Absurd submits to this appetite nonetheless, the only difference between Camus and those whom he thinks commit philosophical suicide being that Camus, in principle, denies what would satiate his appetite. By not only "stepping back" but "stepping out," Camus's reason also takes him beyond the limits of its own efficacy. It is one thing to try to justify some subset of the particular commitments that comprise a life from some broader perspective either within that life or within the social framework that furnishes the stuff of that life's commitments (whether potential or actual), but it is quite another thing to try to justify these commitments from a perspective that is outside of life itself, which is the only perspective that can raise the question of "the meaning of life" as such. Indeed, to raise this question from an external perspective is essentially misconceived, for if something must be justified in terms of something outside it, which, in turn, must be justified by something outside it, and so on, then an infinite regress results and, therefore, absolutely nothing within the chain of justification is ultimately justified.[10] Put more colloquially, when a child continues to ask "why" in response to every answer you give, the child's "whys" will outrun your ability to answer them, and the justifications in response to all of the previous "whys" will ultimately remain unjustified because the anchoring justification is not forthcoming.

Camus recognizes the futility inherent in this problematic, and his project in *The Myth of Sisyphus* is not to reason to the Absurd (which, he acknowledges, others before him have already done) but rather from it. His "absurd reasoning," which begins in this "waterless desert" and is interested "not so much in absurd discoveries as in their consequences" (MS, p. 16), culminates in the conclusion that while the Absurd "merely defines a way of thinking," the ultimate "point is to live" (MS, p. 65). Camus will broach *how one might live* later in the book, but at this point he is content with indicating *why one ought to live*, which responds to the basic problem with which the book began, the question of suicide. Camus's argument along these lines is not particularly strong. He con-tends that I ought to live precisely in order to "keep the Absurd alive," allegedly because I have some obligation to "preserve the very thing that crushes me" (why this is so he does not say), and that to commit suicide is simply to accept this condition rather than to revolt against it (which, along with freedom and passion, are the three consequences that he draws from the Absurd).

More importantly, with respect to our present concerns, which deal with the problem of meaning, Camus maintains that we must learn "to live without appeal" (presumably to either the absent God or some final justification in a chain of existential reasoning) because "belief in the Absurd is tantamount to substituting the quantity of experiences for the quality" (MS, p. 60). His conclusion here, that it is not the best living but the most living that counts, actually does follow from his (existential) premise, the Absurd, which all the more bears witness to the problem with this premise, at least to the extent that it is understood in metaphysical terms, as it often appears to be. After leaping outside of the lifeworld to discover "the meaning of life," a perspective from which not only "life" but all of the things that constitute our lives will have no meaning, Camus then (tentatively) steps back into life so as to preserve the Absurd (because, along with the silent world, our continued existences are one of the two terms that maintain it), and then, armed with the lesson of the Absurd, can only abstractly posit indeterminate "life" itself as a value. Camus's move here, the valorization of life itself, has Nietzschean overtones, but Nietzsche, who would have seen his recourse to the Absurd as a move made in "the shadow of God" (whether spurred by religious *or* secular considerations), would have devolved the responsibility for engendering life-affirming meaning back onto the individual, which, by introducing qualitative distinctions, is the very move that Camus suggests would run afoul of the lesson of the Absurd.

I indicated earlier that validly coordinating engagement and reflection, the immersion in a situation and the step back to reflect on it, is an exceedingly complex problem, and, to this point, it is clear that Camus has not mastered it. To the extent that the Absurd is seen in metaphysical terms, Camus basically careens from pillar to post. Between the leap "outside" (to the position of the absent God, the "nowhere" position, or some combination of the two, as I think is the case for Camus) and the step back "inside" (a position from which no qualitative distinctions can be made), Camus has left us in the existential lurch. In both cases, we have lost the very possibility of giving our lives meaning. Yet, there is a better way to read Camus, a way for which there is ample justification in the text. As Robert Solomon contends, "Camus's book is best understood as giving us a phenomenology, not a way of reasoning," and what is being made is a "powerful appeal to our pre-philosophical feelings."[11] What Camus is giving us, to elaborate somewhat, is his own existential phenomenology, one that is shorn of the more complicated apparatuses that one finds in either Heidegger or Sartre.

Camus's Existential Phenomenology

> The feeling of the absurd is not, for all that, the notion of the absurd. It lays the foundation for it, and that is all. It is not limited to that notion, except in the brief moment when it passes judgment on the universe.
>
> Albert Camus, *The Myth of Sisyphus*[12]

These are the lines that begin the section of *The Myth of Sisyphus* titled "Philosophical Suicide," and they are important because they testify to the claim that Camus is making a "powerful appeal to our pre-philosophical feelings." To this point, I have been suggesting that Camus's "notion of the absurd," which "passes judgment on the universe," is essentially misconceived, but this does not mean that an exploration of "the feeling of the absurd" is also misconceived, for the "feeling of the absurd," at least on certain occasions, is an undeniable feature of the human experience. This feeling was particularly strong in France during the early 1940s, when many of its leading citizens collaborated with the occupying Nazi forces, and it is what prompts Camus. As Camus himself declares in the book's introductory paragraph, he is dealing with "an absurd *sensitivity* that can be found widespread in the age," and he is offering "merely the description, in the pure state, of an intellectual malady," an intellectual malady with which "no metaphysic, no belief, is involved" (MS, p. 2). When considered in terms that are historical and phenomenological rather than metaphysical, Camus's discussion of the Absurd makes good sense, but when he slips into discussing the Absurd in metaphysical terms (as he is not infrequently inclined to do), he himself is guilty of some variant of "philosophical suicide," the very thing against which he rightly rails.

Camus's aim, to provide a "description, in the pure state" of the Absurd, calls to mind the phenomenological movement, which was initiated by Husserl, and his atheistic concern with "the human condition" calls to mind its existential variant, which, in its non-religious aspect, is often associated with Heidegger and Sartre. Although Camus does make a few important comments about Husserl (which tend to bear out the current interpretation), he does not deal with Husserl in any great depth, barely mentions Heidegger (whose existential masterpiece, *Being and Time*, had been published roughly 25 years earlier), and makes no mention of Sartre (who was still writing his existential masterpiece, *Being and Nothingness*). Instead, Camus primarily sets his sights on the religious existentialists, whom, for the most part, he takes to reflect "existential philosophy" on the whole.

In particular, Camus takes on Jaspers, Chestov, and Kierkegaard (who, as we previously saw, is not just the father of existentialism but also the first philosopher to express the concept of "the Absurd"). Taken collectively, the religious existentialists trouble Camus not only because they take the "leap of faith" despite the fact that there is no "immediate evidence" for God's existence, which itself constitutes "philosophical suicide," but also because they make a veritable virtue of the limitations of reason that, by their lights, necessitate the leap in the first place: "Starting out from the absurd over the ruins of reason, in a closed universe limited to the human, they deify what crushes them and find reason to hope in what impoverishes them" (MS, p. 32). Because Camus unapologetically hangs on to individual reason without the rationalistic apparatus that would insure it, he believes that it is only reason itself, however haltingly, that can arise from its own ruins. Such a commitment has Kantian overtones, as the renowned *Critique of Pure Reason* was also a critique *by* pure reason *of* pure reason in the wake of the ruins of reason (which, for Kant, was a medieval transcendent metaphysics that misguidedly purported to prove God's existence). Camus's philosophical commitment here is not just an academic one. Nazism itself arose from the ruins of reason by trumpeting an irrationalism built on blood and soil, and in his *Letters to a German Friend*, written while at *Combat* during the war, Camus speaks to the all-important difference between his own views and his imagined friend's: despite an agreement on the lack of a transcendent meaning, intelligence rather than unbridled instinct must be privileged.

Camus's attack on Kierkegaard is particularly instructive. For Kierkegaard, he correctly indicates, antinomy and paradox are the very criteria of religion, which is why the leap of faith is necessary. Although Kant himself had also reveled in the limits of reason, for these limits "make room for faith," the Kantian God is an arch-rationalist of sorts, and, in any event, it would never have occurred to Kant to question the imperatives not only of reason but of pure practical reason, which he saw as the only possible ground for a genuine morality. Conversely, for Kierkegaard, there is no space for reason, at least not with respect to existential matters, and thus reason must give way. In some sense, as we shall see in the next section, this is unavoidable, but, according to Camus, Kierkegaard turns this inevitability into a virtue, and I think that Camus is right here. Kierkegaard holds out Abraham as "the knight of faith," rather than a mere "knight of infinite resignation," and what conveys this is his willingness to "teleologically suspend the ethical" so as to follow God's command to kill his son. What's more, Camus is right to see Kierkegaard's thought as antinomical. Although the self-styled "champion of subjectivity," when it comes to reconciling with God, Kierkegaard calls for "the sacrifice of the intellect," and, ultimately, his vaunted subjectivity itself. Finally, Camus's criticism of Kierkegaard's concept of the Absurd is also right on the mark, and it is one that Camus himself should keep in mind when he is tempted to turn the Absurd into a metaphysical concept: Kierkegaard "makes of the absurd the criterion of the other world, whereas it is simply a residue of the experience of this world" (MS, p. 38).

Although he does not explicitly consider the rationalists, some subset of whom think that reason can "explain the world," Camus also sees rationalism as a "leap" of sorts, no less justified from the perspective of the immediate evidence. For Camus, then, while on the one hand there is nothing beyond reason, on the other hand there is less to reason than philosophy has generally taken to be the case. Camus's aim, therefore, is to steer between the Scylla of rationalism and the Charybdis of irrationalism, acknowledging both the limits of reason and its (relative) powers. To fall either way off this "middle path," he asserts, is not only to err but to err, paradoxically, in much the same way:

> Reason and the irrational lead to the same preaching. In truth the way matters but little; the will to arrive suffices. The abstract philosopher and the religious philosopher start out from the same disorder and support each other in the same anxiety. But the essential is to explain. Nostalgia is stronger here than knowledge. [The epoch's thought] is constantly oscillating between extreme rationalization of reality which tends to break up that thought into standard reasons and its extreme irrationalization which tends to deify it. But this divorce is only apparent. It is a matter of reconciliation, and, in both cases, the leap suffices. (MS, pp. 47–8)

As a result, the father of the twentieth-century phenomenological movement, Husserl, who was spurred by the desire to ground our knowledge of the objects of our experience, and, finally, the scientific enterprise, is not unlike the father of (religious) existentialism, Kierkegaard, who could not care less about such matters. Both philosophized in "the shadow of God." Yet, crucially, up to a point, as Camus declares, Husserl's phenomenology shares a good deal in common with his own approach. Because phenomenology "declines to explain the world [but] wants to be merely a description of actual experience, it confirms absurd thought in its initial assertion that there is no truth but merely truths," and, indeed, "it certainly seems that in this way nothing contradicts the absurd spirit" (MS, p. 43). So, too, Camus agrees not only with Husserl's emphasis on the notion of "intentionality," the notion that consciousness "intends" (or is actively directed toward) some object of experience, but also with Husserl's renowned "phenomenological reduction," which is a bracketing or suspension of "the natural attitude" that we have toward such objects in order "to get back to the objects themselves." Put less technically, the phenomenological reduction is not unlike the step back, and in this limited sense it is not unlike Camus's perspective in *The Myth of Sisyphus*: "If the theme of the intentional claims to illustrate merely a psychological attitude, by which reality is drained instead of being explained, nothing in fact separates it from the absurd spirit" (MS, p. 44). Indeed, this "draining" of the natural attitude is the philosophical beginning for him as well:

> It happens that the stage sets collapse. Rising, streetcar, four hours in the office or the factory, meal, streetcar, four hours of work, meal, sleep, and Monday Tuesday Wednesday Thursday Friday and Saturday according to the same rhythm – this path is easily followed most of the time. But one day the "why" arises and everything begins in that weariness tinged with amazement. "Begins" – this is important. Weariness comes at the end of the acts of a mechanical life, but at the same time it inaugurates the impulse of consciousness. (MS, pp. 12–13)

There are a number of things worth noting here. First, unlike Camus the detached observer, who wonders about the "inhuman" man on the phone behind the glass partition, this revelatory "why" arises within "the stage sets," not outside of them, and thus is born of a truly phenomenological impulse rather than a philosophically induced metaphysical one. Second, unlike Husserl, Camus does not offer a methodology and cannot account for why the stage sets collapse (which seems to rule out any robust sense of agency, a problem that he shares with Sartre). Third, unlike Husserl's, Camus's phenomenology is clearly existential (rather than epistemological) in nature.

For Camus, where Husserl's epistemologically driven phenomenological project runs off the tracks is in its ultimate aim to get to the "essence" of the objects of perception, or how these objects exist in their "ideality" rather than in their commonplace, everyday "reality" (i.e., in the "natural attitude"). According to Husserl, objects as they exist in their ideality refer back to the transcendental ego, and after executing the phenomenological reduction, there still remains one more reduction to be executed, the transcendental reduction, which puts before us this meaning-conferring transcendental consciousness itself. Although Camus is wrong to associate Husserl's essences with Platonic ones as he does (because, for example, Husserl's transcendental idealism is not making classical metaphysical claims), his basic complaint, that Husserl is restoring "depth to experience," and is, therefore, running afoul of phenomenology's more radical impulses, is not wrong. The very concretion toward which Husserl's phenomenology initially aimed, "the things themselves," ends up running aground in abstraction, which is Camus's point when he declares that "rather than encountering here a taste for the concrete, the meaning of the human condition, I find an intellectualism sufficiently unbridled to generalize the concrete itself" (MS, p. 47).

Camus's preoccupation here with the concrete, and, more generally, the human condition, is also evidenced by Heidegger (who was Husserl's student) and Sartre (who mediates, extends, and, ultimately, transfigures Husserl and Heidegger). Both Heidegger and Sartre are existential phenomenologists, as is Camus, but there are vital differences between their three approaches at even the most fundamental level, a brief summary of which will help to flesh out Camus's own approach. Unlike Camus, Heidegger and Sartre take themselves to be doing "phenomenological ontology," but they have different accounts of what this involves. In general, phenomenological ontology offers an account of Being (the ontological aspect) based on the way in which we are constrained to experience it (the phenomenological aspect). For Heidegger, who describes what he does as "fundamental ontology," phenomenology is chiefly a way into the ontology, and what ultimately motivates his entire corpus is "the question of the meaning of Being." Fundamentally opposed to the Cartesian consciousness-world dichotomy, which one finds in Camus and Sartre, Heidegger states that we *Dasein* (literally translated as "being-there," and meant to be contrasted with the Cartesian conception of human beings as essentially consciousness) have an underlying intuition of Being, and by carefully attending to the nature of our experiences, we can discern its deeper structures. These deeper structures, which are invariable, are what Heidegger describes as "existential."

Understood in this particular way, Camus is not an existentialist, for he would reject not just the idea of these deeper "existential" structures but, more generally, the recourse to ontology itself. Ontology deals with the "essential" structures of Being, and, although Heidegger would vehemently reject the claim, his "existential structures," constitutive of "the meaning of Being" as such, are existential transmutations of Husserl's epistemologically driven "essences." In this way, by Camus's lights, Heidegger also commits "philosophical suicide," for even if he begins from the concrete, he abstractly derives a transcendent meaning to which we ought to conform, which involves an "authentic" comportment. Now, although it derives from the consciousness-world dichotomy that Heidegger rejects, one might argue that Camus's concept of the Absurd is just such an existential, for Camus often speaks of the Absurd as a fundamental constituent of the human experience, and he seeks to make sense of what it means to live in accordance with its logic. However, this is not the case, unless, perhaps, we interpret the Absurd as part and parcel of a Camusian metaphysics, which is the interpretation that I have been arguing against here. As a phenomenologist, Camus might well begin from the Absurd because this is *our* experience of the world, but it is not an existential, for the "absurd sensitivity that can be found widespread in the age," which involves "no metaphysic, no belief" (MS, p. 2), is not historically invariable. In other words, Camus is not ontologizing the Absurd: having described an experience, he is merely seeking to determine what follows from it.

Sartre's phenomenological ontology is much closer to Camus's phenomenology, for the emphasis with Sartre – who sees consciousness ("being-for-itself"), the natural world ("being-in-itself") and other people ("being-for-others") as the three fundamental constituents of Being – is on the phenomenology, and, most of all, consciousness itself. One reason that Sartre provides an ontology is to circumvent the "deworlded" nature of the Cartesian consciousness, which is why Heidegger calls human beings *Dasein*. Still, Sartre does see consciousness, properly understood, as the starting point, which leads him to cleave a middle path: consciousness is not a "substance" as such, for, as he slyly says, it is "nothing" (i.e., it is the nothingness in *Being and Nothingness*), and, therefore, does not stand alone. Rather, it makes itself in the world, to which it stands in a relation of "interiority" (instead of the relation of "exteriority" that exists between consciousness and the world for Descartes). In living its world, however, consciousness is also always beyond it in the sense that the world does not determine consciousness, and thus Sartre contends that we are phenomenologically free (i.e., we are constrained to experience ourselves as free) regardless of the metaphysical fact of the matter. This position is especially close to Camus's. In *The Myth of Sisyphus*, Camus declares (in a section titled "Absurd Freedom") that to remain faithful to his own approach, he will have "nothing to do with the problem of metaphysical liberty," for "'the problem of freedom' as such has no meaning, [and] it is ultimately linked in quite a different way with the problem of God" (MS, p. 56). Crucially, however, Camus goes on to emphasize that "I can experience only my own freedom" (MS, p. 56), which includes "my freedom of action" (MS, p. 57), and that my ability to "take a broad view" of my life "involves the principle of liberation" (MS, p. 59). In other words, on the basis of this experience, which we all live in our day-to-day being, we must understand ourselves as free.

Despite this similarity, Camus and Sartre differ in crucial respects, not the least of which pertains to the Absurd, and the relation here between Camus and Sartre is further complicated by the fact that Sartre's position on it changes over time. In *Nausea*, a novel published in 1938 and reviewed by Camus in 1939, Sartre's conception of the Absurd arises from a radical disjunction between consciousness and the material world, and it is the experience of the world's superfluity, that it is *de trop* (too much), which incites the nausea experienced by the protagonist, Roquentin (while he is in the park, looking at the gnarled root of a chestnut tree). Roquentin's estrangement from the material world differs from Camus's estrangement from the meaningless universe in at least one crucial respect: for Camus, nature is not simply a compensation but is representative of reconciliation as such, and it is thus "on this side" of the divorce that engenders the Absurd. In his review of *Nausea*,

Camus laments that Sartre takes the realization that life is absurd as an end rather than a beginning, which, of course, anticipates his own position in *The Myth of Sisyphus*, but what is of particular interest is his claim that *Nausea* is concerned only with "the mechanical side of existence," for this suggests that Sartre's character is split off from his natural side, from those things such as "beauty, love, or danger" that make life tragic precisely because there is also much that can make it "magnificent" (LCE, p. 201). Consequently, according to Camus, Sartre's characters in *Nausea*, and, more generally, his collection of short stories in *The Wall and Other Stories*, tend to evidence an abstract freedom that can do little more than run up against their own lives, and thus they founder on their own freedom. Bracketing for the meantime the question of whether the same could also be said of Camus, Sartre moves beyond this position in *Being and Nothingness*, in which the root of the Absurd resides in the fact that human beings can never "be what they are" due to the fact that consciousness is always "beyond" whatever it would make of itself in the world. In other words, the operative myth for Sartre is not Sisyphus but Tantalus, for the more we try to make ourselves into something "essential," the more this essential self recedes from our grasp.

In the final analysis, however, what is perhaps most important to emphasize, at least for our present purposes, is that Camus will have no truck with any ontology whatsoever, not even one, like Sartre's, that is phenomenologically driven and primarily heuristic in nature. Camus's prototype in *The Myth of Sisyphus* is neither Husserl, Heidegger, nor Sartre, but rather Nietzsche, and, much like Nietzsche, Camus regards all attempts at philosophical systematization as a form of "philosophical suicide," for no ontology is supported by "the immediate evidence." Nietzsche declares in *Twilight of the Idols* that "the will to a system is a lack of integrity," and what we are getting with Camus is a bare bones, deliberately unsystematic phenomenology, one that refuses to go beyond those deductions from human experience that are more or less "self-evident."

Camus's Sisyphean Ethics

> Your judgment "this is right" has a pre-history in your instincts, likes, dislikes, experiences, and lack of experiences. . . . Let us therefore limit ourselves to the purification of our opinions and valuations and to the creation of our own new tables of what is good, and let us stop brooding about the "moral value of our actions." . . . We want to become those we are – human beings who are new, unique, incomparable, who give themselves laws, who create themselves.
>
> Friedrich Nietzsche, *The Gay Science*[13]

To this point we have been concerned exclusively with the first chapter of *The Myth of Sisyphus*, "An Absurd Reasoning," which is primarily concerned with the question of suicide (understood in terms of both body and mind). The much shorter second and third chapters of the book build from the conclusion of this "absurd reasoning" (that even in the face of the Absurd "the point is to live") to an absurd ethics, which is no longer concerned with the question of whether to live but rather with the question of how to live. Accordingly, the second chapter, "The Absurd Man," offers three existential responses to the Absurd – the Don Juan, the Actor, and the Conqueror – while the third chapter offers a fourth existential response, the one favored by Camus, namely, the Creator and, more specifically, the Self-Creator. This is all very Nietzschean, and it needs to be considered more closely, but first some preliminary comments are in order.

The three existential responses or, as Camus calls them, "styles of life" that comprise the second chapter are clearly not favored by Camus, and any suggestion to the contrary is simply not supported by the text. "These images do not propose moral codes and involve no judgments," he states, for "they are sketches [and] merely represent a style of life" (MS, p. 90). The Conqueror, in particular, is a "style of life" from which Camus intends to distance himself, as is reflected in the fact that (in contrast to the Don Juan and the Actor, which were both parts that he personally played) every paragraph begins with quotation marks. Now, there is surely a nettlesome problem here, but it is to be found not in Camus's celebration of these positions but, rather, in his lack of criteria for unequivocally ruling them out. "In the absurd world the value of a notion or of a life is measured by its sterility" (MS, p. 69), Camus states, and these three "styles of life" are at least "consistent" because they all "think clearly and have ceased to hope" (MS, p. 92). The problem, accordingly, is that lucidity in the face of the Absurd itself implicitly becomes the highest value, but as others have indicated with respect to such lucidity in analyses of "existential authenticity," this criterion does not rule out such nasty types as "authentic torturers." Camus is not unaware of the problem, and at the beginning of the chapter he attempts to do just this, asserting that Ivan Karamazov's infamous "Everything is permitted" must "not be taken in the vulgar sense," and that "'Everything is permitted' does not mean nothing is forbidden . . . for this would be childish" (MS, p. 67).

In sum, Camus maintains, while the Absurd "does not recommend crime," it does "confer an equivalence on the consequences of [our] actions," but "if all experiences are indifferent, that of duty is as legitimate as any other" (MS, p. 67). Admittedly, this is some rather thin stuff, so why does Camus offer it up? I think that there are basically two things going on here. First, as I have emphasized throughout this chapter, the

Absurd can be understood phenomenologically or metaphysically, and it is, decidedly, the phenomenological approach that is to be preferred. Yet, in this context, Camus has implicitly shifted back to a metaphysical view of the phenomenon, the one that saps all meaning from life and, therefore, privileges the quantity of life over the quality of life. If Camus had stuck to his phenomenological guns, his experience of the Absurd might have occasioned a sociohistorical inquiry into the root causes of the experience, but by turning it into a metaphysic there is no impetus for such an inquiry. Second, following in the footsteps of Nietzsche, Camus (who, we must remember, is composing *The Myth of Sisyphus* during World War II) is registering the breakdown of the enlightenment project itself, as the land that gave the world Kant and the categorical imperative opted for Hitler and categorical annihilation instead. Nietzsche had recognized that *the* moral law is nothing more than *our* moral law, and that (contra Kant) "our" moral law is neither universal nor necessary in nature. What we are left with, then, is either his open-ended "imperative" that we each individually "create our new tables of what is good," which is the culmination of the enlightenment's commitment to the free, self-determining individual, or wholesale destruction, which is the culmination of a festering resentment that, in the wake of God's death, fragments into nihilism.

It is this Nietzschean either/or that Camus implicitly takes up in *The Myth of Sisyphus*, but before pursuing Camus's Nietzscheanism, it must be pointed out that there are vital ways in which the two differ. In contrast to Camus, Nietzsche would have had no truck with the Absurd, at least not if understood in metaphysical terms. Nietzsche clearly recognized that even his own project ambled in "the shadow of God," and the Christian commitment to "improving mankind" was one with which he flirted in his anti-Christian project, as *Thus Spake Zarathustra* distinctly testifies. (Indeed, *Thus Spake Zarathustra* helps itself to a good deal of Christian imagery, even if it is inverted.) But fetishizing God's empty throne, which leads to a wholly external viewpoint that saps life of meaning in a vampiric fashion, would have been seen by Nietzsche as a betrayal of what is "this-worldly," the very thing that his own "transvaluation of values" was intended to revivify. Camus is also (at least nominally) committed to what is "this-worldly," but the Absurd, when understood in metaphysical terms, unwittingly undercuts this very commitment.

Now, in contrast to Nietzsche, who goes so far as to occasionally hold up Napoleon and Caesar as self-actualized creators but ultimately gives pride of place to the artist (as exemplified by Goethe), Camus only points to the Don Juan, the Artist, and the Conqueror as "styles of life" that are not incompatible with the Absurd before ultimately giving pride of place to the artist as well. What's more, in contrast to Nietzsche, Camus implicitly retains aspects of a conventional moral orientation, even as, in Nietzschean style, he says that "no code of ethics and no effort are justifiable *a priori* in the face of the cruel mathematics that command our condition" (MS, p. 16). Camus thus goes on to assert that "there can be no question of holding forth on ethics [because] I have seen people behave badly with great morality and I note every day that integrity has no need of rules" (MS, p. 66). This suggests, as we shall see, that Camus is no less concerned with "behaving well" than conventional moralists, although the grounding of this imperative and what constitutes "behaving well" differ. (In terms of Nietzsche, however, this second difference must not be pushed too strongly, not because Camus did not retain his fair share of conventional moral commitments but because Nietzsche also did, as is exhibited in various passages throughout his corpus that celebrate not only honesty but courtesy and kindness.) In the final analysis, however, as the following passage attests, the Camus of *The Myth of Sisyphus* has hitched his moral wagon to Nietzsche's star, and, therefore, it is not unfair to assess his moral position, at least in its broad contours, in much the same way that Nietzsche's moral position is assessed:

> When Nietzsche writes: "It clearly seems that the chief thing in heaven and on earth is to *obey* at length and in a single direction: in the long run there results something for which it is worth the trouble of living on this earth as, for example, virtue, art, music, the dance, reason, the mind – something that transfigures, something delicate, mad, or divine," he elucidates the rule of a really distinguished code of ethics. But he also points the way of the absurd man. Obeying the flame is both the easiest and hardest thing to do. (MS, pp. 64–5)

"Obeying the flame" here refers to the "flame of life," and, like Nietzsche, Camus thinks this should be our highest value. Morally speaking, what does it entail? As a preliminary matter, what it definitely does not entail is a general collapse into hedonism or, indeed, any immediate, impulse-driven way of being in the world, for this presumably would be "the easiest thing to do." As Nietzsche emphasizes time and again, his "higher types" are not "hog-faced pleasure seekers" but rather are quite severe, and, most of all, severe with themselves, for such severity is a necessary condition of "obeying at length and in a single direction," which Nietzsche views as a necessary condition of genuine self-creation. Put differently, "obeying the flame" need not be interpreted in a vulgar way, and it is not necessarily inconsistent with a "really distinguished code of ethics." When John Stuart Mill sought to defend utilitarianism against the charge that it was vulgar, since it is based on "the greatest happiness principle" (i.e., the principle that it is morally incumbent on us to act so as to maximize the happiness of those who will be affected by our actions in morally charged situations), he followed the lead of the

Epicureans, who contend that "it is not they, but their accusers, who represent human nature in a degrading light, since the accusation supposes human beings to be capable of no pleasures except those of which swine are capable."[14] Camus would level a similar sort of charge against his accusers, arguing that it is not necessarily the case that the egoism inherent in "obeying the flame" will manifest itself in vulgar ways.

The deeper problem for Nietzsche, and, derivatively, Camus, is how to make moral sense of "the single direction" that is chosen in the pursuit of genuine self-creation and the "obeying at length" in the pursuit of this single direction. In other words, the deeper problem is the absence of moral criteria that can be brought to bear in evaluating both the single end that is chosen and the means that are employed to realize it. For Camus, as we saw, it is "integrity" (which "has no need of rules") rather than "great morality" that is the key to "behaving well," a point that his protagonist in *The Fall*, Clamence, ostensibly reiterates when he declares that "when one has no character one *has* to apply a method" (F, p. 11). The problem, however, is that "integrity" and "character" might not be the same thing, although the terms are usually used interchangeably. An individual with integrity is whole or well-integrated, as is the Nietzschean individual who obeys at length and in a single direction, but, at least technically, a whole or well-integrated individual is not necessarily a virtuous one, and, therefore, might "behave badly." (Indeed, this is the case with the Don Juan, the Actor, and the Conqueror.) Such an individual, who lacks character, has no need of rules, for the end will determine the means, but if the individual lacks the virtues, it is unlikely (or, at least, it does not reasonably follow) that he will choose both a proper end and the proper means to realize it. Alternatively, although the individual of character also has no need of rules, this is because he has been raised in a social context in which "doing the right thing" is not inconsistent with personal flourishing but, rather, is a condition of it.

The problem, therefore, is not that Nietzsche and Camus reject modern morality, which is based on method (specifically, a rational decision-making process, whether in the form of Kant's categorical imperative or Mill's utilitarian calculus), since, in some sense, both buy into a virtue-based ethics. Rather, the problem is that both Nietzsche and Camus are coming out of a modern problematic in which the well-ordered society that is the indispensable condition of engendering the virtues in the first place has broken down. This is Alasdair MacIntyre's point in *After Virtue*, in which he argues that the modern moral project has foundered because, while we continue to talk about "the good person," we are no longer in a position to make sense of what this means.[15] Without a shared social context, in which there is some agreement concerning what constitutes the human *telos* (i.e., the ultimate human aim or purpose), and, therefore, some basis for judging our actions, there is, according to MacIntyre, no basis for virtue ethics, since what constitutes a virtue depends on the kinds of beings we are. Put differently, the enlightenment emphasis on the free, self-determining individual strips this individual of the very content that can make sense of the good, and what the autonomous individual is left with, as Sartre's version of existentialism, in particular, suggests, is merely the decision itself. Although I think that MacIntyre's account is problematical insofar as he sees this as a necessary rather than historically contingent outcome of the modern project (for I believe that modernity had other resources at its disposal to circumvent this problem), his point is well taken with respect to the (historically contingent) circumstances in which Nietzsche and Camus found themselves. Both Nietzsche's Zarathustra (not to mention his *übermensche*, or "overman") and Camus's "absurd man" are on their own, and their attempts to create themselves *sui generis* are problematical. Accordingly, although Nietzsche and Camus seek a return to the virtues, they do so by way of the breakdown of the modern project, whose faltering structures cannot accommodate the attempt, and thus they appear to be immoralists.

In defense against the particular charge of immoralism, however, Nietzsche and Camus still might have an argument to make. They might argue that, even in the absence of Aristotle's good *polis*, putative self-creators would not capitulate to the vices of their society. Although the complexities of Nietzsche's larger meta-ethical framework are well beyond what can be discussed here, Nietzsche thinks that Judeo-Christian morality is "slavish" rather than "masterly" because it is characterized by resentment and, ultimately, an ascetic ideal, which values self-denial not for the sake of self-denial *per se* but, ultimately, for (an impotent) self-righteousness. In essence, the argument would be that, freed from resentment and the ascetic ideal, putative self-creators would not experience the "return of the repressed," and, therefore, would not be inclined to do the sorts of vicious things that we usually rely on conventional morality to proscribe. In other words, the more "severe" morality that such types have would not dispense with many of the conventional moral proscriptions. At the end of the day, I am not sure this is right with respect to Nietzsche, who often speaks of our innate cruelty, as well as the justifiability of subordinating inferiors, but I do think it is right with respect to Camus (if, for no other reason, because he did not reason it out to its stark end as Nietzsche had). Thus, for Camus's (self-)creator:

A world remains of which man is the sole master. What bound him was the illusion of another world. The outcome of his thought, ceasing to be renunciatory, flowers in images. It frolics – in myths, to be sure, but myths with no other depth than that of human suffering and, like it, inexhaustible. Not the divine fable that amuses and blinds, but the terrestrial face, gesture, and drama in which are summed up a difficult wisdom and an ephemeral passion. (MS, pp. 117–18)

In the final analysis, it must be borne in mind that Camus's moral position in *The Myth of Sisyphus* is only the starting point, and when he later states that the movement from *The Stranger* to *The Plague* "represents the transition from an attitude of solitary revolt to the recognition of a community whose struggles must be shared" (LCE, p. 339), he is tacitly speaking to a transition in his ethical theory, more generally.

The Myth of Sisyphus

The gods had condemned Sisyphus to ceaselessly rolling a rock to the top of a mountain, whence the stone would fall back of its own weight. They had thought with some reason that there is no more dreadful punishment than futile and hopeless labor.

Albert Camus, *The Myth of Sisyphus*[16]

The Myth of Sisyphus ends with five short pages that discuss the ancient Greek myth itself, and in this brief span a number of important themes arise, three of which will be discussed here. As an initial matter, however, the particulars of the myth itself: Sisyphus was among the most cunning human beings, and his contempt for the gods was infamous, but what earned him the punishment of ceaseless, meaningless labor was that he cheated death on two occasions. When confronted by Hades, who was to escort him to the Underworld at the end of his life, Sisyphus tricked Hades into putting the handcuffs that were intended for him onto Hades' own wrists, at which point he imprisoned Hades in his house and, in effect, ended death on earth. The god of war was sent to release Hades, and Sisyphus was dragged back to the Underworld, but not before he instructed his wife not to bury his body. On arriving in the Underworld, Sisyphus implored the gods to let him return home to secure the burial of his body, and they agreed, but, of course, once free of the Underworld, Sisyphus had no intention of returning, and he continued to live for a fair number of years. Eventually, however, the gods caught up with Sisyphus, and he was sentenced to eternally roll a boulder up a mountain for defying them. According to Camus, "you have already grasped that Sisyphus is the absurd hero. He is, as much through his passions as through his torture. His scorn of the gods, his hatred of death, and his passion for life won him that unspeakable penalty in which the whole being is exerted toward accomplishing nothing" (MS, p. 120).

The first issue that the myth raises with respect to Camus's notion of the Absurd concerns the role that the gods play in it. As has already been discussed, Camus's concept of the Absurd arises in "the shadow of [the dead] God," and yet, in this archetypical myth, there is no absence of gods. How, then, is Sisyphus "the absurd hero"? One way to make sense of this incongruity is to distinguish between the Greek gods and the Judeo-Christian God. For the ancients, the gods were players in this world, and while they represented both cosmic and human principles, thus linking humanity with the meaning and purpose of the larger cosmos, they themselves were not foundational. In other words, the mere existence of such gods does not, in and of itself, obviate the problem of the Absurd, since the cosmos itself need not be meaningful or justified. (Indeed, according to Greek myth, the cosmos ultimately sprung from Chaos, a yawning chasm or void, but it did not occur to the ancients to thus call into question its meaning or justification.) With the concept of the one God, and, in particular, the Christian God (given that Yaweh, the Jewish God of the Old Testament, was characterized by certain of humanity's more negative emotions), however, we have the ultimate foundation, the ultimate meaning and justification (one, indeed, that even pre-exists the ancients' idea of Chaos). Ostensibly, it takes this type of God to staunch the problem of the Absurd, and it is with the death of *this* God that the Absurd arises. Now, one might say that even with this foundational God, who not only brought the universe into existence but is omniscient, omnipotent, omnipresent, and absolutely good, the Absurd is still not obviated. Nagel makes this point when he argues that justifications come to an end only when *we* want them to come to an end, and that if we can "step back from the purposes of individual life and doubt their point," we can also step back from "the glory of God" and put it "into question in the same way."[17] In the final analysis, I think that Nagel is right, for to contend that God's divine purpose cannot be put into question is to genuflect to his enormity rather than to his foundational nature, which I have always thought is what really motivates Kierkegaard's "fear and trembling" before God.

The second issue that the myth raises with respect to Camus's notion of the Absurd concerns the role that repetition plays in it. In contrast to both Kierkegaard and Nietzsche, who viewed repetition in a positive light, Camus views it in entirely negative terms. With respect to the myth itself, I think that Camus is justified, but when he analogizes Sisyphus's experience to our own, the attack on repetition loses its justification. Why is this? For both Kierkegaard and Nietzsche, repetition is ultimately forward looking, and by virtue of this directionality, it opens up the possibility of breaking with what has been repeated through the very thought of repeating it. For Nietzsche, the concept of repetition arises in his notion of "eternal recurrence," which is based on the idea that the life we are living is one that we have lived countless times in the past and will live countless times in the future. Crucially, however, although

Nietzsche played with the idea of seeing eternal recurrence in cosmological terms (as is evidenced in his notebooks), in his published writings, he always spoke of it in existential terms, and, in particular, as a kind of regulative ideal. What bearing would this thesis have on your life *if* it were true, he asks. How, then, would you choose to live? The idea here is that we would only will to repeat the lives that we are living *if* we are living our lives in such a way that we could validate them with the "heavy weight" of infinite repetition. The essential point, however, is that Nietzsche contends that if we could not will the eternal recurrence, then we should choose to live our lives *differently*, but if we can say *amor fati*, that we love (our) fate, than we can choose to repeat it. For Kierkegaard, too, repetition is essentially existential. Going even further than Nietzsche, Kierkegaard argues that repetition is a necessary condition of genuine selfhood, for without repetition, life would become empty, meaningless noise, an unintegrated parade of what is different, which is at odds with any notion of integrity (not to mention character, as I previously distinguished the two). Conversely, by repeating the past (which can take the form of habit, or, better, ritual), one assumes it, but one assumes it not for the purpose of experiencing it in the very same way but for transcending it, for forging a new perspective or way of being that integrates it. What is ultimately repeated, then, is the self, which is enriched in the process of repetition. Put differently, the genuine self is neither ever-changing nor eternally fixed.

Of course, this is the hitch for Sisyphus: his life is eternally fixed, at least insofar as he is not free to choose to live it otherwise, for he has been condemned to roll a boulder up a mountain for eternity. For both Nietzsche and Kierkegaard, freedom and choice are intrinsically a part of the way in which they view repetition, and even if the Nietzschean or Kierkegaardian self freely chooses to repeat his prior life in all respects, such that this self's repetition outwardly appears to be no less identical than Sisyphus's, we are still speaking of two entirely different phenomena, as Sisyphus did not freely choose to roll a boulder up a mountain for eternity. To be sure, Sisyphus is free to choose how to think about the life that he is living (a phenomenon that Sartre stresses, and one to which we shall return), but this seems to be the extent of it, and for this reason Camus is right to see Sisyphus's enforced repetition in wholly negative terms, and, indeed, the feeling of the Absurd would seem to follow. But when Camus analogizes Sisyphus, who is "powerless and rebellious," to the modern worker (for whom he sees Sisyphus as the prototype), he is wrong. To see the modern worker as having no more choice about the course of his life than did Sisyphus is to encourage a defeatism that does the worker no favors. The worker who can raise the question of repetition along either Nietzschean or Kierkegaardian lines can choose to try to change his lot in life (and not merely the particulars of his work life) either individually or collectively (as the labor movement, at its best, attempted to do), while to validate this sort of defeatism is to live a life in which one does not take responsibility for oneself, or, to be more precise, one's self. I say the worker who *can* raise the question of repetition here because raising this question points to a particular kind of reflective capacity that is hard won rather than simply given. Thus, Camus is wrong to say that the worker's "fate is no less absurd" than Sisyphus's but that "it is tragic only at the rare moments when it becomes conscious" (MS, p. 121), for even if the worker is engaged in Sisyphean tasks, his fate is only absurd *when* he becomes conscious of it (i.e., only when he reflects on it), and it is tragic only *if* he reflects on it from a particular collection of commitments, the kind of commitments that fundamentally constitute the character of the self that is reflecting. In sum, then, the Absurd arises only on reflection, and then only a certain kind of reflection.

This leads to the third (and, for our purposes, most crucial) issue that the myth raises with respect to Camus's notion of the Absurd, which is the relation between experience and reflection. As Solomon contends, for Camus (and, for that matter, Sartre), experience and reflection, living our lives from the first-person perspective and ruminating on them from the third-person perspective, are the ideal poles that structure the force field within which self-consciousness (and, therefore, the self) is produced, and it is in Camus's exploratory accounts of the phenomenology that attends the varying perspectives that arise within this force field that his philosophical novels truly shine.[18] With respect to this relation between experience and reflection, Camus (and Sartre) is running with a theme that was raised by Nietzsche and Kierkegaard in the prior century, both of whom, in contrast to the broader philosophical tradition, saw reflection as overrated. Here, of course, our concern is the Absurd, and what Camus gives us in the last pages of his discussion of the ancient Greek myth of Sisyphus are two ways of dealing with the Absurd, ways that crudely correspond to these ideal poles. On the one hand, he suggests, Sisyphus's passion causes him to wholly throw himself into his task, and "all Sisyphus's silent joy is contained therein": "His rock is his thing," Camus declares, for when "the absurd man says yes," his "effort will henceforth be unceasing" (MS, p. 123). This "yes" is to life, to experience itself, and, at its extreme, it is what leads Camus to value the quantity, as opposed to quality, of life. On the other hand, he declares, Sisyphus is tragic because he is conscious (that is, reflective): "The lucidity that was to constitute his torture at the same time crowns his victory, [since] there is no fate that cannot be surmounted by scorn" (MS, p. 121). This is, in effect, a "no" to life, a "no" to experience from a perspective allegedly far removed, a perspective from which "the whole shooting match" can be held in utter contempt. This scorn is an expression of the reflectively induced resentment against which both Kierkegaard and Nietzsche railed.

These two proposed responses to the existential problem posed by the Absurd, which are diametrically opposed, thus represent a move to the extremes, but, as we shall see, moving to the extreme that is represented by either one of these constituting poles of human consciousness does not solve the existential problem posed by the Absurd but exacerbates it. With Meursault of *The Stranger* (chapter 3) and Jean-Baptiste Clamence of *The Fall* (chapter 4), we get two characters that exemplify the choices of lived experience, in which the "quality" of life falls by the wayside, and reflection, in which resentment pushes lived experience to the wayside. As Hegel would put it, with these two "forms of consciousness," we get the chance to observe, in unadulterated form, the logic innate to each of these extreme positions as they break down of their own accord. Any viable response to the existential problem posed by the Absurd depends not only on a dialectical relation between lived experience and reflection (that is, a relation in which lived experience and reflection mutually inform one another to yield results that transcend the one-sidedness of each) but a larger social context, and, indeed, this is what we get with certain characters in *The Plague* (chapter 5). This "unfolding dialectic" then sets up a philosophical re-examination of the Absurd, which occurs when we consider Camus's other philosophical work, *The Rebel* (chapter 6).

notes

1   Samuel Beckett, *Endgame* (New York: Grove Press, 1958), pp. 32–3.
2   Karl Marx and Friedrich Engels, *The Communist Manifesto* (Oxford: Oxford University Press, 1992), p. 6.
3   LCE, p. 89.
4   Blaise Pascal, *Pensées*, trans. A. J. Krailsheimer (London: Penguin Classics 1995), p. 66.
5   Friedrich Nietzsche, *The Gay Science*, trans. Walter Kaufmann (New York: Random House, 1974), p. 180.
6   Ibid., p. 181.
7   Søren Kierkegaard, *Concluding Unscientific Postscript to Philosophical Fragments*, vol. 1, trans. Howard V. Hong and Edna H. Hong (Princeton: Princeton University Press, 1992), p. 210.
8   Friedrich Nietzsche, *The Gay Science*, p. 167.
9   Thomas Nagel, *The View From Nowhere* (New York: Oxford University Press, 1986), p. 210.
10 Thomas Nagel, *Mortal Questions* (Cambridge: Cambridge University Press, 1979), p. 12.

11 Robert C. Solomon, *Dark Feelings, Grim Thoughts: Experience and Reflection in Camus and Sartre* (New York: Oxford University Press, 2006), p. 39.
12 MS, p. 28.
13 Friedrich Nietzsche, *The Gay Science*, pp. 263–6.
14 John Stuart Mill, *Utilitarianism*, 2nd edn., ed. George Sher (Indianapolis: Hackett Publishing, 2001), pp. 7–8.
15 Alasdair MacIntyre, *After Virtue*, 2nd edn. (Notre Dame: University of Notre Dame Press, 1984).
16 MS, p. 119.
17 Thomas Nagel, *Mortal Questions*, pp. 16–17.
18 Robert C. Solomon, *Dark Feelings, Grim Thoughts*, pp. 213–18.

further reading

Sagi, Avi, *Albert Camus and the Philosophy of the Absurd*, trans. Batya Stein (Amsterdam: Rodopi, 2002).
Solomon, Robert C., *Dark Feelings, Grim Thoughts: Experience and Reflection in Camus and Sartre* (New York: Oxford University Press, 2006).
Sprintzen, David, *Camus: A Critical Examination* (Philadelphia: Temple University Press, 1988).

life

He wanted to crush himself into that mud, to reenter the earth by immersing himself in that clay, to stand on that limitless plain covered with dirt, stretching his arms to the sooty sponge of the sky, as though confronting the superb and despairing symbol of life itself, to affirm his solidarity with the world at its worst, to declare himself life's accomplice even in its thanklessness and its filth.

Albert Camus, *A Happy Death*[1]

During the years leading up to the publication of *The Myth of Sisyphus*, Camus had either just written, or was in the process of writing, three fictional works, all of which revolved around the theme of the Absurd, or, to be more exact, what it would mean to "affirm life" in the face of the Absurd. The first of these works, the novel *A Happy Death*, was written between 1936 and 1938 but not published during Camus's lifetime, and the last of them, the play *Caligula*, was written in 1938 but only first performed in 1945. The middle work, which is Camus's most famous, and has entered the pantheon of classical literary works, is, of course, *The Stranger*, which was published in 1942.

All three of these works revolve around an attempt on the part of the lead character to make sense of what it means to immerse oneself in life, which, following Nietzsche, Camus sees as the only way to truly affirm it, but each of the three lead characters makes sense of this aim in different ways. Thus, although I shall focus on *The Stranger* in this chapter, as its lead character, Meursault, represents the purified extreme of "lived experience" (which purportedly manifests an unadulterated "yes" to life), I shall also briefly look at the lead characters in *A Happy Death* and *Caligula*, who are also instructive, albeit in different ways. *A Happy Death* was Camus's dry run for *The Stranger*, and the two novels share not only lead characters with identically sounding last names, as Patrice Mersault becomes Meursault (no first name), but also a fair number of scenes and secondary characters. Moreover, Patrice Mersault and Meursault share the same basic aim, "the happy life." Where the two characters differ, albeit only in degree, is psychologically, and it is in their psychological differences that what is most interesting about Camus's early conception of "the happy life" can be glimpsed. Conversely, *Caligula* turns on the daunting recognition that "the happy life" cannot be achieved, and Caligula's response to this is to "affirm life" in a much darker way. If life itself is not only meaningless but capricious, he reasons, then to affirm life is to affirm it in precisely this way, which, for Caligula, takes the form of a frenzy of meaningless, capricious destruction.

Although, in certain respects, Caligula is Meursault's opposite, with Patrice Mersault somewhere between the two, all three characters are alike in that they kill unjustifiably and end up dying themselves. What I would like to suggest here is that this is no accident. To abstractly privilege "life," paradoxically, is to equally privilege death, for all of the particular things that we generally take to make life worthwhile are leveled for the sake of "life" itself, as the excerpt that introduces this chapter aptly reflects. To solipsistically become one with "life" is to become an abstract self, and, ultimately, no self at all, which not only prefigures but implicitly privileges the nothingness that the self becomes in death. In the final analysis, as we shall see, this is the logic innate to the abstract privileging of "life."

From Mersault (*A Happy Death*) to Meursault (*The Stranger*)

Mersault was ridding himself of everything, of himself as well.
Albert Camus, *A Happy Death*[2]

A Happy Death begins with a rather strange murder: Patrice Mersault enters the home of Roland Zagreus, and, after hesitating only momentarily, heads toward a chest, from which he withdraws a suicide note penned by Zagreus, a thick stack of money ("twenty packets of hundreds"), and a revolver. Mersault eyes Zagreus, who silently stares back from his wheelchair, and proceeds to blow Zagreus's brains out. At this moment, Mersault begins to feel feverish, which is a portent of his own death at the end of the novel.

Part I of *A Happy Death*, incongruously titled "Natural Death," builds toward Zagreus's decidedly unnatural death, giving us a sense of both Mersault and the circumstances that lead up to his commission of this murder. Mersault is employed as a shipping clerk, and his aim during office hours is to find "a way of escaping into life" (HD, p. 17). He has a few acquaintances but is generally inclined to spend his Sundays sitting alone on the balcony of his shabby apartment, which he had shared with his mother before her death. Mersault's neighbors "recalled the son's deep feeling for his mother," and, while she was alive, "he had continued to read, to reflect," but her death forced him to get a job (HD, p. 14). Mersault has a girlfriend, Marthe, but he is cool toward her, making clear that he is only interested in the sex, and Marthe, in turn, largely accepts Mersault's coldness, which she does not understand, although she "frequently noticed Mersault's gestures in strangers, in film actors" (HD, p. 28). When Marthe runs across an old boyfriend in Mersault's presence, however, his attitude radically changes, and he jealously demands that she give him a list of the men with whom she has slept. One such man was Zagreus, who had since lost his legs, and Marthe introduces the two men, for she thinks that they have much in common. After an initial meeting that includes Marthe, Mersault returns to Zagreus's home alone, and the two men speak frankly. "To devote myself to impersonality – that's what concern[s] me" (HD, p. 38), Mersault tells Zagreus, as he goes on to relate his fervent desire to live a passionate life. Zagreus acknowledges that the necessity of earning a living precludes such a life, and that money is needed to buy back the time of one's life, at which point he shows Mersault the money, suicide note, and revolver in his chest. Just before Mersault leaves, Zagreus states: "Don't take anything seriously except happiness. Think about it, Mersault, you have a pure heart" (HD, p. 47). The next morning Mersault returns to Zagreus's home and kills him.

Part II of *A Happy Death*, titled "Conscious Death," deals with Mersault's efforts to make good the life for which he has killed. Mersault travels through Europe, but instead of achieving happiness he plunges into despair, as even his longing for happiness progressively diminishes. A letter from two old female friends inviting him to stay with them comes at just the right time, for "poisoned by solitude and alienation," he believes that he needs "to withdraw into friendship and confidence, to enjoy an apparent security before choosing his life," which involved "creating his happiness and his justification" (HD, pp. 79–81). Although Mersault does enjoy his time with his friends, and, indeed, meets Lucienne, whom he marries, he now comes to the conclusion that he must live in solitude to be happy, although once he achieves his solitude, he is disconcerted by it. According to the ever-reflective Mersault, "happiness implie[s] a choice, and within that choice a concerted will, a lucid desire," which must be pressed into the service of detaching himself from all of his old habits (HD, p. 118). Nevertheless, "Mersault, stripped of all his props, still tried to locate them in a life which had nothing but itself to consider" (HD, pp. 119–20). It is only when his "mind denies the mind" that he can "touch his truth and with it his extreme glory, his extreme love" (HD, p. 122). Immersed in nature, Mersault gradually yields to his illness: "his life seemed so remote to him, he was so solitary and indifferent to everything and to himself as well," that he sensed "he had at last attained the peace that he was seeking, that the peace which filled him now was born of that patient self-abandonment that he had pursued and achieved" (HD, pp. 138–9). The way already well prepared, Mersault now dies a happy death, as he returns to the truth of the earth from which he had sprung.

There is a good deal to comment on here, but I shall refrain from doing so until we are in a position to compare Patrice Mersault with Meursault. Still, what I would like to preliminarily suggest is that, from a phenomenological perspective (i.e., from the perspective of a methodical description of the way that the world is experienced), Meursault begins where Patrice Mersault ends. Patrice Mersault, who self-reflectively strives toward impersonality, comes to fruition as Meursault, who appears to be characterized by impersonality and the utter lack of self-reflection that is the condition of impersonality's possibility. While, for Patrice Mersault, it takes a "slow decomposition" to facilitate the "self-abandonment" that will "restore him to the world" (HD, pp. 149–50), Meursault seemingly begins from this oneness with the world, and it is for this reason that he has no first name. Unlike the last name, which identifies us with a family whose ongoing reproduction is of a piece with the (natural) world, the first name is linked with an individual's personality (as is suggested by our more narcissistic movie stars, who in identifying themselves exclusively by their first names are asserting that they are unique, self-generating personalities), and Meursault has no personality.

What's more, by virtue of the fact that, from a phenomenological perspective, Mersault comes to fruition as Meursault, the narrative form must change, for the third-person perspective of A Happy Death could not adequately capture the strikingly impersonal nature of Meursault's experience of the world. Narratively speaking, however, what is unusual about The Stranger is not Camus's mere assumption of the first-person perspective but, rather, the tense in which the story is told, the French passé composé (in English, the present perfect tense). As Sartre says in his review of The Stranger, "it was in order to emphasize the isolation of each sentence unit that Mr Camus chose to tell his story in the present perfect tense," for by making each sentence "a present instant" that "refuses to exploit the momentum accumulated by the preceding ones," the transcendent moment is eliminated: "the transitive character of the verb has vanished [and] the sentence has frozen."[3] The relation between the language in which Meursault tells his story and his impersonality shall be considered in greater detail, but, in the meantime, it should be pointed out that A Happy Death and The Stranger are otherwise structured along roughly the same lines. Like A Happy Death, The Stranger is comprised of two parts, with the first part culminating in the lead character's murder of another (although the first part of A Happy Death also starts with the murder and then makes it intelligible by detailing the events that lead up to it) and the second part culminating in the lead character's own (impending) death.

The storyline of *The Stranger* is straightforward: Part I begins with Meursault's receipt of a telegram indicating that his mother has died and his resulting attendance at her funeral. On returning from the funeral, Meursault, who works as a shipping clerk, immediately recommences his life. He goes swimming the next day, meets his casual girlfriend Marie, who sleeps with him that evening, and spends a boring Sunday by himself (in a scene that is a virtual replay of the one in *A Happy Death*). With the start of the new work week, Meursault encounters the people that constitute his day-to-day existence, such as his boss, his co-worker Emmanuel, the restauranteur Céleste, and his neighbor Salamano, but Meursault also meets for the first time Raymond Sintès, a neighborhood pimp, and the two become friends. During the remainder of the week, Meursault goes about his business, which includes backing up one of Raymond's stories at the local police station, and, on the following Sunday, he and Marie set off with Raymond for the beach house of one of Raymond's friends. Before boarding the bus, they notice a group of Arabs, one of whom has a quarrel with Raymond, and, at the beach, they see the group of Arabs again, at which point a fight breaks out in which Raymond is wounded. Meursault, Raymond, and Raymond's friend withdraw to the beach house, but Meursault decides to take another walk on the beach, where he again comes across Raymond's Arab. During the earlier fight, Raymond had handed Meursault his gun, and now, in an ambiguous situation, spotting the knife that had cut Raymond, Meursault draws the gun, shoots once, striking the Arab, briefly pauses, and then shoots four more times at the motionless body. Part II begins after Meursault's arrest, and is constituted by various official interrogations of Meursault, empty time, and the trial, at which Meursault is found guilty, less for what he did than for who he "is" (or, at least, who he had been, since the legal process changes him). Meursault is sentenced to death, and, shortly before his execution, he is visited on a number of occasions by the priest, who seeks to "save" him. Meursault will have none of this, asserting the sole value of the sensual experiences of this world as against the priest's next world.

Although the storyline of *The Stranger* is interesting enough, what makes this one of the truly great modern works of literature is Meursault's consciousness: his experience of the world, his experience of himself, and the interrelation between these two things capture the extremes of what is a peculiarly modern sensibility.

Meursault: Outsider or Stranger?

The Stranger is, finally, myself in relation to myself, that is, natural man in relation to mind.

Jean-Paul Sartre, "Camus' *The Outsider*"[4]

Camus's *L'Etranger* has alternatively been translated into English as *The Outsider* (England) and *The Stranger* (the United States), and although both translations are technically appropriate, *The Stranger* is far more faithful to the work itself. At the risk of nitpicking, "the outsider" raises the specter of one who is estranged from society, but it indicates nothing about the character of the one who is estranged, while "the stranger" goes further, for it raises the specter not only of one who is estranged from society but of one who is inherently strange besides. This distinction goes to the heart of how to make sense of Meursault, and although it is a distinction that Camus never explicitly makes, he implicitly weighs in by describing Meursault more as "the outsider" than as "the stranger":

> The hero of my book is condemned because he does not play the game. In this respect, he is foreign to the society in which he lives; he wanders, on the fringe, in the suburbs of private, solitary, sensual life. And this is why some readers have been tempted to look upon him as a piece of social wreckage. . . . [I]f one asks just *how* Meursault doesn't play the game, the reply is a simple one: he refuses to lie. To lie is not only to say what isn't true. It is also and above all to say *more* than is true, and, as far as the human heart is concerned, to express more than one feels. This is what we all do, every day, to simplify life. He says what he is, he refuses to hide his feelings, and immediately society feels threatened. . . . For me, therefore, Meursault is not a piece of social wreckage, but a poor and naked man enamored of a sun that leaves no shadows. Far from being bereft of all feeling, he is animated by a passion that is deep because it is stubborn, a passion for the absolute and for truth. This truth is still a negative one, the truth of what we are and what we feel, but without it no conquest of ourselves or the world will ever be possible. . . . One would therefore not be much mistaken to read *The Stranger* as the story of a man who, without any heroics, agrees to die for the truth. I also happened to say, again paradoxically, that I had tried to draw in my character the only Christ that we deserve. (LCE, pp. 335–7)

Meursault is not just "foreign to the society in which he lives," as Camus says here. The renowned opening lines of *The Stranger* – "Maman died today. Or yesterday maybe, I don't know" – evoke a character that is strange by the standards of any society, and not only those of "the society in which he lives." Of course, there exist mother-son relationships that are severely wanting, but Meursault's use of "maman," the French equivalent of "mama" or "mommy," tends to suggest a closeness that belies his casual reportage, and, more generally, the indifference that he exhibits with respect to her death. Indeed, Meursault is strange even by Camus's lights, as is evidenced in two other references by Camus to the mother-son relationship: the first, as we saw, occurs in *Nuptials*, in which Camus speaks appreciatively of the "unreflective" Algerian ethical code that declares "you don't let your mother down" (LCE, p. 87), and the second occurs during Camus's questioning in connection with his Nobel Prize, when he famously states that while he believes in justice, he would defend his mother before justice. What's more, beyond the mother-son relationship, and, indeed, beyond justice itself, Meursault has no commitment to any code of ethics at all, whether reflective or unreflective, collective or individual, which not only puts him at odds with all societies but also with Camus's own starkly individualist ethics of the Absurd in *The Myth of Sisyphus*, as even the Don Juan, the Actor, and the Conqueror live far more coherent lives, not to mention the loftier Nietzschean (Self-)Creator. At first blush, then, Meursault surely appears to be "a piece of social wreckage."

Still, according to Camus, Meursault "doesn't play the game" at least to the extent that he "refuses to lie," which does imply some minimalist ethics. Plainly, however, Meursault does not have any compunction about lying. When Raymond asks Meursault to fabricate a letter for him to woo back one of his prostitutes, who had cheated on Raymond and was brutally beaten for it, Meursault has no problem doing so, although even the sentiment expressed in the pimp's letter is a lie, for Raymond seeks to woo back the woman just to spit in her face. So, too, when Raymond asks Meursault to lie to the police for him in connection with the brutal beating that he had given to her, Meursault agrees to do this and then follows through, simply noting that the police never checked out his statement. Given the context, Meursault's lies surely cannot be justified even by those who believe that lying can be justified when certain beneficial consequences follow. Now, Camus does further qualify what it means to lie by asserting that beyond saying what is not true, lying "is also *and above all* to say more than is true, and, as far as the human heart is concerned, to express more than one feels." In this sense, perhaps Meursault is truthful, for he is true to his feelings, even if not to the letter of the truth, as Conor Cruise O'Brien stated in a relatively early book on Camus's work. Nevertheless, it is not clear that Meursault is true to his feelings, and, indeed, it is not even clear that Meursault has feelings, if by feelings we mean emotions instead of bare, stripped-down sensations. I shall return to this question in the next section.

In the meantime, however, if we are to make sense of Camus's claim that Meursault "is animated by a passion . . . for the absolute and for truth," we must consider it within the context of his broader philosophical position, as it is articulated in *The Myth of Sisyphus*. For Camus, it will be recalled, the Absurd, when comprehended metaphysically rather than phenomenologically, is characterized by consciousness searching for meaning in a universe that refuses to bequeath it, a universe whose indifference toward our need for meaning condemns humanity to living "without appeal." It is for this reason that Camus claims that the Don Juan, the Actor, and the Conqueror represent "styles of life" that are not inconsistent with the Absurd (although, of course, the "style of life" that he prefers is that of the Creator): these are "men who think clearly and have ceased to hope" (MS, p. 92), for "in the absurd world the value of a notion or of a life is measured by its sterility" (MS, p. 69). Although, as we shall soon see, Meursault is a qualitatively more extreme example of hopeless sterility than the Don Juan, the Actor, and the Conqueror, Camus's assertion that he is honest must be understood along roughly the same lines. Meursault not only perceives the futility of hoping (not to mention forging ethical values) in the face of a meaningless universe in which "all experiences are unimportant" (MS, p. 62), but he actually lives his life accordingly. Therefore, when Meursault coolly lies to the police on behalf of Raymond, he is being dishonest in a conventional sense, but from the viewpoint of our metaphysical condition he is being honest, for ultimately, just like the death of his mother, it makes no difference. So, too, when Meursault failed to invest these same happenings with a nonexistent meaning for the prosecutor, judge, and jury, and thus was not only convicted but also sentenced to death, he was established as a martyr whose death would bear witness to the essential truth of the human condition. It is in this way, as Camus puts it, that Meursault is "the only Christ that we deserve." Meursault, in other words, is the metaphysically honest man, which he himself implies in the early morning hours of the day of his execution: "I opened myself to the gentle indifference of the world. Finding it so much like myself – so like a brother, really – I felt that I had been happy and that I was happy again" (S, pp. 122–3).

Is it the case, however, that under the threat of death a metaphysically honest man would refuse to lie to his judges with regard to how he felt about his mother's death? Lying for himself would have been no more nor less a violation of the metaphysical truth that Meursault ostensibly held dear than lying for the neighborhood pimp. Indeed, insofar as Camus contends in *The Myth of Sisyphus* that it is the quantity rather than the quality of life that is to be privileged, Meursault *should* have lied to extend his life, and, in fact, Meursault's archetype, Sisyphus, lied not once but twice to the gods to extend his life. Why, then, didn't Meursault lie? O'Brien's claim that it is because "his own feelings, and his feelings about his feelings, are sacrosanct" is too contrived, and the example that he uses to show Meursault's alleged fealty towards his feelings, that while Raymond beat the Arab girl he did not send for the police because he dislikes them,[5] manifests a more complicated psychological phenomenon. For the present, however, it bears emphasis that the picture of Meursault that I have taken from Camus, that Meursault is a metaphysically honest man, does not justify O'Brien's claim that he is true to his feelings, for the metaphysically honest man is as indifferent to his feelings as the universe is to him. Moreover, if our engagement with the universe is fraught with meaninglessness and ambiguity, as Camus believed, then the relation between the metaphysically honest man and his lifeworld would similarly follow suit, which is just what we see when Meursault kills the Arab.

A more promising way of approaching the question of Meursault's truthfulness is opened up by Solomon, who maintains that

> Meursault neither lies nor tells the truth, because he never reaches that (meta-) level of consciousness where truth and falsity can be articulated. . . . Meursault is a philosophically fantastic character who, for the first part of the novel, is an ideal Sartrean prereflective consciousness, pure consciousness without reflection, always other than, but also nothing other than, what he is conscious of at the moment.[6]

Understood in this way, as it both exists for him and is revealed to us, Meursault's consciousness is tantamount to a "piece of flat, colorless glass,"[7] which is another way of saying that the first-person account that we are getting of what he is experiencing is, in fact, what *he* is experiencing, but what the strangeness of the first part of the novel shows is that the experiences of an ideal prereflective consciousness come to very little. To be sure, Meursault has various pleasant and unpleasant experiences, but these pleasant and unpleasant experiences are limited to sensations, for to talk about experiences that transcend the immediacy of the five senses as either pleasant or unpleasant signifies that one has already engaged in a reflective judgment, which is precisely what Meursault does not do. Thus, Meursault finds such things as drinking coffee and milk, smoking cigarettes, and the look, feel, smell, and taste of Marie's body pleasant, while he finds such things as soggy towels in the men's room and Sundays unpleasant. Yet, when Raymond tells Meursault about beating up one of his prostitutes because "she refused to work" and then asked Meursault "what [he] thought of the whole thing," Meursault relates "I didn't think anything but that it was interesting" (S, p. 32), and when Marie asks Meursault whether he loves her, Meursault relates "I told her it didn't mean anything but that I didn't think so" (S, p. 35). Meursault could not have chosen a more revealing response to Marie, "it didn't mean anything," for at an unremittingly prereflective level nothing can actually mean anything.

From all appearances, then, Solomon's claim would seem to be correct. Meursault is a "philosophically fantastic character" by virtue of his utter lack of reflection, and, especially, self-reflection, the necessary condition of selfhood as such, and being "true to his feelings" amounts to little more than the animal's response to its physical environment. In this sense, the quotation from Sartre that opens this section, that "the Stranger is, finally, myself in relation to myself, that is, natural man in relation to mind," is on target. Meursault appears to be the thoroughly "natural man," and therefore, quite literally, "selfless." However, what if there are aspects of Meursault's consciousness of which even he himself is not aware, aspects that remain undisclosed because he does not reflect on them. The contents of these estranged aspects of his consciousness could not be disclosed to us by virtue of the book's first-person perspective, which limits us to Meursault's highly restricted experience of the world. Theoretically, then, there could be more to Meursault than meets the eye. To confirm whether this is the case, of course, we are relegated to drawing inferences from what is presented to us, but sometimes these are enough to bear fruit, as we shall see in the next section. In the meantime, however, it bears emphasizing that the intense visceral response that Meursault evokes in many who read *The Stranger*, irrespective of whether it takes the form of identification or revulsion (or both), belies the inference that there is nothing more to Meursault, for such a character could not generate this type of response. Indeed, these responses to Meursault suggest that he is the ideal limit of an actual existential temptation, and although he is "philosophically fantastic" precisely because he achieves an extreme that would be off limits to us, his ploy, in a less extreme form, is one of our existential choices and, indeed, is an object lesson with respect to it.

Meursault's "Selflessness"

When I enter most intimately into what I call *myself*, I always stumble on some particular perception or other, of heat or cold, light or shade, love or hatred, pain or pleasure. I never can catch *myself* at any time without a perception, and never can observe any thing but the perception.

David Hume, *A Treatise of Human Nature*[8]

A self-consciousness exists for a self-consciousness. Only so is it in fact self-consciousness; for only in this way does the unity of itself in its other-ness become explicit for it.

G. W. F. Hegel, *Phenomenology of Spirit*[9]

In *The Myth of Sisyphus*, Camus says that "the great philosophical novelists" show a preference "for writing in images rather than in reasoned arguments," which evidences a certain thought that is common to all of them: they are "convinced of the uselessness of any principle of explanation and sure of the educative message of perceptible appearance" (MS, p. 101). For Camus, abstract philosophy falsifies by attempting to go beyond its subject matter rather than allowing its subject matter to speak for itself, and, for this reason, "philosophical novels" can get to the truth in a way that philosophy, which deals in abstract concepts, cannot. What Camus has done in *The Stranger* is to project this commitment on to Meursault. It is Meursault himself who is "convinced of the uselessness of *any* principle of explanation," and, indeed, anything that is even a condition of the possibility of "*any* principle of explanation," and thus, I shall argue, he has *chosen* to live his life on the level of "perceptible appearances" rather than "reasoned arguments." Meursault, in other words, has *chosen* to live his life on the level of pure, unreflective experience, which gives rise to various questions that must be looked at in the course of our consideration of him. In particular, how does Meursault come to cognize the world in this fashion, what is the "educative message" of the perceptible appearance for Meursault, and, ultimately, what is the "educative message" of Meursault's choice for us?

As has already been suggested, from all appearances, Meursault is "selfless" (in the first part of the novel), and it is this selflessness, which results from his refusal to reflect, that enables him to cognize the world in the peculiar way that he does. Thus, if the move from consciousness in general to that specific form of consciousness that we call self-consciousness is the move from having a series of unreflective perceptions to having a reflective conception of oneself and one's perceptions, then what makes Meursault "philosophically fantastic" is his complete reversal of field, his move from self-consciousness back to consciousness in general. In order to make sense of just what this means, it is necessary to briefly look at the relation between selfhood, reflection, and perception.

To begin with, the nature of this thing that we call "the self" is more problematic than our ordinary use of the terms suggests. What is this "self" that we all take for granted? When Hume stated that "when I enter most intimately into what I call *myself* . . . I never can catch *myself* at any time without a perception, and never can observe any thing but the perception," he was arguing that "the self" as such is not something that can be experienced, and thus the term might not actually refer to anything at all. In response to Hume, Kant agreed that "the self" could not be observed in perception, but he argued that Hume presupposed the very thing that he could not find. The "I" that looks into "myself," according to Kant, is not going to find the self in a perception because it is the condition of the possibility of even having a perception. In other words, the "I," which Kant labels "the transcendental unity of apperception," stands behind my perceptions and unifies them, thus enabling me to recognize my continuing stream of disjointed perceptions as mine. Although Kant solves Hume's problem, he gives rise to another, however. This "self," the transcendental unity of apperception, is not the self to which we usually refer, the empirical self or ego, which makes each of us the individuals who we are, but rather an abstract concept that we posit as existing simply by virtue of the way in which we experience the world. For Kant, the empirical self or ego, which (unlike the transcendental unity of apperception) can be made the object of our reflections, is merely the stuff of anthropology. In response to Kant, Hegel contended that the transcendental condition (i.e., the condition of the possibility) of the empirical self or ego is none other than an interpersonal framework, or what Hegel calls Spirit, which roughly is humanity (or, in philosophical terms, "the subject") writ large. Arguing against a long tradition of "state-of-nature" theorists, who presupposed the isolated, autonomous individual or self as the basic philosophical building block (e.g., Descartes, Hobbes, Locke, Leibniz, and Rousseau), Hegel argues that the self, understood in terms of the empirical self or ego, is a product of interpersonal relations and, ultimately, the social world instead of a condition of it. When Hegel says that "a self-consciousness exists for a self-consciousness [and] only so is it in fact self-consciousness, for only in this way does the unity of itself in its otherness become explicit for it," he is saying that each of us is the result of our interactions with other selves and, finally, Spirit, the collective self-understanding (as in "the spirit of the times"), which itself is the result of a long, complex sociohistorical process.

Viewed in Hegel's terms, Meursault's self-consciousness does not exist for another self-consciousness, and due to this fact he himself does not rise to the level of self-consciousness. In other words, Meursault's perceptions are both solipsistic and selfless. When his mother's friends in the old-age home are ushered into the room with the casket, Meursault says that while he "saw them more clearly than [he] had ever seen anyone . . . it was hard for [him] to believe they really existed" (S, p. 9), and when he proceeds to smoke cigarettes, drink coffee, and otherwise remain emotionless, he has an off-the-cuff intuition: "For a second I had the ridiculous feeling that they were there to judge me" (S, p. 10). Of course, given the way that he was conducting himself, any person who was even remotely attuned to what others were thinking would not have had to think twice about this, but for Meursault it scarcely rises to the level of a vague presentiment. So, too, after Marie asks Meursault if he loves her and he replies that he "didn't think so," Meursault only says "she looked sad" before he is promptly distracted by other matters (S, p. 35). Undoubtedly she did look sad, but while this is a veritable epiphany for Meursault, for any person who is even remotely attuned to others it would be painfully self-evident just by virtue of the circumstances. Beyond his obliviousness to others, Meursault is virtually selfless in even the abstract Kantian sense, for although he can technically recount the various sensations he experiences over time as his own, they do not have the feel of a unity for him. As Sartre puts it, Meursault does not experience a "causal link" between, say, telling Marie that he does not love her and her sad look, but instead experiences this and everything else as "the simple appearance of succession": "The world dissolves and is reborn with each pulsation of time."[10]

Meursault thus seems to be the instantiation of Hume's philosophical conception of the "I," the "I" of isolated perceptions that cannot find its "self" in any of them. To live at the level of pure, unreflective experience as Meursault does, however, is not to "get into" the experience, as Camus seems to imply, for if one does not reflect one cannot have a lively sensual experience. Of course, since Kierkegaard, many existentialists have spoken of the death of experience due to reflection, and this is why many have concluded that all variants of existentialism privilege some form of irrationalism, but what virtually all of these existentialists have been attacking is a hyper-reflection that they see as endemic to the modern age, not reflection as such. To step back from one's life completely (as it were) and live it as if from a third-person perspective may well bring about the death of any experience worth having (as we shall see when we consider Jean-Baptiste Clamence of *The Fall*), but to immerse oneself in "life" completely and live it exclusively from the first-person perspective is also the death of experience, for previous reflection constitutes the foundation on which genuine sensual experiences arise. Although a superficial "oneness" with one's experiences can be attained by either a solipsistic withdrawal from the world into the realm of reflection (because the world does not meet our expectations and thus we fabricate a different world) or an unreflective collapse into the world of experience (because the world does not meet our expectations and thus we abandon our expectations), the experience of "oneness" that is the mark of true sensual experiences results from an exceedingly complex interrelation of experience and reflection. Meursault's wholesale collapse into the world, which means that his experiences are the stuff of those life situations that contingently happen to come his way, thus operates as a prophylactic as to the true sensual experience. Meursault's senses might tingle with Marie, but because these sensations are atomized and unemotional one gets the sense that they would tingle no less with an anatomically correct doll.

Now, I previously claimed that Meursault has *chosen* to live his life on this level of pure, unreflective experience, and on two occasions in *The Stranger*, both of which revolved around being questioned by an authority figure, we see that Meursault was not always the unreflective, selfless individual with whom we are confronted at the start of the book. On the first occasion, Meursault's employer confronted him with the possibility of taking a position with a new branch office in Paris. After a short encounter in which Meursault expressed his typical indifference to the proposition, to which the employer responded that he suffered from a grave lack of ambition, Meursault tells us: "I would rather not have upset him, but I couldn't see any reason to change my life. Looking back on it, I wasn't unhappy. When I was a student, I had lots of ambition like that. But when I had to give up my studies I learned very quickly that none of it really mattered" (S, p. 41). On the second occasion, shortly after Meursault killed the Arab, his attorney asked him whether he had experienced grief over his mother's death. Relating the incident, Meursault tells us: "I answered that I had pretty much lost the habit of analyzing myself and that it was hard for me to tell him what he wanted to know. I probably did love Maman, but that didn't mean anything" (S, p. 65). Because he was questioned in these encounters, Meursault was forced to reflect, which means that he was forced to reflect on his underlying choice not to reflect, which would then expose and thus endanger this basic choice of himself in the world. As I shall argue in the next section, Meursault's project is self-deceptive at its core, but in the meantime it should be pointed out that this is the reason that he does not like to be questioned (S, p. 21). Contrary to O'Brien's claim, this is also why Meursault refuses to call the police: it is not just that he "dislikes" them.

Fortunately, Meursault had a job that was compatible with his desire not to be questioned, for his responsibilities largely involved the solitary task of wading through bills of lading, but for such a man, a purported sensualist who loves the sand and the sea, it should be Sunday that is the day on which he truly lives. Yet, Meursault tells us, Sunday is the very day that he cannot abide. On the first Sunday that he recounts, Meursault, after having spent the night with Marie, woke up, saw that she was no longer there, and then was seized by an unpleasant thought: "I remembered that it was Sunday, and that bothered me: I don't like Sundays" (S, p. 21). Meursault went back to sleep, ate lunch, and then felt "a little bored." After reading the newspaper and cutting out an advertisement "just for something to do," he went out to the balcony, where, for the remainder of the day, he focused his attention on the parade of people in the street. At nightfall, as if to make sure that, with no distractions, he had not inadvertently begun to reflect back the self that he had once smothered, Meursault glanced in the mirror, in which he saw only the corner of his table, a few pieces of bread, and his lamp, which relieved him: "It occurred to me that anyway one more Sunday was over" (S, p. 24).

Meursault's failure to see his own reflection in the mirror could not be a more appropriate metaphor for his "selflessness," as viewing my reflection in the mirror is the way in which, quite literally, I inspect my self. For Meursault, of course, there is nothing to inspect, there is no self, and, therefore, he does not see himself in the mirror. As we shall see in Part II, when Meursault is incarcerated, he will start to see his reflection, which is no less appropriate, for while in jail he will become self-conscious. In the meantime, however, it should be clear that Meursault dislikes Sundays because, more than any other day of the week, it is the day on which his consciousness is most likely to be thrown back onto itself, which is part of the back and forth that constitutes self-reflection and, finally, selfhood. Of course, this is not to say that Camus's revelatory "why" in *The Myth of Sisyphus* cannot arise when one is at work, but it is to say that for someone who has "lost the habit of analyzing himself" because he has anteriorly chosen not to analyze himself, the office, with its mind-numbing tasks, can be a very receptive place. Ironically, then, although Camus demands in *The Myth of Sisyphus* that we maintain lucidity in the face of the Absurd and Mersault declares in *A Happy Death* that "happiness implie[s] a choice, and within that choice a concerted will, a lucid desire" (HD, p. 118), Meursault has tacitly adopted a policy of stripping lucidity from desire, which means that he refuses to reflect, refuses to will (beyond satiating his most basic, immediate desires or "physical needs," S, p. 65), and, ultimately, refuses to choose (which itself is a choice). How is such a policy formulated?

Meursault's "Bad Faith"

> [The person] who does not display care and concern for his engagement, who does not accept responsibility for it, is the person most ready to avow such engagements (viz., the youth who admitted that he quite consciously abandoned his aging, ailing mother alone in a car, since, as he readily also admitted, it made no real difference to him what happened to her). The person who cares deeply is, on the other hand, the one most tempted to disavow an engagement.
>
> Herbert Fingarette, *Self-Deception*[11]

Freedom and personal responsibility, and, more importantly, their opposites, the desire to escape from freedom and personal responsibility, are, in many respects, the hallmarks of existentialism, and this is surely true of French existentialism in virtually all of its manifestations. In *The Fall*, the hyper-reflective Jean-Baptiste Clamence says that "freedom is not a reward or a decoration that is celebrated with champagne . . . [but] it's a chore, on the contrary, and a long distance race, quite solitary and very exhausting" (F, pp. 132–3). Nevertheless, Clamence says that there are "no excuses ever, for anyone; that's my principle at the outset" (F, p. 131). By all appearances, Meursault does not even rise to the level at which freedom and personal responsibility are relevant notions at the start of *The Stranger*, and the account that he gives of his life (for which he offers no excuses) surely suggests this, but, as we have seen, this existential comportment itself must be understood as a free choice that was previously made. What I am suggesting, therefore, is that when we meet Meursault he is in self-deception, or, better, bad faith. (As Solomon rightly points out, while self-deception is a so-called paradox that merely goes to the belief in conflicting propositions, the belief in "x" and "not x," and how it is that we can come to lie to ourselves in this way, bad faith goes to the basic nature of our self-consciousnesses and, finally, ourselves.) Indeed, Meursault is not only in bad faith but is in its most extreme form, and it is in this way that he is "philosophically fantastic."

Although Sartre himself offers the most enlightening framework for making sense of the phenomenon of bad faith, I shall largely bypass its complexities, for it is inextricably intertwined with his phenomenological ontology, which is well beyond what can be considered here. Still, I shall draw in a more basic way on his insights, as well as the insights of other philosophers who work in this area, to show that Meursault is in a "radical" form of bad faith. To begin with, then, it is by virtue of our human capacity to "step back" from the "contents" of our consciousnesses at any point in time (i.e., from what it is that we are conscious of at any given moment) that enables us to speak of ourselves as free. Despite the seeming "logic" of my situation, in the very process of thematizing it, which is this "step back," I experience myself as free to choose how to conduct myself, and thus free to do other than that which I am heavily inclined to do. This space, which is the ground of my free choice, is not absolute, however. Although I am free to choose how to conduct myself with respect to the facts of this situation (for the facts never overdetermine how I might choose to approach them), it is, nevertheless, the facts of *this* situation that limit the range of my possible choices (and thus limit the range of those things that I might achieve through any one of these choices). Therefore, I am both free and unfree: I am absolutely free to choose how to approach the facts of any situation but I am unfree in terms of having to (freely) choose within some limiting factual situation, whose parameters might leave me with unsavory choices in terms of the kinds of ends that I might seek to achieve.

Now, structurally, this complex interrelationship finds direct expression in discussions of the self. When we speak of the self we speak of those qualities that we associate with ourselves, qualities that refer to the "facts" about us. Nevertheless, for Sartre, and, for that matter, virtually all of the existentialists, there is no inherent self but only what we have freely made of ourselves through our past choices, and what we will freely make of ourselves through our future choices. At any point in time, then, I must live my life in terms of a fundamental tension: I must live the facts that constitute myself insofar as the facts that constitute my past are what they are (e.g., my date of birth, my family, where I grew up, and what I have made of myself through all of my past choices, more generally), but I must also live my freedom by recognizing that I can always go beyond these facts that constitute myself in the future, all the while admitting that these facts (like the "situation" above) represent the necessary starting point at any given moment for all of my future projects. Thus, on Sartre's account, bad faith is the product of overemphasizing either the "facts" about me (my "facticity") or my freedom (my "transcendence," in the sense that I am always beyond my facticity). If I justify not coming to the aid of another by simply pointing to my history and stating that "I am a coward," I am overemphasizing my facticity at the expense of my freedom even if I do always engage in this sort of cowardly behavior, and if I depict myself as brave (or at least not a coward) despite the fact that I have a history filled with cowardly acts, I am overemphasizing my freedom at the expense of my facticity.

All persons in bad faith fall one way or the other off the tightrope that is good faith (and, indeed, it may well be the case that good faith is unachievable, given the kinds of beings that we are, although this question need not concern us). Despite the dual nature of bad faith, however, there is one basic characteristic that all individuals in bad faith (irrespective of whether they are fleeing from freedom or facticity) share in common: they are emphasizing some human qualities at the expense of other human qualities. To flee from freedom for facticity is to concretize those human qualities with which one currently identifies at the expense of those with which one might have come to identify (if one had stayed open to them), while to flee from facticity for freedom is to abstract from those human qualities that one currently evidences in favor of those that one has not yet evidenced (and, indeed, may never evidence). Moreover, the particular set of human qualities that a person chooses (or refuses to choose) at any point in time, whether the person is explicitly aware of these choices or not, is consonant with that person's self-conceptions, which are the result of one's fundamental choice of oneself in the world. Ultimately, then, what makes Meursault an example of "radical" bad faith, and thus "philosophically fantastic," is his unerring refusal to choose any human qualities whatsoever: Meursault has rejected nothing less than the intrinsic human responsibility of selfhood, thus negating the innate tension between freedom and facticity that gives both of them their very meaning.

The key to sustaining such a project (even in its less radical, human forms) is the refusal to reflect (and, especially, to self-reflect). As Herbert Fingarette contends in *Self-Deception*, bad faith is made possible by the basic distinction between prereflective and reflective consciousness. Prereflective consciousness is continuously engaged in the world at innumerable levels, and it is well beyond our capacity to be aware of all of our engagements. (For example, while the pencil sitting directly in front of my keyboard has been in my visual field for quite some time, I became aware of it only when I reflectively articulated its existence for the purpose of using it in this sort of example.) It is only when we "spell out" our engagements (i.e., reflect on them) that we truly become aware of them. Crucially, however, we do not spell out at random but, rather, implicitly seize up a situation to determine whether, given our underlying self-conceptions and the projects that arise from them, there is a compelling reason to spell out something or avoid spelling it out. (In my parenthetical example, there was no reason to spell out the existence of the pencil in front of me until I searched for an example to make clear the problem of bad faith, a task that is tied up with my underlying commitment to writing this book, and, more generally, identifying myself as a philosopher.) Accordingly, a repeated failure to spell out a particular engagement in the world does not arise from an inability to spell it out but, rather, "it is the adherence to a policy (tacitly) adopted. 'He cannot admit it, cannot let himself become conscious of it,' here means 'He will not'; but the 'will not' refers to a general policy commitment and not an *ad hoc* decision not to spell it out."[12]

Meursault's "general policy commitment," which is to selflessness itself (or, as Mersault states it, "impersonality"), demands that he spell out nothing whatsoever. As a result, Meursault comes across as a slab of malleable clay, a piece of *pre*-social human wreckage that utterly lacks in all causal efficacy and, therefore, exists for the indifferent universe to do with him as it will. It is not just that Meursault denies his particular choices, but, more radically, he denies (at least for him) the very concept of choice. Nevertheless, Meursault does makes choices, even if he does not articulate them as such, and all of these choices, in turn, relate back to his most fundamental choice, his general policy commitment toward selflessness, which is born of the belief that in an indifferent universe nothing makes any difference. Such a general policy commitment might be viewed as a form of suicide, or, if you will, "metaphysical" suicide, since, historically, the stuff of metaphysics includes such matters as the nature of freedom, personal responsibility, and self-identity, which are precisely the sorts of things that Meursault rejects in the face of what he (like Camus) takes to be an indifferent universe. An indifferent universe is an indifferent universe *for us* (or, at least, for Camus), however, and, as we saw in the last chapter, it is the result of our own projections in the wake of God's death. By an exceedingly odd reversal, then, the universe, as it is represented by the ubiquitous sun, comes to take on the personality that Meursault drains from both himself and those with whom he comes in contact.

In a way that qualitatively differs from everything else, it is the relentless, unfathomable sun that dominates the two events that lead to Meursault's demise. First, at his mother's funeral, at which Meursault doubts the existence of those around him, who sound like "parakeets" (S, p. 5), he speaks of the sun as he speaks of nothing else. He not only ceaselessly speaks of the heat, light, and discomfort that it generates, but, in a highly uncharacteristic fashion, he also speaks of its effects in a reflective way: "with the sun bearing down, making the whole landscape shimmer with heat, it was inhuman and oppressive" (S, p. 15). Second, it is the obtrusiveness of the sun that plays the determining role in the events that culminate in the Arab's death: "The sun was the same as it had been the day I'd buried Maman. . . . All I could feel were the cymbals of sunlight crashing on my forehead and . . . everything began to reel. The sea carried up a thick fiery breath. It seemed to me as if the sky split open from one end to the other to rain down fire. My whole body tensed and I squeezed my hand around the revolver" (S, pp. 58–9). What's more, toward the end of his trial, when the Judge asked Meursault what his motive for the crime had been, he tentatively placed the blame where he thought it belonged: "Fumbling a little with my words and realizing how ridiculous I sounded, I blurted out that it was because of the sun" (S, p. 103).

For Meursault, who is purportedly the "metaphysically honest man," the sun functions in a way that is diametrically opposed to the way that it functions for Plato. In *The Republic*, Plato suggests that the sun is the sensible correlate of the intelligible Idea of the Good, which is the condition of revelation and what grounds the Forms that we intellectually intuit (and the Forms, in turn, undergird all of our sensible truths). More simply put, the sun, as the sensible analogy of the intelligible Idea of the Good, is the ultimate foundation of meaning and truth. Contrarily, for Meursault, who sees the universe as "indifferent," the experience of the sun is the experience of pure meaninglessness and ambiguity, which is why it is "inhuman and oppressive," "crashing on his forehead" instead of enlightening his mind, and the scene with the Arab typifies this relation. Yet, all of this (including, one might argue, metaphysics itself) is in bad faith. Whether he killed the Arab in self-defense or not, it is Meursault, not the sun, that is the cause of the Arab's death. As Meursault's own account clearly evidences, he is making choices right up to the time that he kills the Arab, and even if he is unaware of these choices by virtue of his refusal to either reflect or spell out, he is still responsible for them by virtue of his anterior general policy commitment, his basic choice of selflessness. Indeed, it is this underlying commitment to selflessness instead of an "indifferent universe" that is the ultimate condition of the meaninglessness and ambiguity that Meursault discerns.

If we return to "the scene of the crime," then, we see, generally speaking, that Meursault is not just following the path of least resistance, is not just being buffeted by the universe, but is (purposely) acting against the grain. On returning from the altercation with the Arabs, in which Raymond was slashed, Meursault chooses not to follow Raymond up the stairs of the bungalow, although his "head [is] ringing from the sun," because he is "unable to face the effort it would take to climb the wooden staircase." Instead, in spite of the "intense" heat and "blinding stream" of light, which he could have escaped by going inside, he decides to walk back to the beach: "To stay or to go, it amounted to the same thing. A minute later I turned back toward the beach and started walking" (S, pp. 56–7). Predictably, as Meursault walked on the beach, he found the sun intolerable. Nevertheless, he tells us, "all that heat was pressing down on me and making it hard for me to go on. . . . I gritted my teeth, clenched my fists in my trouser pockets, and strained every nerve in order to overcome the sun" (S, p. 57). As Meursault progresses, he sees Raymond's Arab, which causes him to be "a little surprised," since "the whole thing was over, and I'd gone there without even thinking about it" (or, at least, spelling it out). At this point, the Arab, seeing Meursault, goes to the knife in his pocket, and Meursault, in reaction, grips Raymond's revolver. Now, in the midst of the heat, Meursault declares: "It occurred to me that all I had to do was turn around and that would be the end of it. But the whole beach, throbbing in the sun, was pressing on my back" (S, p. 58). There is now one last opportunity for Meursault to avoid a confrontation with the Arab, and he stood impassively, but not for long: "It was this burning, which I couldn't stand anymore, that made me move forward. I knew that it was stupid, that I wouldn't get the sun off me by stepping forward. But I took a step, one step, forward," and the Arab drew his knife. At this point, "the trigger gave; [Meursault] felt the smooth underside of the butt," and he "then fired four more times at the motionless body" for no apparent reason (S, p. 59).

Meursault's own rendition of the events immediately preceding the Arab's death indicate that he is making choices throughout this episode (even if he does self-deceptively state that "the trigger gave" rather than "I pulled the trigger"), as is illustrated by the fact that he is atypically battling *against* his vaunted "physical needs." Of course, by virtue of the psychic disintegration that arises from his radical form of bad faith, the project of selflessness, he cannot articulate why he made these choices, and, therefore, he attributes them to something outside of himself. Still, it is Meursault himself who is exclusively responsible for orchestrating the events that led to the death of the Arab, not a cruel metaphysics. As Aristotle would say, even if Meursault's actions were done "in ignorance" (i.e., even if we accept the idea that he was strictly ignorant of what he was doing when he killed the Arab), he must still be held responsible, for he was responsible for his choice of himself as a selfless being, which, as the root cause of this ignorance, makes it unjustifiable. Put differently, to choose to remain wholly prereflective and, therefore, to choose to spell out nothing – perhaps in the belief that a total plunge back into "life" is the best existential choice in the face of a morally compromised reality (as we have seen Camus himself imply with respect to Meursault in one of his less auspicious statements) – not only makes us prereflectively complicitous with the morally compromised reality from which we seek to escape but also does nothing to assuage our own personal guilt, as Meursault himself will come to realize.

Accordingly, while, in one sense, the extensive secondary literature on *The Stranger* that sees the novel's blind spot in terms of the harsh reality of French colonialism in Algeria is right, in another, deeper, sense it is missing the point. To be sure, there would be something extremely strange about any *pied-noir* that would be oblivious to the social and political realities of Algeria in the 1940s, a mere decade before an especially bloody anti-colonial war, but, of course, strange is precisely what Meursault is. It is true, as these critics contend, that when Meursault says such things as the Arabs "were staring at us in silence, but in that way of theirs, as if we were nothing but stones or dead trees" (S, p. 48), he is unwittingly recapitulating a deep social pathology, but, of course, Meursault describes everyone else, from the senior citizens whose existence he doubts (and who sound like parakeets) to "the robot woman" that he sees on two occasions, in much the same fashion. The fundamental point here is that by unreflectively plunging back into "life," it is not abstract, indeterminate "life" into which Meursault is returning but, rather, the life of a social context that is no longer thematized as such. Indeed, since the Meursault who makes this choice of himself is the Meursault who was produced within the crucible of the very social context from which he seeks to escape, the more successfully he refrains from reflecting on these background circumstances, the greater the probability that he will recapitulate them without, quite literally, "a second thought." Accordingly, if it is the case that Meursault strikes a disconcerting chord with his social critics, it is not because he is your standard colonizer but because his psychodynamics reflect, albeit in purified form, the run-of-the-mill bad faith that might be the condition of living one's life under such circumstances.

Meursault's Rebirth and Death

> But everybody knows life isn't worth living.
>
> Albert Camus, *The Stranger*[13]

Part II of *The Stranger*, which begins with Meursault freshly incarcerated and ends on the brink of his execution for killing the Arab, is primarily about Meursault coming to self-consciousness, for while in prison he is forced to reflect, and in this way selfhood is engendered. As Meursault comes back to himself, we are in a better position to see what inspired his radical bad faith in the first place, which, to say it preliminarily, is not so much a desire for life as a desire for death. In this way, he is just like his predecessor, Patrice Mersault.

Early on, while alternatively being questioned by the examining magistrate and his own lawyer, Meursault evidences his characteristic indifference toward his mother's death, the Arab's death, and the fact that Christ had died for his sins. This indifference is still due to the fact that he is selfless, which naturally makes him a curiosity, and thus the examining magistrate initially informs Meursault that "what interests me is you," which leads Meursault to tell us that "I didn't really understand what he meant by that" (S, p. 66). Yet, predictably, this interest soon turns to disdain, as the examining magistrate tells Meursault that "I have never seen a soul as hardened as yours" (S, p. 69), and subsequently, during the trial, the prosecutor says that after having looked into Meursault, "the truth was that [he] didn't have a soul and that nothing human, not one of the moral principles that govern men's hearts, was within [his] reach" (S, p. 101). Because what we ordinarily mean by the soul is actually a person's character, and character presupposes selfhood, what they are saying is, strictly speaking, true. Yet, by virtue of his continuing selflessness, what Meursault mostly is during the early stages of his incarceration is not soulless but rather (socially) oblivious, as is exhibited in a brief exchange with some Arab prisoners, which, in his recounting, assumes almost comic proportions: "[The Arabs] laughed when they saw me. Then they asked me what I was in for. I said I'd killed an Arab and they were all silent. A few minutes later, it got dark" (S, p. 72).

For Meursault, however, the condition of selflessness is about to change, for there are (at least) two aspects of his incarceration that all but ordain it. First, a day in prison for Meursault is akin to a Sunday on which he could not leave his apartment and expose himself to some form of undemanding stimulation, such as the beach or a movie. In prison, moreover, he could not even repair to his bedroom with Marie or to his balcony, where he could distract himself by watching the people on the street. Like Sundays, then, "once again the main problem was killing time" (S, p. 78), a problem to which prison could offer no answer. Under these conditions, consciousness may have nothing to focus on but itself. Second, unlike his life in the external world, where his unreflective consciousness was able to glide through a vast array of superficial social interactions largely unscathed, while in prison (and, especially, while on trial) Meursault becomes the center of attention, and his consciousness is forced back onto itself because that is where those around him are concentrating. Thus, when the prison guard informs Meursault that he has been in prison for five months, which seemed like "the same unending day," he tells us that "I looked at myself in my tin plate [and] my reflection seemed to remain serious even though I was trying to smile at it." It will be recalled that Meursault did not see himself in the mirror during the first part of the novel, but now the project of selfless-ness is doomed, and, therefore, Meursault begins not only to see himself (albeit incongruously) but also to "hear the sound of [his] own voice" (S, p. 81). In fact, during the early, naïve stages of this psychic rebirth, Meursault tells us that he begins to feel like "one of the family" and enjoys nothing better than being slapped on the back and called "Mr Antichrist" (S, pp. 70–71).

With the start of the trial on a day "with the sun glaring outside," the focus on Meursault intensifies, as "they [a]re all looking at him," and he, correspondingly, "had the odd impression of being watched by [him]self" (S, pp. 82–5). The court is packed not only with the personnel that make up the legal machinery, but also with reporters, a vast collection of potential witnesses against him (including the senior citizens from his mother's home and the people that comprised his daily existence), and, lastly, the general public, which, for Meursault, is embodied by the odd little robot woman whom he had previously watched and is now both watching and judging him. As the parade of witnesses testify more about the facts of the "soulless" existence that Meursault had lived than about the facts surrounding the Arab's death, Meursault comes to realize "how much all these people hated [him]," which leads to the following revela-tion: "For the first time I realized that I was guilty" (S, p. 90). Meursault's feeling of guilt here does not result from a premonition of "legal" guilt (although "legally" he will be found guilty) because, as has been indicated by others, in French colonial Algeria it is unlikely that Meursault would have even been tried for killing an Arab, especially given the operative legal facts. These facts suggest, moreover, that Meursault's feeling of guilt does not result from a feeling of "moral" guilt, and, indeed, it could be reasonably argued that Meursault should not feel morally guilty because he had killed in self-defense. (The same Arab had knifed his friend earlier in the day and was again going back to his pocket for the knife. The addi-tional four shots might be explained by adrenaline.) Meursault's feeling of guilt here is a feeling of "existential" guilt, the sort of guilt that arises from being "human," which, on the model of Christian metaphysics, might be understood in terms of "original sin." Indeed, put in Christian terms (and, as previously contended, Camus's problematic, the Absurd, arises from Christian metaphysics), Meursault's push for selflessness is a futile attempt to undo the original fall, when Adam becomes self-conscious by eating from the apple of knowledge. It is for this hubris that Meursault is finally convicted, and, understood in these terms, perhaps rightfully so.[14]

With respect to Meursault's ultimate conviction on existential rather than legal or moral grounds, I say "rightfully so" here because, as I have been arguing throughout, many of Camus's metaphysical positions make good sense when grasped phenomenologically. In a certain sense, all of us should feel existentially guilty, as is evidenced by the fact that we all, ineluctably, wear clothing and eat food produced by badly exploited human beings, many of them children. Or, put simply, we are all part of the social food chain, which is exactly what Meursault self-deceptively tries to deny with his inhuman bid for pre-social, selfless innocence (which then absolves him of the responsibility for changing these social conditions, thus lessening this ultimately ineradicable guilt). As a result, Meursault is easily depicted as a "monster" by the prosecutor (S, p. 102) and, therefore, easily convicted. Now fully self-conscious (or, at least, as self-conscious as "normal" folk get), Meursault has nothing but time to reflect on the trial and his impending death as he awaits execution in his prison cell. He is mortified by the obliviousness that he had shown with respect to the operations of the legal machinery that would convict him, the "arrogant certainty" of this legal machinery, and the idea of his own death, which would cause him to "get so cold that [he] would curl up into a ball under his blanket" (S, pp. 108–10). Clinging to hope, he also indulges in the fantasy that his appeal will be successful, which causes wild joy to well up in him. Yet, ultimately, it is when Meursault considers "the worst," the denial of his appeal, that he gives the game away, the impulse that had motivated his bid for selflessness from the very start: "Well, so I'm going to die . . . [b]ut everybody knows life isn't worth living" (S, p. 114). It is roughly at this point that, after having been repeatedly rebuffed by Meursault, the prison chaplain unexpectedly barges into the cell, thus occasioning in Meursault one more conversion of sorts.

The appearance of the unwanted chaplain causes Meursault to reaffirm his innocence, but this time reflectively, if not downright philosophically. Striking a Nietzschean pose, Meursault repeatedly rejects the chaplain's increasingly emotional appeal that he turn to God, provocatively refuses to admit that he even knows what sin is, and generally reaffirms this world, the world of Marie's face, the sun, the sand, and the sea, against the Christian other-worldly. "Do you really love this earth as much as all that?," the chaplain asks, to which, crucially, Meursault makes no reply (S, p. 119). It is at this point that Meursault "snaps," and, "yelling at the top of his lungs" that the chaplain was already "living like a dead man" (S, p. 120), reaffirms his life. If we listen closely to what Meursault is screaming, however, we can hear that it is not life but, rather, death that he is affirming, and we can see that Meursault, too, had been living like a dead man: "I had been right, I was still right, I was always right," for "nothing, nothing mattered, and I knew why. So did he. Throughout the whole absurd life I'd lived, a dark wind had been rising toward me from somewhere deep in my future," which had "leveled whatever was offered to me at the time" (S, p. 121). Meursault is basically conceding here that it was resentment, a resentment directed at "life" itself, that motivated his bid for self-destructive selflessness.

Calling his life "absurd," as Camus would have it in *The Myth of Sisyphus*, Meursault can be seen careening here from his purportedly Nietzschean commitment to affirming *this* life, which is suggested when he tells the chaplain that the only afterlife he would desire is "one where I could remember this one" (S, p. 120), to his anti-Nietzschean resentment, since, presumably, nothing would "matter" any more in the "remembrance." As Camus points out in *The Myth of Sisyphus*, the Absurd is characterized by antinomy, which, to be sure, is represented in these contradictory positions. At the end of the day, however, there can be no effective plunge back into life from the Absurd, and to start from the Absurd is to start from an insurmountable resentment, as is shown in Meursault's concluding wish: "I had only to wish that there be a large crowd of spectators the day of my execution and that they greet me with cries of hate" (S, p. 123).

What can be concluded from both Meursault and, for that matter, Patrice Mersault is that privileging abstract, indeterminate "life" is only the flip side of privileging death. When Camus refers to Meursault as "a poor and naked man enamored of a sun that leaves no shadows" despite the fact that he unreflectively kills the Arab (and otherwise engages in shameful behavior), and when he has Zagreus tell Mersault that he has "a pure heart" one day before Mersault reflectively blows his brains out, he is suggesting that the former is entirely "self-presencing," a being who is perfectly in the moment and at one with "himself" (which really means that he has no self), while the latter is "pure" because he has aspirations along these lines. Yet, as the quotation that opens this chapter suggests, this desire to be one with "life" acts as a Trojan horse for the Freudian idea of *thanatos*, the death drive, the desire to give up life's struggle and return to nature. The vivid expression of this drive in both characters exposes, in turn, what is, finally, their fierce hostility toward "life," which results from their (resentful) embrace of Camus's metaphysical concept of the Absurd. Meursault's last remark reflects this hostility, although he (and Mersault) often give lip service to the idea of "happiness." The final character that we shall consider, Caligula, has no such illusion concerning happiness, and thus he throws himself into life with a destructive fury.

From Meursault to Caligula

Universal freedom, therefore, can produce neither a positive work nor a deed; there is left for it only negative action; it is merely the fury of destruction . . . The sole work and deed of universal freedom is therefore death, a death too which has no inner significance or filling, for what is negated is the empty point of the absolutely free self. It is thus the coldest and meanest of all deaths, with no more significance than cutting off a head of cabbage or swallowing a mouthful of water.

G. W. F. Hegel, *Phenomenology of Spirit*[15]

Although Camus composed *Caligula* in 1938, the play was not performed until 1945, and during this period he revised it intermittently. In 1938, Camus had not yet begun working on either *The Stranger* or *The Myth of Sisyphus*, but by 1945 both of these works had been long published, and, more importantly, Camus had undergone the Nazi occupation (as well as his stint as the editor of the resistance newspaper *Combat*), which had a profound effect on his sensibilities. As a result, although Camus chiefly saw *Caligula* as the last work in his "Absurd cycle," this depiction does not do justice to the distinctive role that it plays in the evolution of his thought, as it betokens his break with the abstract, romantic, solipsistic commitment to "life" evidenced in *A Happy Death* and *The Stranger*. As Camus himself will retrospectively put it in a 1957 Author's Preface:

> Obsessed with the impossible and poisoned with scorn and horror, [Caligula] tries, through murder and the systematic perversion of all values, to practice a liberty that he will eventually discover not to be the right one. He challenges friendship and love, common human solidarity, good and evil. He takes those about him at their word and forces them to be logical; he levels everything around him by the strength of his rejection and the destructive fury to which his passion for life leads him. But if his truth is to rebel against fate, his error lies in negating what binds him to mankind. One cannot destroy everything without destroying oneself. (CTOP, pp. v–vi)

As this passage suggests, the resentment that implicitly motivates the abstract plunge into "life" is made explicit in *Caligula* (even though Camus continues to see it as the result of a "passion for life"), as are the consequences of the choice to live life accordingly. To be sure, Camus does not give up on the Absurd as his theoretical starting point, for he contends here that Caligula's "truth is to rebel against fate," but what Caligula makes exceedingly clear is that an abstract, romantic, solipsistic approach to the problem of the Absurd is not a viable one.

Camus loosely bases *Caligula* on Suetonius's *Twelve Caesars*, which discusses the life of the historical Caligula, Gaius Caesar Augustus Germanicus, who briefly ruled the Roman Empire in the century following Christ's death. Like the historical Caligula, Camus's Caligula is defined by his unparalleled depravity, but if this depravity can be unproblematically attributed to insanity in the case of the historical Caligula, in the case of Camus's Caligula matters are rather different. If his depravity is also the result of insanity, his insanity, in turn, is the result of what might strike us as a comparatively banal insight: "Men die; and they are not happy" (CTOP, p. 8). As Camus demonstrates, Caligula's renunciation of what the youthful Scipio characterizes as his (previous) concern with the suffering of others (CTOP, p. 10) is not for the sake of happiness, or even for an absurd happiness (whatever this might mean) but, rather, for the sake of a resentment engendered by the belief that happiness is unachievable. This is the theme that motivates the play, and unlike *The Stranger*, in which we get merely the truncated perspective of Meursault, in *Caligula* we get a variety of perspectives, three of which (the perspectives of Scipio, Cherea, and Caligula himself) represent aspects of Camus's own complex, multifaceted perspective.[16]

Caligula begins with the ruling circle apprehensively discussing the possible effects of Drucilla's death on the young emperor Caligula. From the conversation, it can be gathered that the group, which includes various patricians, Cherea, Scipio, and Helicon, sees Caligula as fairly pliable, but fears that the death of Caligula's sister (who was also, reportedly, his mistress) might effect his emotional state and, therefore, cause problems for the efficient administration of the Empire. On his return, Caligula bears out this fear but in an unanticipated way. The death of his sister does not lead to a particularized, debilitating grief but to a generalized, frenetic one. As Caligula puts it, "her death is not the point; it's no more than the symbol of a truth that makes the moon essential to me" (CTOP, p. 8). Caligula's demand for the moon, which reflects a demand for the impossible (that the arch-bureaucrat Helicon will mechanically seek to satisfy regardless of the cost), is his destructive response to death and unhappiness. This destructiveness plays out as follows: if the moon is off limits even to Caligula, a limitless freedom is not (*his* "freedom has no frontier," CTOP, p. 14), and this limitless freedom is employed with increasing fanaticism in its pursuit. By a peculiar inversion, however, when the impossible ideal that transcends arbitrary fate is not achieved, the limitless freedom turns around into its opposite in an attempt to mimic that which it cannot transcend: "There's no understanding fate," Caligula states, and "therefore I choose to play the part of fate" (CTOP, p. 44). This false transcendence ultimately turns on the one employing it, however, and thus Caligula's destructiveness is ultimately self-destructiveness. Accordingly, when Caligula states near the end of the play that "only the dead . . . are of my kind" (CTOP, p. 68), he not only embodies Camus's claim that "one cannot destroy everything without destroying oneself" but testifies to the misguided notion of freedom that underpinned his actions, which he explicitly acknowledges immediately before his assassination: "I have chosen a wrong path, a path that leads to nothing. My freedom isn't the right one" (CTOP, p. 73).

Caligula's increasing depravity throughout the play, his desire to use his freedom to "play the part of fate," is another variation on a dynamic that we saw unfold in both *The Stranger* and *A Happy Death*. In nearly every respect, Meursault and Caligula seem to be polar opposites, as Meursault, a poor working-class guy, chooses to be unreflective for the sake of happiness, while Caligula, the emperor of the Roman Empire, chooses a hyper-reflectivity in the face of what he takes to be an unachievable happiness. Yet, Meursault's ultimate motivations, I have suggested, are not unlike Caligula's. Meursault chooses not to reflect out of a contempt for the very social conventions that Caligula finds contemptuous, which both flout, and out of a despair in the face of the very absurdist metaphysics that drive Caligula insane. Moreover, like Caligula, Meursault "plays the part of fate," as is evidenced by the way that he describes his role in the death of the Arab (which he attributes to "the Sun," his metaphor for fate), and, like Caligula, he is indifferent to his impending death. In contrast to Meursault and Caligula, Patrice Mersault is an amalgam of sorts. Like Meursault, he is a working-class guy committed to happiness, but, like Caligula, he is reflective, and thus his cold-blooded murder of Zagreus has Caligula-like resonances. Yet, like both Meursault and Caligula, he, too, ultimately opens himself up to a "happy" death.

Interestingly, in *Caligula* there is a character who might be deemed a successor to Patrice Mersault and Meursault – Scipio. Like his predecessors, Scipio is young and devoted to "Nature," albeit in a richer, more expansive sense (he is an aesthete in the broadest sense of the term), and, like his predecessors, but with far greater insight, he recognizes that he bears certain similarities to Caligula. When Cherea asks Scipio to take part in the assassination of Caligula, he begs off, declaring that "something inside me is akin to him, [since] the same fire burns in both our hearts" (CTOP, p. 56). Unlike his previous works, however, Camus refuses to give pride of place to this fire at the expense of everything else. By virtue of Scipio's ambivalence in the face of Caligula's numerous atrocities (which include the gratuitous murder of his own father), Scipio is relegated to irrelevance, as he is unable to align himself either with Caligula, whose evil he recognizes, or with those who would do Caligula harm. So, too, if the restorative power of nature (the sun, the sand, and the sea) is no longer a panacea, neither is sexuality. While both Patrice Mersault and Meursault (ostensibly) take delight in sex, the same cannot be said for Caligula. The joys of sex, as they are embodied in Caesonia, Caligula's somewhat older mistress, contain no real attraction for Caligula, and, at best, are only momentary distractions. Sex, as Caligula puts it, is a "joyless pleasure" (CTOP, p. 70).

The most significant character in *Caligula* is Cherea, whose views most faithfully reflect Camus's at this point. Camus now thinks that nihilism reflects the ultimate logic of the Absurd, and, therefore, it must be attacked in practice, but in theory he continues to think that this logic is unimpeachable. Accordingly, Cherea, who would "rather be left to his books" (CTOP, p. 6) but ends up as the brains behind the conspiracy to kill

Caligula, concedes that Caligula's philosophy is "logical from start to finish," but he maintains, nevertheless, that "where one can't refute, one strikes" (CTOP, p. 21). This is a rather peculiar claim (since some things that cannot be refuted are truly justifiable and, therefore, should not be attacked), and it is expressed even more clearly in Cherea's confession that his "plan of life may not be logical, but at least it's sound." Cherea's "plan of life" is simply "to live and to be happy" (CTOP, p. 51), but, as he says, it is inconsistent with Caligula's "inhuman vision in which [his] life means no more than a speck of dust" (CTOP, p. 22). Cherea's view here is much stronger than he suggests, and if it seems illogical (although "sound") to him it is only because he misguidedly accepts Caligula's delineation of the Absurd.

Early in the *Nicomachean Ethics*, Aristotle famously states that one cannot ask for greater precision with respect to a given subject than that subject inherently permits, which was meant to signal that the ethics he was about to offer would not bear up to the same kind of logical analysis that could more fruitfully be brought to bear with respect to his other philosophical explorations. His point is well taken, and it applies here. When Cherea states that it is "intolerable to see one's life being drained of meaning" (CTOP, p. 21), he is correct, and there is nothing "illogical" about his commitment to a happy, meaningful life. If his views are "sound," however, it is not because they are the result of valid argumentation from true premises (which is the technical definition of "soundness") but because experience suggests that they are an indispensable condition of human flourishing. Conversely, if Caligula's views are "logical," it is only because they follow from his premise, the Absurd, but this premise, which Cherea also accepts, is false. Cherea realizes that neither life nor happiness "is possible if one pushes the absurd to its logical conclusions" (CTOP, p. 51), but why begin with the Absurd at all. As we observed in the last chapter, interpreting the Absurd in metaphysical terms is a mistake engendered by inappropriately taking an objectifying perspective on our lives (i.e., "the view from nowhere"), and Caligula's nihilism is the inevitable result of taking this perspective.

Finally, what Caligula shows is that even the one value that Camus does embrace in the face of the Absurd, "life," or, to be more precise, life understood exclusively in terms of quantity (with absolutely no reference to quality), cannot hold up. Caligula seems to take Camus's view when he asserts, in response to Cherea's contention that "some actions are . . . more praiseworthy than others," that "all [actions] are on an equal footing" (CTOP, p. 52), but if this is true, then it follows that murdering is no more nor less praiseworthy than any other action. However, if this is true, then it must be because life itself is valued no more nor less than anything else, or, to be more precise, like everything else, "life" is not valued at all. As Nietzsche asserted, the problem of nihilism is that "the highest values devalue themselves," and Caligula reflects the truth of this with respect to the value of "life," which, although the condition of value, cannot have any value in itself if none of the things that constitute it have any value.

notes

1   HD, p. 75.
2   Ibid., p. 25.
3   Jean-Paul Sartre, "Camus' *The Outsider*," in *Literary and Philosophical Essays*, trans. Annette Michelson (New York: Criterion Books, 1955), p. 41.
4   Jean-Paul Sartre, "Camus' *The Outsider*," p. 29.
5   Conor Cruise O'Brien, *Camus* (London: Fontana Modern Masters, 1970), p. 22.
6   Robert C. Solomon, *Dark Feelings, Grim Thoughts: Experience and Reflection in Camus and Sartre* (New York: Oxford University Press, 2006), pp. 15–16.
7   Ibid., p. 19.
8   David Hume, *A Treatise of Human Nature* (London: Penguin Books, 1969), p. 300.
9   G. W. F. Hegel, *Phenomenology of Spirit*, trans. A. V. Miller (Oxford: Oxford University Press), p. 110.
10 Jean-Paul Sartre, "Camus' *The Outsider*," p. 42.
11 Herbert Fingarette, *Self-Deception* (London: Routledge and Kegan Paul, 1969), p. 148.
12 Ibid., p. 48.
13 S, p. 114.
14 I am particularly indebted to the insights of Robert Solomon here. See *Dark Feelings, Grim Thoughts*, especially pp. 26–7.
15 G. W. F. Hegel, *Phenomenology of Spirit*, p. 359.
16 David Sprintzen argues that the major figures in *Caligula* are all alter egos of Caligula. There is some truth in this, but it also seems to be the case, as we shall see, that for some of these figures Caligula is an alter ego as well. See David Sprintzen, *Camus: A Critical Examination* (Philadelphia: Temple University Press, 1988), p. 72. What is quite clear is that the views of Scipio, Cherea, and Caligula are all views that Camus himself entertains.

further reading

O'Brien, Conor Cruise, *Camus* (Glasgow: Fontana/Collins, 1970).
Solomon, Robert C., *Dark Feelings, Grim Thoughts: Experience and Reflection in Camus and Sartre* (New York: Oxford University Press, 2006).

scorn

There is no fate that cannot be surmounted by scorn.

Albert Camus, *The Myth of Sisyphus*[1]

Although, paradoxically, Patrice Mersault, Meursault, and Caligula all purposefully reject their previous lives for (abstract) "life" because they resent life, Caligula clearly differs from Patrice Mersault and Meursault in numerous respects, two of which are particularly significant for our purposes. Prior to this choice, both Patrice Mersault and Meursault self-deceptively believe that transcendence can be found in (abstract) "life," while Caligula knows that resentment motivates this choice and that its end product is death. (Of course, Caligula is also guilty of self-deception, as nihilism is neither transcendence nor a "logical" substitute for it, but this is a different matter.) Moreover, in varying degrees, both Patrice Mersault and Meursault negate their reflective selves (in the belief that transcendence can be achieved only if the reflective self that separates us from pure experience is negated), while Caligula's nihilism calls for the absolutization of the reflective self, which throws itself into life with a destructive fury that will terminate only on "making the impossible possible" (CTOP, p. 13). Like Caligula, who is an intermediary figure, Jean-Baptiste Clamence of *The Fall* absolutizes his reflective self for nihilistic purposes, and, like Caligula, his "consolation [is] scorn" (CTOP, p. 38), which, as we saw, is Camus's alternative to "life" as an existential response to the Absurd. Unlike Caligula, however, at no point does "fire burn in [his] heart" (CTOP, p. 56), for with Clamence we get a cold, hyper-reflective withdrawal from life.

The Fall, published in 1956, was Camus's last novel, and it is the only one of his works that I shall consider drastically out of sequence. If one were to consider Camus's miscellaneous works solely from the perspective of his own experiences, this chronological deviation would be a mistake, for Clamence's psychology is meant to reflect both Camus's own psychology and the psychology of those on the French intellectual left who marginalized him for his philosophical and political positions, both practical (on the Cold War and the Algerian War) and theoretical (particularly in *The Rebel*). What's more, Clamence characterizes himself as "an empty prophet for shabby times" (F, p. 117), and the times in which Camus is composing *The Fall* undoubtedly qualify. Nevertheless, it would be a mistake to particularize the book with respect to the French intelligentsia or France of the mid-1950s, as neither finds explicit expression in *The Fall*. While Clamence has a history that is worth considering (to the extent that we can actually discern it), he essentially represents the bourgeois self, and while the times in post-War France are shabby, they essentially represent the breakdown of the modern project (which, it will be remembered, is what initially gives rise to the Absurd). Ultimately, then, *The Fall* is about the fault lines innate to the modern self, as well as the kind of psychological ploy to which it resorts in its resentful desire to prop itself up.

This psychological ploy, as I already suggested in my passing reference to Clamence, is a cold, hyper-reflective withdrawal from life, and as an extreme (if not "philosophically fantastic") example of this ploy, Clamence might be thought of as Meursault's opposite. While Meursault personifies the purified extreme of lived experience, which involves a resentful immersion in so-called "life" (brute experience shorn of all reflection) to negate the flagging self with its assorted responsibilities, Clamence personifies the purified extreme of reflection (reflection largely shorn of ongoing experience), which involves a resentful withdrawal from life to insulate and, finally, absolutize the flagging self through scorn. Life is not even nominally affirmed by Clamence, as it is by Meursault and Patrice Mersault (and, indeed, even by Caligula in his depraved way), but is, rather, rejected. Yet, as is the case with the privileging of life, this rejection of life is abstract, and as is the case with the negation of the self, the absolutization of the self ultimately privileges death, as any life worth living is left behind. When Clamence marvels before the "most beautiful negative landscape," a "soggy hell" within which "space is colorless and life dead" (F, p. 72), he could be speaking about his own life, which is all but dead, and if he does not commit suicide, it is probably because, as Kierkegaard suggests in *The Present Age*, reflection gets in the way.

""Jean-Baptiste Clamence""

> I know what you're thinking: it's very hard to disentangle the true from the false in what I'm saying. I admit you are right. I myself . . .
>
> Albert Camus, *The Fall*[2]

On meeting Jean-Baptiste Clamence in "Mexico City," one of the sleaziest bars in Amsterdam's notoriously sleazy red light district, he informs us that he was once an esteemed lawyer in Paris whose specialty was noble cases but that he is now a "judge-penitent" who plies his trade in this very bar. What, precisely, a judge-penitent is, and how this previously esteemed Parisian lawyer comes to ply this trade in a sleazy Amsterdam bar, is what this novel is about. Although there is absolutely nothing direct about the way in which we come by this information (for Clamence's second-person perspective monologue is, as we shall see, a veritable model of what Kierkegaard would depict as "indirect communication"), it is relatively clear from the start that, as the novel's title suggests, Clamence has experienced a fall from grace.

Who Clamence is (both before and after this fall) depends on how you define "is" (in the words of former US President William Clinton), and a good deal of the novel revolves around the uncertainties that surround this genuinely existential question. To begin with, Jean-Baptiste Clamence is not his original name, and whether it is even now his legal name is unclear (thus the first set of quotation marks around his name in the title of this section). Furthermore, as the excerpt that opens this section indicates, Clamence readily acknowledges not only that he might not be giving us the truth about himself all of the time (or, perhaps, any of the time), but that he himself is unclear as to the truth or falsity of some (or, perhaps, all) of what he is saying (thus the second set of quotation marks around his name). Accordingly, in contrast to Meursault, whose consciousness is tantamount to a "piece of flat, colorless glass" (which itself was the result of a previous decision not to reflect), Clamence's consciousness is tantamount to the endless mirrors in an amusement park fun house, in which distorting mirrors reflect the images of distorting mirrors. With every twist and turn, who Clamence "is," and, ultimately, who *we* "are," becomes further obscured.

When Clamence first introduces himself to the unsuspecting patron of Mexico City, who is everyone and no one but at this very moment "you [the reader] first of all" (F, p. 73), he seeks to help you obtain a drink from "the worthy ape" that is working behind the bar, confessing that he is "drawn by such creatures who are all of a piece." Such "creatures," indeed, are not unlike Meursault, who was also "all of a piece," but now, fully dragged into the social world, as we all are, they are mere "primates," who at least lack "ulterior motives" (F, pp. 3–4). Still, Clamence says, to be "double," which is the condition of having ulterior motives, is ultimately to be human, and he has chosen a quintessentially human occupation: "My profession [as a judge-penitent] is double, that's all, like the human being" (F, p. 10). For Clamence, all things human are double, and nothing is as it appears, least of all himself. Thus, after the third of three disturbing events that engender his "fall," he tells us that "my reflection was smiling in the mirror, but it seemed to me that my smile was double" (F, p. 40), and when he considers his "sign" ("his true profession and identity"), he tells us that it is "a double face, a charming Janus, and above it the motto of the house: 'Don't rely on it'" (F, pp. 46–7). Lastly, it must be pointed out that Clamence's "house," Mexico City, is located in hell, as "Amsterdam's concentric canals resemble the circles of hell," and Mexico City is in "the last circle" (F, p. 14), which, in Dante's *Inferno*, is the nastiest one of all. Ultimately, however, if it feels as if we are in hell, it is not because of where we are but because of who we are with, for all of the reflections in this fun house are Clamence's: "The portrait I hold out to my contemporaries becomes a mirror" (F, p. 140).

What we are caught in here is a hyper-reflectivity in which the experiences that constitute life basically disappear, which is the reason that the experiential "stuff" of Clamence's personal stories is totally historical. Paradoxically, then, although Meursault (and Patrice Mersault) seeks to negate the self while Clamence seeks to absolutize it, Clamence strives toward impersonality no less than Meursault (and Patrice Mersault). For Clamence, however, it is memory rather than brute experience that takes the place of meaningful living. Once supported by "an extraordinary ability to forget" (F, p. 49), which, according to Nietzsche, is a vital human attribute because it is essential to action and, therefore, life (or, at least, a life that is well lived), Clamence now "chews a bitter resentment" (F, p. 54). (Drawing on Nietzsche's famous remark that Mirabeau could not forgive because before he could forgive he invariably forgot, Clamence informs us that "I wasn't good enough to forgive offenses, but eventually I always forgot them.") Yet, although Clamence is bogged down by his memory, unable to act at all, he does not exclusively live in the past, for, as Nietzsche puts it, his resentment has become "creative." In other words, Clamence is a "man with a plan." Geared toward a "negative" future in which "salvation" will come to pass when we all "sleep on the floor" (F, p. 32), Clamence has already dropped to the floor, and he now seeks transcendence not by his own actions but, instead, by judging our actions, or, to be more precise, by judging our failure to properly appreciate the moral import of our actions.

Momentarily bracketing Clamence's motivations here (which shall be considered in due course), the underlying basis for this gambit is, essentially, twofold. First, Clamence exploits the complex, dynamic interrelationship between reflection and experience that is innate to all human beings (including both Meursault and Clamence). Because there cannot be an absolute identity between reflection and experience, since our reflection on our experiences necessarily transcends the experiences that are reflected on, human beings are unavoidably "double," which means that they can never be "just themselves." Nevertheless, Clamence convicts us for lacking "sincerity," which, as Sartre points out, presupposes this unachievable self-coincidence. Second, Clamence exploits the opacity of our own motivations, which is a philosophical problem that goes all the way back to Plato. The basic idea here is that human beings are ultimately, *necessarily* egoistic, irrespective of how their motivations might appear to both others and themselves, which means that our "altruistic" actions are really no less (and, perhaps, even more) self-interested than those actions that we explicitly recognize as such.

Who we actually are, in sum, is no simple matter, and what Clamence is trying to convey is that all our names belong in quotation marks, a position that was graphically reaffirmed by the recent French (poststructuralist) philosopher Jacques Derrida, who "signed" his name to certain works in just this way.

Clamence's Fall

Pride goeth before destruction, and a haughty spirit before a fall.

The Bible, Proverbs 16:18.

Structurally, *The Fall* is akin to *The Stranger*, but, phenomenologically (i.e., from the standpoint of the lead character's experience of the world), it is one step removed. By virtue of killing the Arab, which leads to his downfall, Meursault goes from a wholly prereflective figure immersed in "life" to a reflective figure that (largely) reaffirms life, while by virtue of the three events that lead to his fall, Clamence goes from a reflective figure living (by all accounts) a meaningful life to a hyper-reflective figure that (largely) leaves life behind. With Meursault, we saw that a prior choice not to reflect hung behind the prereflective figure that we first meet, and that this choice, motivated by resentment and made in bad faith, set him up for his downfall. Of course, what we must now determine is whether there is anything in Clamence's personal history that set him up for his fall. To make this determination is no easy task, for unlike Meursault, who unreflectively disgorged this kind of information on a few occasions, which means that there is no question as to its truth, Clamence hyper-reflectively chooses what to tell us, and then carefully crafts it for his own purposes. As he himself concedes, "it's very hard to disentangle the true from the false in what [he's] saying." Still, there is a way to proceed. Although Clamence's "methodology" is perverse, his interest, to put himself in a position to judge us, is direct enough, and "declarations against interest" are every bit as reliable in his case as they are in more run-of-the-mill ones.

Before his fall, as we know, Clamence was a revered lawyer in Paris who specialized in noble cases. Aside from "widows and orphans, as the saying goes," his preferred cases included "noble murderers, as others are noble savages" (F, pp. 17–19), the more believable Meursaults of the world. What's more, as Clamence describes it, "[he] was always in harmony" (F, p. 27), and a better description of the flourishing human being could not be found, for unlike human beings who are "all of a piece," the concept of "harmony" acknowledges the multiple aspects that make up the truly actualized human being, which apparently Clamence was. Well built, good looking, extremely intelligent, able to seduce at will, and accomplished in things as diverse as the fine arts and sports, Clamence "looked upon [him]self as something of a superman" by virtue of "being so fully and simply a man," and he "held sway bathed in a light as of Eden," with "no intermediary between life and [him]" (F, pp. 27–8). Nevertheless, Clamence declares, "at the same time [he was] satisfied with nothing," as "each joy made [him] desire another" (F, p. 30).

Clamence attributes his fall from (relative) grace to a series of events that he recounts in reverse order. The event that actually pushes him over the edge, which is the most innocuous of all, occurs one night while standing on a bridge overlooking the Seine. Enlivened by the feeling that he "dominated" what he oversaw, Clamence hears two bursts of laughter behind him, which precipitates a panic attack that causes him to see his "double smile" in the mirror (F, pp. 38–40). Reeling from this laughter, which triggers a severe depression, Clamence's "extraordinary ability to forget" goes by the boards, as "gradually [his] memory returned" (F, p. 50). Clamence recalls a number of everyday events, but now in a more jaded way, as he comes to "humbly admit" that he "was always bursting with vanity," as "I, I, I" could be seen as "the refrain of [his] whole life, which could be heard in everything [he] said" (F, p. 48). For instance, he recalls treating women badly, exploiting them for his own pleasure, and "no man is a hypocrite in his pleasures" (F, p. 66). Clamence also recalls two events, in particular, that utterly undermine his ability to think of himself as a "superman." First, he recalls an event with a rude motorcyclist, whom he confronts, only to be punched in the head from behind by another motorist. Although he concedes that this is probably "a totally insignificant story," he tells us that this "collapse in public" disabused him of the idea that he could "dominate in all things" (F, pp. 54–5). Second, and more importantly, he recalls an event that had taken place two to three years earlier, when, crossing one of the same bridges spanning the Seine, he passed a young woman leaning over the guardrail and then, when roughly 50 yards away, heard what he took to be the sound of a body hitting the water. Immobilized by fear, he eventually went on his way, and proceeded to tell no one of the incident (F, p. 70). With these recollections, Clamence unravels. The laughter becomes all but ubiquitous, he feels "vulnerable and open to public accusation" (F, p. 78), he begins to obsess about death (F, p. 89), and he then throws himself into a life of debauchery, which helps numb the pain, "as each excess decreases vitality, hence suffering" (F, p. 105). Ultimately, however, Clamence cannot elude his pain, and one day, while on an ocean liner, he sees "a black speck on the steel-gray ocean," at which point he concludes that he "had to submit and admit [his] guilt" (F, p. 109).

So, why does Clamence fall? The events that he recounts – what he takes to be the sound of the young woman's body hitting the water, being sucker-punched in public, and the sound of (unattributable) laughter – are not enough to topple a "superman." (Indeed, as Clamence admits with respect to the first event, which is the one that most disconcerts him, it may well be the case that the woman didn't jump, and, in any case, that there was little he could have done about it even if she had.) Of course, it might be argued, the higher that one is, the more that one sticks out, the more vulnerable one is and the farther one has to fall, and there is undeniably an element of truth in this. Yet, these incidents do not seem to be enough. Of course, there is always the possibility that Clamence is lying to us with respect to the "basics." Perhaps he was not as successful as he claims or the events that triggered his fall were more severe than he describes, or, more radically, perhaps his account is pure fabrication. Of course, we are in no position to rule this out, since there is no trustworthy third-person perspective in the novel, but it does not seem to be the case, for if it were, the novel would not be especially interesting or, for that matter, worth taking seriously. The "bare" facts can be taken at face value, but it is their interpretation that might be distorted, which is just the point that Clamence is trying to make with us. When Nietzsche says that "there are no facts, only interpretations," his point is not that there are no underlying factual occurrences but, instead, that these "bare" facts mean very little (if, indeed, anything at all), and that it is only when we "take them up" and, thereby, (ineluctably) interpret them that they come to be meaningful. Thus, the problem with trusting Clamence does not pertain to the "bare" facts but to his interpretation of them.

Moreover, while the "bare" facts refer to past occurrences, interpretations refer to future commitments. We interpret on the basis of who we seek to be (individually and collectively) or what we seek to bring about. Clamence, as we know, seeks to bring about our fall, and what he seeks to do is interpret the facts in such a way as to maximize this possibility. This requires two things. First, as Clamence himself states, the image that he creates of himself must be universal: "I construct a portrait which is the image of all and of no one" (F, p. 139). Second, this "image of all and of no one" must, nevertheless, be compelling: if Clamence was not a "superman," then we would be able to find ways to distinguish ourselves from him, thus insulating ourselves from his game. If he had an Achilles heel that made him fatally vulnerable, one that we ourselves do not possess, then we could distance ourselves from his portrait. Ultimately, then, the question as to why Clamence falls is a question of whether this extremely accomplished man had a particular Achilles heel or was simply "human all too human" (the universal Achilles heel).

Of course, it is this second conclusion toward which Clamence attempts to "skillfully navigate" us, for it is in this way that Clamence can show that "we are in the soup together" (F, pp. 139–40), but I shall argue that it is actually the first conclusion that we should draw.

"Pride goeth before destruction, and a haughty spirit before a fall," according to Proverbs 16:18, and if Clamence has an Achilles heel, it is undoubtedly pride. Indeed, Clamence not only does not deny this pride but goes so far as to play it up, although, of course, he plays it up in such a way as to suggest that it is of the universal, human-all-too-human variety. If we are to say that Clamence's fall is due to an overweening personal pride, which would effectively pluck you and me out of the soup (unless, of course, we, too, are subject to this vice), we must find some account of the facts of his life in Paris (rather than his self-interested retrospective characterization of it) that bespeaks this pride. Such an account would be a dependable one in this house of mirrors, for although we are getting all of our facts from Clamence, this would be a declaration by Clamence against his own interest, which is to show that we are all motivated by the same sort of pride that he alone has been insightful enough to diagnose. Fortunately, such a declaration against interest is to be found, namely, in Clamence's assorted claims to the effect that he *always* "needed to feel above" (F, p. 23), for here he is speaking of a less than noble sentiment that *explicitly* motivated him *before* the events that precipitated his fall.

To make the point more clearly, this sort of claim must be contrasted to other claims that, on the surface, appear to be the same. For example, when Clamence speaks of the good feelings that he got from helping the elderly and infirm across busy intersections, his story accords with his interest, for, presumably, we get good feelings from doing such things as well. Having set us up, Clamence can then lower the boom by attributing a vulgar motivation to his action. Thus, he tells us, once after helping a blind man across the street, he tipped his hat to the man (despite the obvious fact that the blind man could not appreciate this), which allegedly attested to the fact that what "really" motivated him was vanity, a desire to look good to the public (F, p. 47). Of course, this is an easily explainable mistake, given that he was undoubtedly conditioned to act in such a way under these kinds of circumstances, but Clamence will not entertain this possibility, and, by implication, neither should we with respect to our own prior good deeds, whether we committed a *faux pas* while carrying them out or not. What Clamence is doing here (and, indeed, what he is doing to Clamence of "pre-fall" Paris, more generally) is equivalent to what he (perversely) tells us the living do to the dead: "Once you are dead, they will take advantage of it to attribute idiotic or vulgar motives to your actions" (F, pp. 75–6). Crucially, however, when Clamence speaks of his desire to be at the peaks gazing down on "the human ants" (F, p. 24), he is not retrospectively affixing a vulgar motive to an action that might have been well motivated but, rather, is speaking of a vulgar sentiment that he actually had at the time, which cuts against his present interest, for it is a sentiment that you and I might not actually have. This gives us, as cynical politicians say, the basis for "plausibly denying" that we are actually as vain as he was, which thwarts his ploy.

Ultimately, because people who are both more and less virtuous than Clamence do not go into an existential tailspin in response to circumstances that are far more distressing than those he experiences, we should not fall for his attempt to convince us that he is an Adam, pope, or Christ for our shabby times, and, indeed, Camus would be the first to agree (even if he did concede that Clamence manifests a fair number of his own character traits). Clamence does manifest a certain pathology indigenous to our modern(-cum-postmodern) times, but it is surely not universal, and, even among the afflicted class, the bourgeoisie (whom Clamence exclusively seeks out), it surely is not inexorable. In any case, by virtue of his own "admission of guilt," Clamence literally and figuratively inverts his life in accordance with the "high-low" fixation that had tacitly dominated it even before "the fall." From his sun-drenched penthouse in Paris, "the city of light," he moves to a shabby apartment in dark, damp Amsterdam, which is below sea level, and retiring from his profession as a lawyer of noble causes, which "satisfied most happily that vocation for summits" (F, p. 25), he becomes a judge-penitent who admits to being the lowest of the low, but views *this* as "a height to which [he is] the only one to climb," one from which he can "dominate at last, but forever" (F, p. 142).

The Roots of Clamence's Resentment

The Enlightenment has always aimed at liberating men from fear and establishing their sovereignty. Yet the fully enlightened earth radiates disaster triumphant.

Max Horkheimer and Theodor W. Adorno, *Dialectic of Enlightenment*[3]

My original fall is the existence of the Other.

Jean-Paul Sartre, *Being and Nothingness*[4]

In much the same way that it is hard to unravel the true from the false in what Clamence says, it is hard to unravel the discrete but interweaving influences (both conceptual and sociohistorical) that have gone into the formation of his pathological psyche, which, like Meursault's, is mired in bad faith. Nevertheless, I would like to suggest, there are two basic influences, a loss of meaning and a loss of community, which are both interrelated and share the same fundamental cause, the breakdown of the modern project. The best place to start, however, is by considering yet another literary figure, "the Underground Man" (from Dostoyevsky's *Notes from Underground*). It has often been claimed that the Underground Man is the model for Clamence, and, indeed, these two figures bear numerous striking similarities: like Clamence, the Underground Man has resentfully retreated to the margins of life, reveling in a self-debasement that sees its own self-reflection as a sickness from which it cannot flee, and, like Clamence, the Underground Man sees this sickness as a peculiar form of transcendence. In the final analysis, however, although, formally speaking, the Underground Man might well be the archetype for Clamence, their positions are the result of very different perspectives, but these differences are illuminating for our current purposes.

Unlike Clamence, a cosmopolitan mid-twentieth-century Frenchman who personifies bourgeois cynicism in the face of the modern project gone amiss, the Underground Man, a mid-nineteenth-century ex-bureaucrat living in semi-feudal Russia, offers a theoretical critique of the modern project's basic conceptual assumptions, contending, in essence, that its very aims are misguided. Largely rejecting the idea of progress, the Underground Man questions the ability of science and reason to deliver "the good life," which requires nothing less than the "improvement" of humankind (an idea that Nietzsche also questions): "You want to cure man of his bad old habits and reshape his will according to the requirements of science and common sense. But what makes you think that man either can or *should* be changed in this way?"[5] Even if science and reason could construct "the utopian palace of crystal," which, supposedly, would bring about "the days of bliss," people would act perversely out of utter boredom, and, ultimately, their "most advantageous advantage," the ability to freely, impulsively act in the way that they *feel* like acting rather than the way that reason dictates. To act in this way, the Underground Man asserts, "leaves us our most important, most treasured possession, our individuality," and it is in the service of our individuality that he "sticks his tongue out" at the utopian palace of crystal. Conversely, to fail to act in this way (i.e., to live in accord with the logic of the modern project) is tantamount to a living death, and *Notes from Underground* concludes with the lament that "today we don't even know where real life is, what it is, or what it's called . . . and we long to turn ourselves into something hypothetical called the average man. We're stillborn . . . [and] we'll invent a way to be begotten by ideas altogether."[6]

Although Clamence's critique of the modern project is basically by his own example (i.e., "the whys and wherefores" of his own existential choices), he, too, occasionally criticizes it, although his criticism usually takes the form of an offhanded comment rather than a more rigorous analysis. For example, early in *The Fall* Clamence nonchalantly states that "I live in the Jewish quarter or what was called so until our Hitlerian brethren made room. What a cleanup! Seventy-five thousand Jews deported or assassinated; that's real vacuum-cleaning. I admire that diligence, that methodical patience! When one has no character one has to apply a method" (F, p. 11). For many theorists, Nazism manifested both the conceptual and sociohistorical limits of the modern project, and this passage cryptically captures much of their critique. Beyond the fact that Nazism arose in one of the world's most culturally and technologically advanced societies, what was so troubling about it, at least from a conceptual perspective, was that the sociopolitical irrationality it embraced seamlessly dovetailed with the sort of technological rationality that was supposed to liberate humanity. In other words, the Nazis' horrific "vacuum-cleaning" operation was, nevertheless, quite "methodical." Furthermore, it was argued, this sociopolitical breakdown was the ultimate logic of the modern project itself, which, in effect, privileged subjective reason over the ethical imperatives of our concrete existences, and then attempted to ground our moral imperatives in the very same abstract reason. Indeed, although motivated by very different moral commitments, Kant's categorical imperative and Mill's utilitarian calculus are alike in that they both constitute a "method" for deciding how to act, a method that essentially stands in for those virtues of character that were indicative of the ethical person in the ancient and medieval worlds. (This practitioner of "abstract reason" is the "average man" against whom the Underground Man protests.) Divorced from a concrete form of social life that could offer compelling reasons to act ethically (not to mention define what is "ethical" in the first place), many modern thinkers came to believe that such reasons could no longer be provided, which is Clamence's exact point when he asserts that "every reason can be answered with another one and there would never be an end to it [but] power . . . settles everything" (F, p. 45). What this suggests is that Clamence is beset by the problem of nihilism, which Nietzsche rightly defines as follows: "The highest values devalue themselves. The aim is lacking; 'why?' finds no answer."[7] Put simply, nothing means anything, for there is nothing that can conclusively justify itself, much less anything else.

Crucially, however, Clamence (like Camus) continues to buy into the rationalism of the modern project, even as he founders in its wake. Although Clamence is surely speaking sarcastically when he says that he "admires" the "methodical patience" of the Nazis, as his ensuing claim that "when one has no character one has to apply a method" testifies, he no longer has any character himself, and for this reason applies his own method (which shall be detailed below). Describing himself as "an enlightened advocate of slavery," since "without slavery . . .

there is no definitive solution" (F, p. 132), Clamence's "answer" to the breakdown of modernity, which no longer has God to step into the breach to restore moral order and, above all, (existential) meaning, is to copy the religious problematic but without God, moral order, or meaning. "One must choose a master, God being out of style" (F, p. 133), he asserts, for "the essential is that everything should become simple, as for the child, that every act should be ordered, that good and evil should be *arbitrarily*, hence obviously, pointed out" (F, p. 135). Understood in terms of the previous discussion of the Absurd, Clamence's resentful comportment here takes place in "the shadow of God." With "the death of God," it was thought that humanity could ascend to His vacant throne (and, some might contend, Clamence's earlier hubris could be understood in terms of this aspiration), but the very idea that there is a vacant throne to which we should ascend presumes the "view from nowhere," which, as we saw, falls squarely within the "shadow of God" problematic.

Clamence's brand of humanism, in short, finds itself in the lurch, and his "answer" to the seemingly intractable problem of nihilism sits halfway between the answers offered by Nietzsche and Dostoyevsky. Although the Underground Man's hostility toward the modern project evinces Dostoyevsky's own views, what does not come out in *Notes from Underground* is Dostoyevsky's ongoing commitment to Christianity (specifically the Russian Orthodox Church), which was part and parcel of the concrete form of life that he struggled to defend against modern rationalism. In other words, if, according to Dostoyevsky, we no longer actually know where "real life is, what it is, or what it's called," it is because we have driven Christianity out of the picture. Of course, for the cosmopolitan Clamence, who unequivocally (if, perhaps, ambivalently) accepts the "death of God," Christianity is not the answer, but his own nihilistic answer to nihilism exhibits a nostalgia for it. Conversely, according to Nietzsche, who also believes that "real life" has been driven out of the picture, Christianity is the culprit, and if modernity is to make good its promise, it will be through its own privileged category, "the individual." Although Nietzsche foresaw modernity's breakdown, he believed that it might open the way for masterly types, who, utterly unconcerned with the judgments of others, would each see themselves as the ground of their own (respective) values and, thereby, realize themselves (thus harmonizing with his directive to "become who you are"). Clamence, as we shall see, is a creator of values, and, as such, nominally responds to the problem of (existential) meaninglessness, but his values reflect a resentment that is provoked by the judgments of others, which makes him not masterly but slavish.

Indeed, far more than this loss of (existential) meaning, which did not seem to encumber Clamence all that much during his high-flying days in Paris (perhaps because he found meaning in his vain effort to always be "well above the human ants"), it is an obsession with the judgment of others that precipitates his fall. Although the modern project plainly emphasized the rights of "the individual," it was not meant to be at the expense of the community, which was deemed a necessary condition of the individual's self-realization (as was also the case for the flourishing person in Aristotle's *polis*). Not only was the notion of social reconciliation central in the works of Marx (communism) and Hegel (the State), but even in Kant's decontextualized, liberal moral theory it was presumed in the regulative ideal of a "kingdom of ends," in which all rational wills would cohere. What's more, it is well reflected in the French Revolution's demand not only for liberty and equality but also fraternity. With the collapse of the modern project, as is epitomized by Nazism, however, the commitment to community (or, at least, any community worthy of the name) is undermined, and in this way Clamence is a creature of his times. During World War II, Clamence lived under France's collaborationist Vichy government before being incarcerated in a Nazi prisoner-of-war camp, all of which constituted a regression to a kind of Hobbesian state of nature for which the rule is "every man for himself," and it is while in the prisoner-of-war camp that Clamence, who is named pope by his fellow prisoners so as to administer to "the community of [their] sufferings," purportedly instantiates this rule: "Let's just say that I closed the circle the day I drank the water of a dying comrade" (F, pp. 125–6).

In sum, Clamence is an essentially modern man who is no longer able to take the promise of modernity seriously, and, therefore, his response to the modern dilemma is peculiarly modern. Clamence asserts that freedom is "a chore . . . too heavy to bear" (F, p. 133), and thus he becomes an "*enlightened* advocate of slavery" (F, p. 132). Nevertheless, he also asserts that "the essential is being able to permit oneself everything" (F, p. 141). Clamence believes in equality, but it is an equality in which each person is subject rather than sovereign and there are "no excuses ever, for anyone," since "everything is simply totted up" (F, p. 131). Nevertheless, in this "democracy of guilt" (F, p. 136), he alone is the one to "dominate" (F, p. 142). Clamence believes in fraternity, but it is a fraternity in which each person is motivated by the fear of the other's judgment rather than mutual affection. Nevertheless, if in this fraternity it is "all together . . . but on our knees and heads bowed" (F, p. 146), he alone is "the judge-penitent," the only one with the moral standing to raise his head high (albeit with knees still on the floor) for the purpose of judging his brothers and sisters. What is left for Clamence, in other words, are the distillates of the modern project's highest values, which, severed from the fount of anything that might help to constitute "the good life," turn into a grotesque parody. Split off from a community in which he could meaningfully actualize himself by virtue of identifying with some manner of collective self-understanding, Clamence makes use of a subjective reason that is life-denying rather than life-affirming, one in which "self-actualization" pathetically consists of picking off isolated passers-by so as to one-up them and, thereby, be in a position to scorn them. In this way, Clamence (resentfully) tries to make good Camus's contention that "there is no fate that cannot be surmounted by scorn" (MS, p. 121).

Clamence's Revaluation of the Revaluation of Values

> Let us articulate this *new demand*: we need a *critique* of moral values, *the value of these values themselves must first be called into question* – and for that there is needed a knowledge of the conditions and circumstances in which they grew, under which they evolved and changed . . .
> Friedrich Nietzsche, *On the Genealogy of Morals*[8]

In accordance with Nietzsche's demand, Clamence brings about a revaluation of values that were themselves a revaluation of values, and, in the process, cleverly weaves different aspects of what Nietzsche labels the two basic types of morality, master and slave. Nevertheless, although this is also in accordance with Nietzsche's general policy prescription, the values that Clamence brings about are diametrically opposed to Nietzsche's own objectives.

It is frequently taken to be the case that Nietzsche was hostile toward morality, which is not quite right, for he believed that morality was an ineluctable part of human existence. To live is to value, and from our values our morality arises. What Nietzsche was actually hostile toward was Judeo-Christian morality, in particular, and the two basic reasons for this hostility are linked. Fundamentally, Nietzsche thought that Judeo-Christian morality was life-denying, and, therefore, nihilistic, in its emphasis on repressing our natural instincts and valuing the other-worldly. Since there are certain types of people whose deficiencies find their overcoming in its (nominally) self-abnegating tenets, however, he did not reject Judeo-Christian morality altogether, and, moreover, in certain respects he saw it as a training ground for a higher morality. What troubled Nietzsche most about Judeo-Christian morality was its claim to universality (i.e., its claim to be applicable to all people notwithstanding the many significant differences that exist among them), for in this way it suppresses those human excellences that might otherwise be exhibited by the more gifted among us. That is, by claiming to be a "one size fits all" morality, Judeo-Christian morality not only protects those for whom it is intrinsically suitable from those for whom it is not (i.e., their betters) but effectively makes all human beings inferior by sup-pressing the gifts of those with the intelligence, strength, courage, and capacity to stand apart from the masses in the pursuit of (their own) excellence. (This is not to say that Nietzsche advocated the violation of those fundamental proscriptions that make up "conventional" moral-ity, for "excellence" largely presupposes that we will not kill, steal, or bear false witness, even as it transcends these proscriptions.) What's more, when Nietzsche speaks of Judeo-Christian morality, he speaks not just of its religious variant but of secular ones that stem from it. Although Kant's deontology and Mill's utilitarianism differ in that the former emphasizes our duty to refrain from certain acts irrespective of the consequences while the latter (largely) emphasizes consequences (the maximization of happiness) irrespective of the acts required to pro-duce them, they are alike in that both moralities claim to be universally applicable. In this way, indeed, both moralities also arise in "the shadow of God."

According to Nietzsche, Judeo-Christian morality, as well as its enlightenment legatees, are "slavish" in nature. As an initial matter, both Judaism and Christianity actually arose among slave populations: the Jews were not "chosen" during the high-flying days of kings Solomon and David but rather when they were in the mud pits of Egypt, and Christianity first flourished among Roman slaves. More important, however, is Nietzsche's *concept* of slave morality, which he sets forth in one of the most important passages in *On the Genealogy of Morals*:

> The slave revolt in morality begins when resentment itself becomes cre-ative and gives birth to values: the resentment of natures that are denied the true reaction, that of deeds, and compensate themselves with an ima-ginary revenge. While every noble morality develops from a triumphant affirmation of itself, slave morality from the outset says No to what is "outside," what is "different," what is "not itself"; and *this* No is its creative deed. This inversion of the value-positing eye – this *need* to direct one's view outward instead of back to oneself – is of the essence of resent-ment: in order to exist, slave morality always first needs a hostile external world; it needs, physiologically speaking, external stimuli in order to act at all – its action is fundamentally reaction.[9]

According to Nietzsche, those who "lack" (intelligence, strength, courage, and the capacity to stand apart from "the herd"), and, therefore, do not have recourse to "the true reaction, that of deeds," are able to "com-pensate themselves with an imaginary revenge" by envisioning that God will ultimately redeem their weaker position. Whether it is the Old Testament's implacable God, Yaweh, who metes out justice to all who transgress the Law, or the New Testament's somewhat more loving God, who, nevertheless, can eternally damn the transgressor's soul, God underwrites those who "lack," for it is to redeem *their* values that He is conjured up in the first place. These values, the consequence of resentment having "become creative," are themselves the product of a "revaluation of values," which Nietzsche characterizes as the greatest act of "spiritual revenge." While master moralities are defined by "good" and "bad," in that what are "good" are the masters' traits and what is "bad" is the lack thereof (thus master morality is a "triumphant affirmation of itself"), slave moralities are the result of a revaluation of this value structure, such that "the lack" that defines what master morality sees as bad becomes "good" and the traits that master morality defines as "good" become *evil* (and, therefore, are subject to God's punishment). Slave morality thus turns value on its head, as not only the excellences that defined master morality become evil but the slave becomes "good" simply by virtue of lacking the traits that could make one evil. In this way, "No" is slave morality's "creative deed," as it affirms itself only by what it is not (i.e., in terms of the excellences that it lacks).

Now, Clamence epitomizes this "revaluation," albeit once removed, for the values that he revalues are themselves the slaves' revalued values. As was discussed earlier, Clamence (and, in fact, his European compatriots, more generally) must struggle with the breakdown of the modern project, a breakdown that Nietzsche had predicted roughly 50 years before the fact. Nietzsche believed that such lofty enlightenment values as liberty, equality, and fraternity were themselves a product of resentment and, with the widespread recognition that "God is dead," would come to be historically transfigured in appalling ways. After this comes to pass – that is, after the highest values have, in fact, devalued themselves – a new set of values is needed, and it is Clamence that megalomaniacally steps into the breach: "Fortunately, I arrived! I am the end and the beginning; I announce the law. In short I am a judge-penitent" (F, p. 118). Clamence's "announcement of the law" is Nietzsche's resentment having once again "become creative," and the values that it gives birth to are a peculiar amalgamation of Nietzsche's master and slave moralities.

Nominally, Clamence's ambition here, which is to become a new master, twists away from slave morality's self-abnegating strictures and betokens a return to a more masterly morality, but, in fact, it is actually a radicalization of slave morality, an unmasking of "the will to power" that, according to Nietzsche, motivates all human beings, whether masterly or slavish. Clamence thus depicts *his* revaluation of values as follows: "We should, like Copernicus, reverse the reasoning to win out. Inasmuch as one couldn't condemn others without immediately judging oneself, one had to overwhelm oneself to have the right to judge others" (F, p. 138). Paradoxically, what this means is not just that Clamence can judge others with impunity after properly repenting, but, like the masters prior to the slaves' revaluation of values, he can now judge without any limits on his own actions, for as we saw "the essential thing is being able to permit oneself everything" (F, p. 141). Thus, if the slaves' revaluation of values turns what the masters saw as "bad" into "good" and what the masters saw as "good" into "evil," Clamence's revaluation of values holds that the slaves themselves are "evil" (because they deceitfully believe that they are "good" when they are no less egoistically motivated than the masters they condemned) and that those who forthrightly do "evil" are "good" (because what is now "good" is only the "sincere" confession that one is "evil"). In this way, the masters' excellences go by the wayside entirely, and the only thing that is left of the slaves' moral position is the forthright acknowledgment that there is no genuinely moral position left, which, in some sense, actually brings slave morality to fruition by more or less absolutizing the notion of "original sin." Indeed, even *Christ* "knew he was not altogether innocent" (F, p. 112).

In the final analysis, Clamence aims to judge without being open to judgment, which is a ploy that is slavish at its core, given that more masterly types are unconcerned with the dynamics of judging and being judged. In earlier times, the biblical admonition "Judge not, that ye not be judged" (since we all live in glass houses) might have carried some weight, but with the death of God (and the breakdown of the modern project, which, functioning in the shadow of God, sought to reconcile humanity on secular grounds), judgment falls to every one of us, and every one of us in this community of the estranged is infinitely less merciful than God would have been. "Don't wait for the Last Judgment [as] it takes place every day" (F, p. 111), Clamence proclaims, and, in fact, he takes his own advice, adopting the "gunslinger's Golden Rule: Judge others before they judge you."[10] Clamence's ploy, in other words, is to steal judgment, which is symbolized by his possession of the stolen masterpiece "The Just Judges." By stealing judgment, which allows him to rise above his contemporaries, Clamence puts himself in a position to scorn the entire "human race, you [the reader] first of all" (F, p. 73), as well as his own fate, which, of course, is Camus's recommendation in *The Myth of Sisyphus*. This is the ultimate pay-off. As should now be abundantly clear, however, this is a slavish scorn, for while Nietzsche periodically speaks of a noble scorn for what is inferior (i.e., a scorn for what is "bad"), such a scorn is not motivated by resentment, as the recourse to scorn in order to surmount a despised fate most surely is.

Clamence's Bad Faith

Responsibility must be accepted. . . . This acceptance is evident if there is genuine care or concern of the kind which is peculiar to moral responsibility. There are many marks of such concern beyond the obvious – caring behavior. There may be inner moral conflict, self-restraint, remorse, guilt, or other such manifestations.

Herbert Fingarette, *Mapping Responsibility*[11]

In the last chapter, we saw that existentialism, generally speaking, rejects the idea that there is an inherent self. Although there are certain invariant "facts" about each of us (e.g., our dates of birth, our biological parents, certain physical traits, and the occurrences that make up our pasts), these "facts" are quite thin, and when we speak of the facts about us in a more conventional vein, they are mostly sedimented by layers of interpretation, which are the product of prior choices (of ourselves) that were freely made. Thus, human beings must live in a fundamental tension that is delineated by the complex interrelationship between our invariant facts (i.e., "facticity") and our freedom (i.e., "transcendence," in the sense that we are always beyond our "facticity"), and "bad faith" derives from overemphasizing one of these at the price of the other. Meursault, as we saw, was in "radical" bad faith, for in rejecting transcendence entirely, he rejected nothing less than the intrinsic human responsibility of selfhood, thus negating the innate tension between freedom and facticity that gives both of them their very meaning. Although not quite to the same degree, and from the other side of the coin, much the same could be said of Clamence.

It would thus be too crude to say that Clamence entirely rejects his facticity in the same way that Meursault entirely rejects his transcendence (i.e., his freedom to make *something* out of himself), for Clamence incessantly speaks to the previous facts of his life, while Meursault, who is wholly prereflective, does not seem to rise to a level at which the concept of freedom can even be made intelligible. Clamence is, rather, involved in a more sophisticated operation, trading on the ambiguities that exist between the invariant facts and the facts as (freely) recounted. As we saw, Clamence does not reject the invariant facts – we can be confident that he did, indeed, help a blind man across the street – but once the present recedes into the past there is, at least ideally, some "objective" fact of the matter in terms of not just the actions that one has committed (which are publicly verifiable) but also the motivations that actually hung behind them (which are not). Of course, disentangling our often diverse motivations with respect to any particular action is no simple matter, and, indeed, perhaps our true motivations with respect to any particular action can never be absolutely known (as this would suggest the possibility of some wholly objective, third-person God's eye view). Yet, even so, Clamence has basically stripped down his prior actions to their barest, most invariant aspects and then reconstituted them in accordance with his *current* motivation, his project of making himself (and, finally, you) look as compromised as he possibly can. In any meaningful sense, then, Clamence really does reject his facticity, playing off the ambiguity of prior motivations and the freedom to now reconstitute them as he chooses. While nominally taking absolute responsibility for his previous actions, therefore, he actually takes no responsibility for them at all, for the dynamic tension that ideally typifies the relation between our facticity and our freedom falls away, as does the possibility of any robust self.

What's more, like Patrice Mersault, Meursault, and Caligula before him, Clamence is in bad faith because he deceitfully believes that he can achieve happiness irrespective of his relation to other people, and, indeed, just like these previous characters, he proclaims his happiness under circumstances that speak for themselves in terms of the self-deceptive nature of this belief:

> Intoxicated with evil words, I am happy – I am happy, I tell you, I won't let you think I'm not happy, I am happy unto death! (Clamence; F, p. 144)

> For I *am* happy ... Beyond the frontier of pain lies a splendid sterile happiness. Look at me. (Caligula; CTOP, p. 71)

> I felt that I had been happy and that I was happy again ... I had only to wish that there be a huge crowd of spectators the day of my execution and that they greet me with cries of hate. (Meursault; S, p. 123)

> Conscious yet alienated, devoured by passion yet disinterested, Mersault realized that his life and fate were completed here and that henceforth all his efforts would be to submit to this happiness and to confront its terrible truth. (HD, p. 140)

To this point, we have considered solitary characters who tend to conflate happiness and death, but what must be emphasized here is that in 1956 Camus is well aware of the limits of this position, which means that Clamence must be understood as a mere caricature of it, while in his younger works (*A Happy Death*, *The Stranger*, *Caligula*) it is one that he actually holds himself. As was stated earlier, *Caligula* makes clear the problematical nature of this position, and Camus subsequently informs us that it is at this point that he moved "from an attitude of solitary revolt to the recognition of a community whose struggles must be shared" – that is, "in the direction of solidarity and participation" (LCE, p. 339).

scorn

notes

1   MS, p. 121.
2   F, p. 119.
3   Max Horkheimer and Theodor W. Adorno, *Dialectic of Enlightenment*, trans. John Cumming (New York: Continuum, 1991), p. 3.
4   Jean-Paul Sartre, *Being and Nothingness*, trans. Hazel Barnes (New York: Washington Square Press, 1956), p. 352.
5   Fyodor Dostoyevsky, *Notes from Underground*, trans. Andrew R. MacAndrew (New York: Signet Classics, 1961), p. 109.
6   Ibid., p. 195.
7   Friedrich Nietzsche, *The Will to Power*, trans. Walter Kaufmann and R. J. Hollingdale (New York: Random House, 1967), p. 9.
8   Friedrich Nietzsche, *On the Genealogy of Morals/Ecce Homo*, trans. Walter Kaufmann (New York: Random House, 1967), p. 20.
9   Ibid., pp. 36–7.
10 Robert C. Solomon, *Dark Feelings, Grim Thoughts: Experience and Reflection in Camus and Sartre* (New York: Oxford University Press, 2006), p. 210.
11 Herbert Fingarette, *Mapping Responsibility: Explorations in Mind, Law, Myth, and Culture* (Chicago: Open Court Press, 2004), p. 2.

further reading

O'Brien, Conor Cruise, *Camus* (Glasgow: Fontana/Collins, 1970).
Solomon, Robert C., *Dark Feelings, Grim Thoughts: Experience and Reflection in Camus and Sartre* (New York: Oxford University Press, 2006).

solidarity

You never believed in the meaning of this world, and you therefore
deduced the idea that everything was equivalent and that good and evil
could be defined according to one's wishes. . . . I, believing I thought as you
did, saw no valid argument to answer you except a fierce love of justice
which . . . seemed to me as unreasonable as the most sudden passion.
Where lay the difference? Simply that you readily accepted despair and I
never yielded to it. Simply that you saw the injustice of our condition to
the point of being willing to add to it, whereas it seemed to me that man
must exalt justice in order to fight against eternal injustice, create happiness
in order to protest against the universe of unhappiness. . . . Refusing to accept
that despair and that tortured world, I merely wanted men to rediscover
their solidarity in order to wage war against their revolting fate.

Albert Camus, *Letters to a German Friend*[1]

In *The Plague*, published in 1947, one of the lead characters, Raymond
Rambert, readily admits that there is nothing shameful in desiring
happiness, but he declares that "it may be shameful to be happy by
oneself" (P, p. 209). Rambert might well be right, but he understates
the problem, for the examples provided by the previous characters that
we have considered suggest that being happy by oneself might also be
unachievable. Who and what we are is utterly intertwined with the social
world, and as Meursault and Clamence, in their different ways, demonstrate, the more one withdraws from an unhappy world, the more, it would
seem, the unhappy world comes back to thwart one's personal plans.
This is a lesson that Camus himself learned only too well during the
Nazi occupation of Paris, and even if some form of solitary happiness is
achievable, it would seem that Camus, like Rambert (who initially seeks
happiness at all costs), comes to hold that it is, nevertheless, shameful.

If we pick up the chronological thread of Camus's work (which, it will
be remembered, was abandoned to better make good the conceptual problem of a solitary response to the modern problem of existential meaning
and, ultimately, the Absurd), we see subtle shifts from *Caligula* (which
reflects the exhaustion of the Sisyphean paradigm) through *Letters to a
German Friend*, *The Misunderstanding*, and, finally, *The Plague*. *Letters*

to a German Friend, which consists of four so-called letters from Camus to an imaginary German friend, appeared (pseudonymously) in the Resistance newspaper *Combat* between July 1943 and July 1944. Although these "letters" were politically motivated in the most basic sense, as their primary aim was to inspire the French during the Nazi occupation, they reflect the development of Camus's theoretical perspective. As the opening quotation suggests, Camus does not renounce the "metaphysics of the Absurd," for he does not claim that he had been wrong to hold that "everything is equivalent," which is simply another way of saying that there are no principled qualitative distinctions, the basic position that he took in *The Myth of Sisyphus* and represented through Meursault and Caligula. (Indeed, "that good and evil could be defined according to one's wishes" in the face of the Absurd is Caligula's veritable leitmotif.) Yet, Camus now changes his perspective, if not his basic position. In some sense, he now takes the position of Cherea, who does not dispute Caligula's so-called "logic" but rather its "soundness," or, in other words, the practical upshot of its employment. Cherea, it will be remembered, fears "that inhuman vision in which his life means no more than a speck of dust" (CTOP, p. 22), and he states that neither life nor happiness are possible "if one pushes the absurd to its logical conclusions," one of which is the claim "that all [actions] are on an equal footing" (CTOP, pp. 51–2).

Camus's change in perspective here is not without good philosophical precedent. When Kant purported to have made good Newton's physics in *The Critique of Pure Reason*, he theoretically precluded the possibility of a free, efficacious subject, but when he then moved to the question of morality in the *Foundations of the Metaphysics of Morals* and *The Critique of Practical Reason*, he nevertheless presupposed this free, efficacious subject in establishing the ground of morality, essentially arguing that theoretical and practical philosophy are different perspectives that, while irreconcilable, are still both valid. (To be more exact, Kant laid the groundwork for this position in the latter part of the *Critique of Pure Reason* itself.) It was Kant's view that because we must act under the idea of freedom, then for *practical* purposes we are *necessarily* free, which, in turn, has normative implications. Something similar is taking place in Camus's change of perspective. Theoretically, he does not deny the Absurd, which has its own inherent "logic," but, practically, as Cherea points out, the Absurd cannot be "soundly" lived, if, in fact, it can be lived at all. To try to live the logic of the Absurd, as Patrice Mersault, Meursault, and Caligula do, is, indeed, a category mistake of sorts (akin to the Kantian subject trying to live its existence as a determined being in Newton's causally determined universe), for to act, in some sense, is already to belie it. (In the face of an indifferent universe, why do *anything* at all, and how do we justify what we do? To reject meaning and strive toward happiness in supposed conformity with the Absurd, as both Patrice

Mersault and Meursault do, is already a meaningful choice, and happiness is surely a value.) Put simply, the Absurd, as a *theoretical* perspective, cannot be lived (although it might help to "inform," as the laws of nature certainly help to inform the practical decisions of Kant's free, efficacious subjects). If, for *practical* purposes, what we strive for is (existential) meaning and happiness, what is clear is that these things cannot be achieved by the solitary individual *or* by incongruously sticking to the absurdist (theoretical) perspective. For *practical* purposes, we must collectively strive for (existential) meaning and happiness, as these things are achievements of the human collective. Thus, Camus states in *Letters to a German Friend*:

> I continue to believe that this world has no ultimate meaning. But I know that something *in it* has a meaning and that is man, because he is the only creature who insists on having one. This world has at least the truth of man, and our task is to provide its justification against fate itself. And it has no justification but man . . . (RRD, p. 28; italics added)

From this perspective, the human (i.e., practical) perspective *in* the world (in which it is "human evidence [that] we must preserve," RRD, p. 14), the position of Camus's hypothetical German friend, who "chose injustice and sided with the gods" (i.e., the theoretical perspective), evidences a "logic [that is] merely apparent" (RRD, p. 28). As we shall come to see, although Camus now views the logic of the Absurd as sophistical when applied to practical concerns, the Absurd will continue to strongly inform what we might start to call his evolving ethics, in which "friendship, mankind, happiness, [and] our desire for justice" (RRD, p. 14) figure prominently. At this point, however, the Absurd will no longer be used to motivate his philosophical positions but, instead, it will be used to deflate those grandiose political philosophies whose cosmic pretensions "merely appear" to do justice to these concerns. What's more, happiness will no longer be something that is immediately achievable by the individual but rather will serve as a collective, regulative ideal:

> Our difficult achievement consisted in following you into war without forgetting happiness. And despite the clamors and the violence, we tried to preserve in our hearts the memory of a happy sea, of a remembered hill, the smile of a beloved face. For that matter, this was our best weapon, the one that we shall never put away. For as soon as we lost it we should be as dead as you are. (RRD, p. 29)

With these changes in perspective on concepts that had long played a central role in his thought, changes that are all beholden to a demand for lucidity that begins from unrepentantly humanistic premises, Camus comes to the position that "there are means that cannot be excused" under any circumstances (RRD, p. 5). This position, which, in some sense, will come to underlie his ethics, will also put him at odds with most of the French intelligentsia on some of the most intractable political problems of his time.

Misunderstandings

> I was looked at, but I wasn't *seen*.
>
> Albert Camus, *The Misunderstanding*[2]

If *Caligula* reflects the breakdown of the Sisyphean paradigm and *Letters to a German Friend* signals a socioethical turn based on humanistic premises, *The Misunderstanding*, a play that was first performed in 1944, reflects Camus's initial move (at least in his literary works) toward a concern with the socioethical. This concern, however, is expressed only negatively, as the play, which Camus justifiably calls "claustrophobic" and "gloomy" (thus mirroring life in Paris under the Nazi occupation), reflects the catastrophic consequences of an inability to recognize or to be recognized and, therefore, an inability to communicate. Thus, Camus states, "the play's morality is not altogether negative," given that "it amounts to saying that in an unjust or indifferent world man can save himself, and save others, by practicing the most basic sincerity and pronouncing the most appropriate word" (CTOP, p. vii).

The Misunderstanding is set in a shabby inn located in a cold, desolate Czechoslovakian valley, and its plot is a simple one. Jan, who had left his mother and sister (Martha) many years earlier, pseudonymously registers at their inn in the hope of reestablishing relations with them, which includes helping them out financially. On entering the inn, he is not recognized by either one of them, and he decides to keep his identity a secret, hoping that they will come to recognize him. At a time when he is alone in the lobby, save for the Old Manservant who aids his mother and sister in running the inn, Jan's loving wife, Maria, meets him, and he instructs her to stay at another inn until the situation has resolved itself. Maria protests, sensing that this seemingly harmless deception will lead to disastrous results, but she dutifully goes along with his plan. As it turns out, his mother and sister, who are resentful to their cores, have murdered wealthy, single male patrons in the past, and they intend to kill Jan in order to finally escape their hardscrabble lives. Although the Old Manservant is aware of their plans, he says nothing, and the mother and sister proceed to poison Jan, dumping his corpse into the river. When the pair realize what they have done after going through the dead man's papers, the mother commits suicide by throwing herself in the same river, and then Maria, on returning to the inn, confronts Martha, who remains unrepentant. After Martha leaves, Maria is distraught, and she asks the Old Manservant for help, who ends the play by responding "no."

Although Martha depicts the murder of Jan as "a misunderstanding" when confronted by Maria (CTOP, p. 129), Camus's own depiction of the murder as a mere "misunderstanding" is, I think, a misguided one. Presumably, Jan's life would have been spared if he had "practic[ed] the most basic sincerity and pronounc[ed] the most appropriate word," but even this is not absolutely clear, for although the mother sadly declares right before her suicide that "a mother's love for her son is now my certainty" (CTOP, p. 120), Martha maintains that "if I'd recognized him, it would have made no difference" (CTOP, p. 123). Crucially, however, if it had been *anybody* else, there would have been no question whatsoever of carrying out the murderous plot. Therefore, rather than see the play in terms of a breakdown in language (although, with the exception of Maria, it is true that the others do not appropriately express themselves), it is better to see it in terms of a breakdown in recognition. Martha herself blithely tells Maria that "in the normal order of things no one is ever recognized" (CTOP, p. 132), and if one is not recognized, just for being a human being, then whether one is able to appropriately express oneself is beside the point. Many of the Nazis' victims surely did not lack for the ability to appropriately express themselves, and during the course of the play Martha rebuffs all routine human inquiries by Jan, presumably adhering to her mother's opinion that "it's easier to kill what one doesn't know" (CTOP, p. 79). When one chooses to "turn [one's] heart to stone" (CTOP, p. 133), as Martha cynically advises Maria to do toward the end of the play, one does not genuinely "know" anything, no one is "recognized," and all language, regardless of how eloquent, falls on deaf ears.

As for the four major characters themselves, only two are of particular interest, as Maria and the mother are fairly one-dimensional. Much like Caesonia in *Caligula*, Maria represents the needs of love, and the mother represents a world-weary cynicism, self-deceptively justifying her murderous plot on the ground that "it's hardly a crime" because "life is crueler than we" (CTOP, pp. 80–81). The two characters that best reflect the movement in Camus's thought are Jan and Martha. Although Jan is unduly rigid, and, indeed, is unreasonably closed off to the justifiable concerns of Maria, who only asks that he make clear who he is lest there be a misunderstanding, he represents the acknowledgment that there is more to a well-lived life than happiness (which, we have every reason to believe, he has with Maria). He asserts that "happiness isn't everything, [for] there is duty, too" (CTOP, p. 84), and, moreover, that "one can't remain a stranger all one's life," for while "a man needs happiness, he also needs to find his true place in the world" (CTOP, p. 87). Conversely, the unhappy Martha, who is every bit as one-dimensional as her mother, is of interest because she seems to represent the last gasp of Camus's earlier willingness to justify the resentful pursuit of happiness at all costs: "What is human in me is what I desire, and to get what I desire, I'd stick at nothing [and] sweep away every obstacle on my path" (CTOP, p. 105), she declares, but now this position seems little more than monstrous, as is her inhuman reply to Maria's accusations, namely, that "you have no right to sit in judgment" (CTOP, p. 129). In the past, Camus seemed to tolerate, if not support, the right of outraged innocence to express itself in anything but innocent ways. Patrice Mersault is deemed "pure" and "innocent" even as he blows Zagreus's brains out in the pursuit of his own happiness, Meursault is deemed an "innocent waif" even as he callously objectifies others, and even the sociopathic Caligula is "understood" by the people around him, including the innocent Scipio who "shares his pain" because "the same fire burns in both [their] hearts" (CTOP, p. 56). With Martha, this comes to an end, as self-justifying resentment, which closes itself off to the very happiness that it purportedly seeks, is shown to be as ugly as Nietzsche had always understood it to be.

The last character in the play, the Old Manservant, who is barely more than a specter, in many ways attests to the play's transitional nature. In response to the common interpretation that this character (who refuses to rectify the misunderstanding or ameliorate Maria's pain) represents implacable fate, Camus declares that "if he answers 'No' . . . this is because . . . at a certain level of suffering or injustice no one can do anything for anyone, [as] pain is solitary" (CTOP, p. viii). It is just this attitude that Camus will reject in *The Plague*, for in the face of implacability (whether metaphysical or social) what is called for is not a solitary revolt but one undertaken in solidarity.

The Moral of the Plague – Metaphysical, Sociohistorical, or Characterological?

> Absurd. If one kills oneself, the absurd is negated. If one does not kill oneself, the absurd reveals on application a principle of satisfaction that negates itself. This does not mean that the absurd does not exist. It means that the absurd is *truly* without logic. This is why one cannot *truly* live on it.

> The greatest saving one can make in the order of thought is to accept the unintelligibility of the world – and to pay attention to man.
>
> Albert Camus, *Notebooks*[3]

These entries in Camus's *Notebooks*, written around the time that he was composing *The Plague* and commingled with entries concerning the novel, reflect the shift in perspective that I analyzed at the beginning of this chapter. Moving in the direction of solidarity, Camus does not reject the Absurd as a theoretical principle but, rather, as an animating practical one, for "one cannot truly live on it." Crucially, however, while the Absurd is no longer the animating practical principle, in the sense that Camus no longer explores ways of living in accord with its "logic," it lives on in his thought as a practical problem even after he begins "to pay attention to man," as his claim in the excerpt that opens this chapter evidences: "I merely wanted men to rediscover their solidarity in order to wage war against their revolting fate." Understood in the context of *Letters to a German Friend*, this "revolting fate" (to which his "German friend" submits in despair) is "the metaphysics of the Absurd," now understood as a practical problem, and Camus has come to believe that effectively "waging war" against it (as well as revolting historical "fates") requires human solidarity.

According to Camus, "*The Plague* [can] be read on a number of different levels, [but] has as its obvious content the struggle of the European resistance movements against Nazism" (LCE, p. 339). Yet, many French critics denigrated *The Plague* on precisely these grounds, arguing that a plague is a deceptive metaphor for the Nazi occupation, as a struggle against microbes is a far different matter than a struggle against other human beings. In response to Roland Barthes, who asked "what would the fighters against the plague do confronted with the all-too-human face of the scourge," Camus asserts that "terror has several faces," and "the reproach . . . that *The Plague* can apply to any resistance against any tyranny," and thus fundamentally "rejects history," is not a "legitimate" one, "unless it is proclaimed that the only way of taking part in history is to make tyranny legitimate" (LCE, p. 340). Accordingly, Camus rejects the claim that *The Plague* "lays the foundation for an ahistorical ethic and an attitude of political solitude" and, as we have seen, says that it involves "a community whose struggles must be shared," which reflects a movement in "the direction of solidarity and participation" in his own works (LCE, p. 339).

There is much to unpack here, and the stakes are high, for both the criticism and Camus's response to it contain the germ cells (if you will) of the arguments that will come to surround *The Rebel*, as well as Camus's positions on the Cold War and the Algerian War. To begin with, however, it is not unfair to say that Camus is not adequately responding to his critics here. Aside from his claim that *The Plague* signals an evolution in his work from solitary to collective revolt, which is true enough but beside the point, he is invalidly equating the struggle against the plague with a struggle against tyranny. Assuming, for the sake of argument, that one is confronted with a regime that cannot reasonably be characterized as anything but a tyranny (and this is clearly not always the case), the moral (rather than instrumental) question of how to deal with it is not nearly as straightforward as the moral question of how to deal with the plague. To eradicate the plague, and, therefore, bring about a state of affairs in which both individuals and the larger community are free of it, is an unqualified good, while to eradicate a tyranny might not be. Human suffering is reduced by eradicating a plague, while the same is not necessarily the case when eradicating a specific tyranny. Indeed, when Jean Tarrou, who conceives of the plan to organize sanitation squads to deal with the plague, says that his aim in life is "to have no truck with anything which, directly or indirectly, for good reasons or for bad, brings death to anyone or justifies others' putting him to death" (P, pp. 252–3), he evidences the difference that exists between fighting a plague and fighting fascism, for he could not have organized the analogue to a sanitation squad, a resistance cell, in accord with this principle.

Accordingly, although Camus is right when he asserts that *The Plague* can be understood "on a number of different levels," his critics are also right when they assert, in essence, that these different levels – metaphysical, sociohistorical, and characterological (i.e., individuals with their dispositions of character) – do not seamlessly dovetail. In the next three sections, I shall analyze the novel's metaphysical, sociohistorical, and characterological themes (the last of which, I shall argue, begins to lay the foundation for what I take to be Camus's developing phenomenological ethics.) Before proceeding, however, I shall outline the book's plot, which is easy enough. Oran (which is located on the Algerian coastline) falls prey to an outbreak of the bubonic plague, and as the disease progresses, which leads to a quarantine of the city, individuals respond in different ways. Doctors set themselves to the tasks of coming up with a serum (Dr Castel) and tending to the sick (led by Dr Bernard Rieux, whom, we find out near the end of the novel, is the narrator). Bureaucrats fumble (though one, M. Othon undergoes a conversion of sorts). Priests (like Father Paneloux, who also undergoes a conversion of sorts) continue to sermonize. Sanitation squads are set up, operated, and complemented by concerned individuals (to begin with, Jean Tarrou, who is not even a citizen of Oran, and Joseph Grand, who, like Rieux's mother, embodies the dignity of the ordinary). Individuals continue to strive for a now unattainable happiness (such as Raymond Rambert, a journalist who throws his lot in with the sanitation squads exactly when his unlawful escape from the city becomes a real possibility). And, lastly, there are those who would profit from the misery (such as Raoul, Gonzales, and, most of all, Cottard). Ultimately, whether the efforts to staunch the plague have any effect at all is unclear, but the plague runs its course and the city reopens with a big celebration.

The Plague and Metaphysics

> All entities whose kind of Being is of a character other than Dasein's must be conceived as *unmeaning*, essentially devoid of any meaning at all. . . . *And only that which is unmeaning can be absurd.* The present-at-hand, as Dasein encounters it, can, as it were, assault Dasein's Being; natural events, for instance, can break in upon us and destroy us.

> *Death, as the end of Dasein, is Dasein's ownmost possibility – non-relational, certain and as such indefinite, not to be outstripped.* . . . The more unveiledly this possibility gets understood, the more purely does the understanding penetrate into it as the possibility of the impossibility of any existence at all.
>
> <div align="right">Martin Heidegger, <i>Being and Time</i>[4]</div>

For those even remotely acquainted with Heidegger, a discussion of his philosophy in a section examining metaphysical questions would seem to be little more than perverse, for more than any other philosopher in the western tradition, he repudiated metaphysics. According to Heidegger, metaphysics found its foremost expression in Descartes's philosophy, which is based on a subject-object paradigm that revolves around the question of how the ideas in one's mind match up with the external world, and he thought that this paradigm was not only mistaken but also destructive. Accordingly, Camus's neo-Cartesianism, in which the Absurd derives from the rupture between consciousness and an indifferent world, would have been repugnant to him if he had been aware of it. Yet, in the first of the two passages above, Heidegger speaks of natural events breaking in upon us and destroying us as "absurd," which is precisely how the plague presents itself, and, in the second passage, he speaks of *Dasein* as a "being-unto-death," who in acknowledging death as its "ownmost possibility" is able to heed the "call of conscience," which is precisely what the more virtuous characters in *The Plague* are able to do. (The term *"Dasein,"* literally translated as "being-there," is meant to juxtapose a "worlded" conception of human beings against Descartes's "deworlded" subject or consciousness). As a result, keeping in mind the fundamental structural differences between Camus's neo-Cartesian "metaphysics of the Absurd" and Heidegger's anti-Cartesian "fundamental ontology," which ultimately aims to recover "the meaning of Being," an analysis of certain parts of *The Plague* in Heideggerian terms can be very fruitful.

"A pestilence isn't a thing made to man's measure," and, therefore, although "pestilences have a way of recurring in the world . . . we find it hard to believe in ones that crash down on our heads from a blue sky." In other words, a plague is a "monstrous" phenomenon, for its size and destructiveness is beyond the pale of human comprehension, and thus it seems to be horrifyingly unnatural (even if nothing is more "natural" than the microbes that constitute it). For this reason, Camus contends, when it comes to pestilences, "everybody" is a "humanist," since ("wrapped up in themselves") everybody "disbelieves in pestilences" (P, p. 37). Camus's point, I take it, is that human beings necessarily start from their (collectively engendered) individual experiences of the world, which hang together on the basis of certain fundamental expectations (one of which might be some idea of "cosmic justice"), and there are certain kinds of phenomena, such as pestilences, that cannot have meaning for us because they are so at odds with the fabric of our experience that they call into question the very meaningfulness of the (our) world. Such phenomena *deconstruct* the (our) world, or, as Heidegger puts it, they are an "unmeaning" that can "break in upon us and destroy us" not only physically but also socioculturally. Indeed, on Camus's account, Heidegger himself is a "humanist," for although Heidegger attacked "humanism," declaring that all forms of it are bound up with a metaphysics, as a phenomenologist he must start from the human being's (*Dasein's*) experience of the world. And the human being's (*Dasein's*) experience of the world, in turn, is only made possible by what Heidegger labels "*das Man*" (i.e., "the One"), the anonymous but omnipresent background practices and understandings that constitute our social world. If *das Man* cannot take into account certain kinds of phenomena because they do not cohere with respect to its existing practices and understandings, then these phenomena are absurd.

What must be reemphasized is that it is not the mere fact of death that makes the plague absurd but, rather, the scale of death. Indeed, as Heidegger points out, death itself certainly does not lack for meaning, as *das Man* furnishes a "tranquilizing" interpretation of it that is generally unquestioned. According to Heidegger, a primordial, visceral experience of our own (individual) impending deaths is covered up all the time by the platitudinous "one dies," which, of course, is true, but what the platitude covers up is the fact that we die alone, and, therefore, that we should live distinctly, in the sense that each of us should want to be more than a simple amalgam of the (collectively engendered) characteristics that comprise the anonymous *das Man*. If we have the courage to experience the anxiety of acknowledging that we die alone – that our deaths are "non-relational" – then we might also have the impetus to strive to live authentically, and not simply in accordance with the dictates of *das Man*. Now, the problem with the plague is that it levels death not just for any or all *Dasein* (individual human beings) but for *das Man* (humanity as such), and thus precludes the very possibility of making our lives and deaths meaningful. In other words, to acknowledge one's impending death should lead one to strive to live authentically, which means heeding "the call of conscience" and making a difference in the world, but it is "the world," grasped phenomenologically, that is precisely what the plague destroys. The plague thus reveals to us, in a particularly graphic way, "the possibility of the impossibility of any existence at all."

Ironically, then, when confronted with a monstrous phenomenon such as the plague, the acknowledgment that we are beings-unto-death can have the effect of effacing our individuality, which (at least in such aberrant times) is directly at odds with Heidegger's claim that it opens us up to the possibility of living more authentic individual lives. As Camus points out, individuality takes it on the chin: "No longer were there individual destinies, only a collective destiny, made of plague and the emotions shared by all" (P, p. 167); "none of us was capable any longer of any exalted emotion, [and] all had trite, monotonous feelings" (P, p. 181); "they took an interest only in what interested everyone else, they had only general ideas, and even their tenderest affections now seemed abstract, items of the common stock" (P, p. 183); and finally, the dead were "flung into the death-pits indiscriminately" (P, p. 175). What's more, according to Camus, "plague had leveled out [all] discrimination," and even philosophers, whose job involves making conceptual discriminations, can fall prey to this leveling. Crucially, however, although this last point, in particular, might be true within the context of a plague, it is also where the analogy between a plague and Nazism starts to break down. During a plague, discrimination with respect to such matters as "the quality of the clothes or food" people buy might lessen (P, p. 184), but the moral lines are relatively clear, and most people do not fall prey to the kind of base opportunism that is engaged in by the profiteering Cottard. Conversely, while Nazism is as close to an unqualified social evil as plague is to an unqualified natural evil, none other than Heidegger himself, one of the most prominent philosophers of the twentieth century, was seduced by its ideology and sycophantically lobbied the Nazis for the rectorship of Freiberg University – something that, presumably, the plague's more transparent "ideology" of death would have never prompted him to do.

In any case, according to Heidegger, the ability to attain existential authenticity depends on a disclosedness of Being, which, in turn, presents a more originary, primordial Truth (capital "T"). Even assuming that a "self-presencing" human being (i.e., one who lives "in the moment" and does not "re-present" experience on the Cartesian model) could attain this primordial Truth, it is, if not fleeting, resistant to communication, as the language used by *das Man* will invariably level it down. Despite the different frameworks (both conceptual and stylistic), a similar sort of problematic, albeit toward different ends, is broached in *The Plague*. One of the key characters in the novel is Joseph Grand, a man with "all the attributes of insignificance" (P, p. 44). Largely distinguished by the plodding way in which he records the plague's statistics and an excruciating idiosyncrasy, "an almost finical anxiety over his choice of words" (P, p. 33), he is, nevertheless, trying to write a novel, but he cannot get beyond the initial sentence, as "evenings, whole weeks, [are] spent on one word, [or] sometimes on a mere conjunction" (P, p. 103). Yet, through Rieux, Camus designates this decent but feckless character as the novel's hero: "the narrator commends to his readers, with, to his thinking, perfect justice, this insignificant and obscure hero who had to his credit only a little goodness of heart and a seemingly absurd ideal, and this will render to the truth its due" (P, p. 137). Why, then, to Rieux's (and Camus's) thinking, is Grand *the* hero? He may have agreed to help the sanitation squads "without a moment's hesitation and with the large-heartedness that was second nature with him" (P, p. 134), but given the efforts of others, such as Tarrou, who devised the sanitation squads and died from the plague because of it, Grand's efforts seem rather scant. And what does any of this have to do with Heidegger's primordial Truth?

The simple answer, to begin with, is that Grand's "absurd ideal," which does not enable him to get beyond the first sentence of his novel, is nothing other than Truth (with a capital "T"), or, put more precisely, the recognition that Truth (with a capital "T") is ultimately unachievable but that to strive toward it (with this understanding) is, nevertheless, an existential imperative. It is for this reason that, when Rieux tells Grand that the "opening phrase had whetted his curiosity [and] he'd like to hear what followed," Grand "told him he'd got it all wrong" (P, p. 104). What Rieux does not appreciate here are Grand's lofty "metaphysical" aspirations, his desire, never to be realized, for at least one thing, one sentence, to capture Truth (with a capital "T"). For Rieux, who categorically rejects Father Paneloux's eternal verities exactly because "he speaks with such assurance of the truth – with a capital T" (P, p. 126), Grand is much more honest. While Father Paneloux nonchalantly speaks of "truth – with a capital T" in the abstract, Grand tries to speak of it in the concrete language of literature, and, indeed, he is always trying to make his one sentence "more concrete" (P, p. 134). Understood in this way, if Meursault was the metaphysically honest man during Camus's Sisyphean period, Grand (who retains his solidarity with his comrades) is his successor (and, indeed, it will be remembered that Meursault also rejected the abstract eternal verities of the priest who came to his prison cell on the eve of his execution). Of course, here the analogy between plague (the metaphysical) and Nazism (the sociohistorical) again starts to break down, for although Grand, with his commitment to striving toward an unattainable Truth (with a capital "T"), can unproblematically work with the sanitation squads in an attempt to eradicate the plague, he would be utterly paralyzed when confronted by the ethical quandaries that necessarily face any resistance fighter worth his or her salt.

Now, at first blush it would appear that the Truth (with a capital "T") that Grand is after has absolutely nothing to do with Heidegger's primordial Truth. Grand is looking for words that function transparently, as a sort of "photograph" of reality (P, p. 135), which clearly invokes the Cartesian representational model that Heidegger finds so disturbing. In other words, according to Heidegger, the problem with the metaphysical tradition, as exemplified by Descartes, is that it sees us, first and foremost, as knowers who "re-present" the world in our heads and then question how these "re-presentations" correspond to the external world. (Indeed, tacitly rejecting Grand's "photograph" metaphor, Heidegger speaks disapprovingly of our metaphysical era as "the age of the world picture.") It is not that Heidegger rejects everyday claims about the world (such as the claim that it is raining outside) as having any relation to questions about truth, but these kinds of "correspondence" claims, he emphasizes, are merely of a derivative nature, and what he rejects is the primacy that they are accorded by the metaphysical tradition. Such primacy obscures the fact that we are, first and foremost, engaged in the world, non-cognitively using the entities that make it up, and that it is the background of our collective practices and understandings (*das Man*) that brings an intelligible world into being (and, therefore, makes "correspondence" claims possible in the first place).

Having made this distinction, however, Grand's attempt to "photograph" reality with his words must be understood metaphorically, and his struggle for truth must be understood in terms of the kind of primordial existential Truth toward which Heidegger's search for "the meaning of Being" points. In accordance with Heidegger's thought, Grand is not trying to "photograph" the world so much as "presence" it, and, in accordance with Heidegger's thought, he recognizes that language, which is the common (leveling) property of *das Man*, is not up to the task. Yet, in one absolutely crucial respect, Grand parts company with Heidegger's thought. Although Heidegger says that the background of our collective practices and understandings (*das Man*) is what brings an intelligible world and, therefore, truth into being in the first place, he also holds open, as we saw, the possibility of an authentic existential comportment, in which the self uniquely presences itself to the world of its experience and, in this way, allows it to disclose itself in accordance with a more primordial Truth. The modest Grand, in both his person and in his project, tacitly rejects this possibility, as does Camus himself. Camus believes that abstract Truth (with a capital "T") can be used to justify repugnant ideas, actions, and occurrences by those who take themselves to be in possession of it (as is the case with Father Paneloux, whom we shall consider shortly), and Heidegger's own dalliance with Nazism, which he thought would help to make good the truth of Being, bears out the danger of this hubris in even the most brilliant among us. In his later works, Heidegger seems to recognize this problem, as he emphasizes "the ontological difference" (i.e., the difference between the being of beings like *Dasein* and Being), and states that "Being reveals and conceals itself," which is more modest in that it undermines the idea that anyone (Heidegger included) can get a stranglehold on the primordial Truth of Being.

Like Heidegger, Father Paneloux moves from an arrogant to a more modest philosophical stance without changing his fundamental belief system. However, what induces his move is not a recognition that his more arrogant stance was inadvertently complicit with human evil (as was, ostensibly, the case with Heidegger) but, instead, a recognition that natural evil is not necessarily in accord with Divine Justice. These phenomena, human and natural evil, are the two subsets of a dilemma in the philosophy of religion known as "the problem of evil," which, in general terms, can be depicted as follows: If God is omniscient, omnipotent, and all good, then the world should not have evil in it, but since the world has evil in it, then it must be the case that there is no God. The theist's first response to the problem of evil generally deals with the problem of human evil, and it is a reasonably compelling one: If human beings are to be genuinely moral, then they must be free (for programmed robots might always do what morality requires but could not be deemed moral beings), and if human beings are free, then they can choose to do evil acts. This does not account for the problem of natural evil, however, and for the theist this subset of the problem is tougher sledding. The seventeenth-century philosopher G. W. Leibniz had attempted to address the problem of evil by arguing that we live in the best of all possible worlds (a general principle for which more current philosophers have laboriously argued), but this argument rings hollow, as Voltaire scornfully brings home with his portrayal of Dr Pangloss in the novel *Candide*. (While Voltaire thinks that Leibniz's theodicy is absurd, given such events as the Lisbon earthquake of 1755, which killed tens of thousands in a matter of seconds, he was a deist and, therefore, did not deny the existence of God.) More in line with Kierkegaard than with Leibniz, Father Paneloux's response to the problem of natural evil is somewhat more compelling.

Father Paneloux's movement from an arrogant to a more modest philosophical stance (or, to be more precise, from an arrogant to a more modest Christianity), is evinced in the two sermons that he gives to the beleaguered people of Oran. To begin with, as Rieux points out, he "spoke in a gentler, more thoughtful tone" in the second sermon, and "instead of saying 'you' he now said 'we'" (P, p. 222). Paneloux's movement, from fire-and-brimstone to empathy and from "you" to "we," is not the product of massive death, which does not confound this God-fearing Christian, who *knows* that Oran's evildoers have only reaped what they have sown ("Now you are learning your lesson"), but, rather, the product of just one death, a young boy (the son of M. Othon, the local magistrate), whose innocence is beyond question. On facing the boy, who is strewn across the hospital bed "in a grotesque parody of crucifixion," and listening to "the angry death-cry that has sounded through the ages of mankind" (P, pp. 215–16), Paneloux prays for his life but to no avail. Obviously at a loss after the boy's death, Paneloux weakly suggests to Rieux that "perhaps we should love what we cannot understand" (P, p. 218), which smacks of the sort of Leibnizian rationalization that so infuriated Voltaire, and Rieux, sounding the theme of Ivan Karamazov in *The Brothers Karamazov*, unequivocally rejects this position: "Until my dying day I shall refuse to love a scheme of things in which children are put to torture" and "salvation's much too big a word for me" (P, pp. 218–19). Chided by Rieux in a way to which he cannot tolerably respond, Paneloux comes to recognize that he has no greater understanding of Divine Justice than anyone else, and that such occurrences can in no way be justified. Thus, in his second sermon, Paneloux rhetorically asks "for who would dare to assert that eternal happiness can compensate for a single moment's human suffering," and, conceding that such occurrences are inscrutable, declares that if one has made "the essential choice" to believe in God, then one must will God's will even if it is the plague, for faith is an "all or nothing" proposition (P, pp. 224–5). At the end of the day, then, rejecting both Leibniz's theodicy and Voltaire's deism, Paneloux essentially deals with the problem of evil on Kierkegaardian grounds: for one who has made the leap of faith to believe in God, notwithstanding the absence of good reasons for doing so, a "teleological suspension of the ethical" is demanded (i.e., a suspension of the ethical in the name of this higher end). Yet, unlike Kierkegaard's Abraham, who had to suspend the ethical in terms of his actions so that he could comply with God's command that he kill his son, Paneloux more modestly asks that we suspend the ethical in terms of what we expect of this omniscient, omnipotent, and all-good God, who, nevertheless, wills what we take to be evil things.

The Plague and Social Banality

> . . . he was summing up the lesson that this long course in human wickedness had taught us – the lesson of the fearsome, word-and-thought-defying *banality of evil*.
>
> Hannah Arendt, *Eichmann in Jerusalem*[5]

Camus starts *The Plague* with a discussion of the city of Oran itself, and for a town that is mostly distinguished by its undistinguished "ordinariness," he lingers on the point. "Everyone is bored," we are told, and when they are not working they look to "cultivate habits." Principally, however, Oran's citizens "work hard, but solely with the object of getting rich" and, therefore, their "chief aim in life is, as they call it, 'doing business.' " What Oran's citizens lack, to be more precise, is imagination, and what Camus seeks to convey is "the banality of the town and of life in it." Still, this banal city, which has a "smug, placid air," is "completely modern," and herein lies the deep sociohistorical problem. It is from this "completely modern" banality that the plague of Nazism (and, more generally, totalitarianism in its various fascist and communist forms) arises, and it is because of this "completely modern" banality that men and women "had not the faintest reason to apprehend . . . the premonitory signs of the grave events" that were about to transpire (P, pp. 3–6). Moreover, even after the plague runs its course, these sociohistorical preconditions still remain, as Camus asserts in the final sentence of *The Plague*: "the plague bacillus never dies or disappears for good," for "it can lie dormant for years and years" embedded in the most familiar places, and "perhaps the day would come when, for the bane and enlightening of men, it would rouse up its rats again and send them forth to die in a happy city" (P, p. 308).

Camus's parting shot here, that *perhaps* the plague will come again to be "the bane and *enlightening* of men," reflects his view that while it has just extracted itself from a totalitarianism of its own making, enlightenment thought continues to be in need of "enlightening" with respect to itself, and that *perhaps* the only way this will happen is through further misery resulting from lessons not learned. In other words, Camus believes that there is a subterranean affinity between enlightenment thought (or, at least, certain aspects of it) and totalitarianism, and it is arguably the most likeable and laudable figure in *The Plague*, Tarrou, who makes this point (in a conversation with Rieux): "Let me begin by saying I had plague already, long before I came to this town and encountered it here, which is tantamount to saying I'm like everybody else, only there are some people who don't know it, or feel at ease in that condition" (P, p. 245). Tarrou's essential point, which shall be fleshed out in the next section, is that what he previously took to be a justified use of violence (since it was for justice's sake) is no less a plague than the plague (Nazism) that he is currently fighting, and his rejection of plague in all of its forms is what leads him to state, as we have seen, that his aim in life is "to have no truck with anything which, directly or indirectly, for good reasons or for bad, brings death to anyone or justifies others' putting him to death" (P, pp. 252–3). Of course, this is where the use of the plague as a metaphor for Nazism breaks down, and it is the basis for some of the criticisms that we have already seen leveled against the novel. As I claimed earlier, I think that there is more than a grain of truth in these criticisms, but Camus looks at this relation in much greater theoretical detail in *The Rebel*, and it is in this context (in the next chapter) that it is more properly taken up. In the meantime, it should be reemphasized, the aim of *The Plague* is less about what it is that beleaguers us than about how we forge, or fail to forge, links of solidarity to respond to it, whether it be human or natural evil. Accordingly, in this section, I shall consider those characters who break the links of solidarity in the face of evil, while in the next section, I shall consider those characters who forge them.

As I pointed out at the beginning of this section, Camus thinks that those who play a role in cultivating the sociohistorical preconditions for the plague (fascism) do so unwittingly, but he also thinks that those who deliberately side with the plague (fascism) once it is in full force do so unwittingly as well. Although Camus does not belabor this point, he attributes the shortcomings of the scrofulous Cottard, who is the closest thing in the novel to a straight up Nazi collaborator (or, at least, an ardent supporter of the Vichy government), to "an ignorant, that is to say lonely, heart" (P, p. 302). I believe that this is an overly generous characterization on Camus's part, and I shall consider it momentarily. Initially, however, I would like to briefly consider the type who manifests only an habitual lack of imagination, the type that actually is only unwittingly complicit with evil by virtue of a certain kind of (bourgeois) sociohistorical conditioning, and, therefore, when it gets clearer on matters, will do the right thing. The embodiment of this position is the provincial magistrate, M. Othon. To use the name of Sinclair Lewis's title character, at the beginning of the novel, M. Othon is a Babbitt, a haughty, mediocre man who unreflectively mimics conventional morality. M. Othon finds Paneloux's first, condemnatory sermon "absolutely irrefutable" (P, p. 100), and he tells Tarrou that "it's not the law that counts [but] the sentence," which leads Tarrou to designate him as "Enemy Number One" (P, p. 146). Moreover, playing the part of the austere enforcer of dinner-table manners, he belittles his children in a public restaurant, making his boy, in particular, "a little more shrunken than before" (P, p. 116). Still, like Paneloux, who is "better than his [first] sermon" (P, p. 150), M. Othon is better than his rigid persona. He takes fairness seriously, conceding that since "there is one rule for all alike" his family ought to be quarantined after his son is diagnosed with the plague (P, p. 212), which, despite its rigidity, suggests at least the possibility of a genuine ethical comportment. And, after his son's death, M. Othon not only manifests "a sudden gentleness" but decides to remain with the quarantine after he is cleared to return home, which is a truly noble act (P, p. 259). Through the experience of personal suffering, then, M. Othon moves from Paneloux's accusatory "you" to a fraternal "we," and, in this way, he evinces the possibility of breaking out of the straitjacket of a banal bourgeois morality to assume this more genuine ethical comportment.

Matters are significantly different when it comes to Cottard, however. Although Cottard surely reflects what Arendt terms "the banality of evil," his banality is not the manifestation of a misguided ethical comportment, as is the case with M. Othon, but, instead, of a basic lack of any ethical comportment at all. Cottard, who has no first name (presumably because he is the generic stand in for all collaborators), flourishes during the plague. He declares that he "was never fitter in [his] life" (P, p. 80); he is "puzzled" by Rambert's desire to leave the besieged city (P, p. 144); and, monetarily, he is profiting from the misery of others, "making money hand over fist in small, somewhat shady transactions" (P, p. 260). In short, as Tarrou writes in his diary, Cottard is "the living image of contentment" (P, p. 194). Still, through Tarrou's diary, Camus speaks of Cottard compassionately, suggesting that his love for the plague is the result of his own feeling of social isolation, since with everyone in the same boat, suffering from mental distress and a fear of one's neighbor, he fits in: "obviously he's in the same peril of death as everyone else, but that's just the point; he's in it *with the others*" (P, p. 195). Like elsewhere, the use of the plague as a metaphor for the Nazi occupation breaks down here, for, seen as a collaborator, Cottard is not "in the same peril of death as everyone else." Indeed, he is not "in it with the others," as he himself attests in a rather telling claim: "They're fretting simply because they won't let themselves go, and I know what I'm talking about" (P, p. 198). Because he does not have a conscience, much less a "clean" one (P, p. 196), Cottard can let himself go, and (to follow Clamence's logic) it is only in this sort of race to the bottom that he rises to the top, for the bottom is where he began.

Ultimately, the "problem" with Cottard is that he stands for too much, and thus he does not actually stand for anything at all. He is the only major figure in the book to deliberately align himself with the plague, while those who collaborated with the Vichy government constituted a large, highly differentiated group. Like Camus, we would surely be right to show compassion to some segment of this group, who, confronted with awful options, made choices that did not flow from their basic characters. Cottard, however, is from another segment of this group, a segment for whom the plague itself flowed from their very characters, which is why they flourished in it. This group deserves no compassion, unless compassion is to be indiscriminately lavished on all, which, I must confess, even if it is the most enlightened approach (as, I assume, Camus takes it to be), is beyond my own capabilities.

The Plague and Character: Camus's Emerging Phenomenological Ethics

The evil that is in the world always comes out of ignorance, and good intentions may do as much harm as malevolence, if they lack understanding. On the whole, men are more good than bad; that, however, isn't the real point. But they are more or less ignorant, and it is this that we call vice or virtue; the most incorrigible vice being that of an ignorance that fancies it knows everything and therefore claims for itself the right to kill.

Albert Camus, *The Plague*[6]

Rieux, in particular, functions more or less as Camus's spokesperson, and this passage, part of a lengthier one in which "the narrator" modestly downplays the praiseworthiness of the sanitation squads in order not to pay "indirect but potent homage to the worse side of human nature" (P, p. 131), is, as we shall see, pure Camus. What's more, there are features of Rieux's life that bear striking similarities to Camus's own life, not the least of which is his relationship to his mother. Rieux is not the only character who both serves as a spokesperson for Camus's beliefs and bears striking similarities to his life, however, for the same can be said of Tarrou and Rambert. These three characters, I would suggest, represent the three principal touchstones of Camus's emerging phenomenological ethics: a commitment to understanding, happiness, and the reduction of human suffering.

As the anonymous narrator, Rieux opens *The Plague* with the declaration that he will not take into account "the differences in outlook" concerning the story he is about to tell but, rather, he will confine himself to mere reportage: "[The narrator's] business is only to say: 'This is what happened'" (P, p. 6). How seriously Camus takes this "objective" position is unclear, however, as he certainly does not believe that "the God's eye view" his notion of the Absurd (negatively) holds open is a view that any one of us can ever achieve. Indeed, as we saw, Rieux himself rejects this position. After Paneloux's first sermon, Rieux says that he can "speak with such assurance of the truth – with a capital T" because "he hasn't come in contact with death," and, in response to Tarrou's question concerning whether he believes in God, Rieux says "no," and that he essentially takes himself to be relegated to blindly "fighting against creation as he found it." Nevertheless, like Camus, Rieux holds open "the God's eye view" standpoint, operating, even if only implicitly, in Nietzsche's "shadow of God": "Since the order of the world is shaped by death, might it not be better for God if we refuse to believe in Him and struggle with all our might against death, without raising our eyes toward the heaven where He sits in silence." But as this suggests, unlike Camus (and, for that matter, Tarrou, as we will see), God's empty throne, other than simply existing for him, plays no role whatsoever in his thought. In the end, his eyes focused on the tangible plane of our all-too-human existence, all that Rieux "knows" is that "there are sick people and they need curing," and, as for the rest, he admits that he is "fumbling in the dark, struggling to make something out" (P, pp. 126–7).

To make sense of this seeming disparity between Rieux's self-styled pose as an objective reporter and his renunciation of any viable standpoint from which to make good this objectivity, we should see him as one who is totally committed to remaining on the plane of "the concrete, which means simply describing (rather than explaining) what *he* saw as faithfully as possible." In this way, he is like Meursault, albeit, of course, a markedly more sophisticated version. Like Meursault, Rieux is put off by "the abstract," although, given his sophistication, he realizes that "to fight abstraction you must have something of it in your own make-up" (P, p. 91), and, like Meursault, Rieux is somber and unemotional, as he even forgets that his wife is fighting for her life in a sanitarium outside of the city limits (P, p. 156). Moreover, like Meursault, who claimed that he once took life seriously but this changed after he was forced to give up his studies, Rieux tells us that as a young doctor the sight of death caused him to be "outraged by the whole scheme of things . . . [but] I grew more modest, only I've never managed to get used to seeing people die, [and] that's all I know" (P, p. 128). Reminiscent of Sisyphus, Rieux's scorn of death, and, more generally, "suffering," which he credits with being his teacher (P, p. 129), compels him to fight an uphill battle against the plague, and, by Rieux's lights, there is nothing especially complicated or praiseworthy about this compulsion:

> Many fledgling moralists in those days were going about our town proclaiming that there was nothing to be done about it and we should bow to the inevitable. And Tarrou, Rieux, and their friends might give one answer or another, but its conclusion was always the same, their certitude that a fight had to be put up, in this way or that, and there must be no bowing down. The essential thing was to save the greatest possible number of persons from dying and being doomed to unending separation. And to do this there was only one resource: to fight the plague. There was nothing admirable about this attitude; it was merely logical. (P, p. 133)

Indeed, Rieux thinks that this response is as straightforward as knowing that "two and two make four" (P, p. 132). We shall return to Rieux's ethic here later in this section.

Like Rieux, Tarrou is surely spurred to action by suffering, but, for Tarrou, the character who is most compromised by Camus's use of the plague as a metaphor for the Nazi occupation, suffering must be understood within a larger theoretical framework. When he is asked by Rieux why he decided to get involved, given that he is not even a citizen of Oran, Tarrou answers "my code of morals," and when Rieux follows up by asking him what that "code of morals" is, Tarrou swiftly replies "comprehension" (P, p. 130). For Tarrou, "comprehension" means understanding brute suffering within a larger theoretical framework so that in our effort to ameliorate suffering, we do not merely end up exacerbating it. This larger theoretical framework, which is informed by both sociohistorical and metaphysical considerations (that shall be looked at in turn), makes Tarrou not only the most interesting and well-rounded character in the novel but also the one that is, ultimately, closest to Camus himself.

As we have already seen, Tarrou confesses that he had been infected by the plague – or, to be more precise, its sociohistorical variation, the inclination to inflict suffering and, ultimately, death – long before he journeyed to Oran, and that unlike those who were either ignorant of this fact or completely at ease with it (M. Othon and Cottard, respectively), he "always wanted to get out of it" (P, p. 247). When he was young, Tarrou tells Rieux, he was gifted and complacent, but he had a "great change of heart" the day he watched his father, a prosecuting attorney, handle a death penalty case. Much like M. Othon, Tarrou's father had previously seemed no worse than harmlessly unimaginative, but on seeing him aggressively seek the death penalty for a petrified defendant, Tarrou was repulsed, construing the process as "murder in its most despicable form." Concluding that the social order itself is based on the death penalty, Tarrou joined revolutionary groups that would "fight the established order," only to recognize that he was no less complicit in murder, and that despite the well-reasoned arguments of the groups for whom he was killing, he could not "accept any argument that justified the butcheries" he had to carry out. Tarrou thus concludes that "we all have plague," as in one way or another we all (directly or indirectly) cause death, and what he seeks is the peace of mind that he has lost, which means having nothing to do with anything that can cause the death of another. He "leaves it to others to make history" (since he will not kill), refuses to "pass judgment" on anyone (as is shown by his amiable dealings with Cottard), and aims to become "a saint without God" (P, pp. 245–55). Undoubtedly, Camus has in mind the more aggressive attempts to make history here, but preventing those who would kill to make history can require killing itself, which should, but does not, disarm Tarrou, for establishing the sanitation squads is untenable in light of the novel's overarching metaphor.

In his desire to be a saint without God, moreover, Tarrou gives evidence of an ongoing metaphysical element in his thought, one that arguably distinguishes it from Rieux's thought by only a hair but can lead to real practical differences. Rieux, as we saw, had once been "outraged by the whole scheme of things" but "grew more modest," and while implicitly holding on to the standpoint of God's empty throne, he determined that it was better to "struggle with all our might against death, without raising our eyes toward the heaven where He sits in silence." In short, as we saw, God's empty throne plays no role whatsoever in his thought. Tarrou also was "outraged by the whole scheme of things" and, having recognized that killing is ubiquitous, became "more modest," albeit, like Rieux, with an ongoing commitment to struggle against suffering and death. Like Rieux, moreover, Tarrou holds on to the standpoint of God's empty throne, but for Tarrou it is not implicit but rather explicit, as this standpoint pervades his thought. Thus, while Rieux (not unlike Meursault) confesses to an inability to make sense of all things transcendent, this is at the heart of Tarrou's approach, and, indeed, it might be why he is a richer character than Rieux. As was previously discussed, it is a category mistake to try to live the Absurd (i.e., to live in accord with the "logic" of the Absurd grasped theoretically), for this gives rise to severe deformations in subjectivity, as is shown by Meursault and Caligula. Yet, when the Absurd informs our practical perspective, it functions as a deflator of sorts with respect to our most grandiose plans, whether sociopolitical or existential. As even Thomas Nagel admits, "absurdity is one of the most human things about us, a manifestation of our most advanced and interesting characteristics,"[7] and with Tarrou (unlike Rieux) these characteristics are revealed as humor and irony. Viewed in this way, Tarrou's existential quandaries make for a better life, and although Rieux is thinking of his dead friend when lamenting "the bleak sterility of a life without illusions" (P, p. 292), it is his own life that would have been the more appropriate object of concern.

While neither Rieux nor Tarrou are especially happy guys, as the commitment to reduce suffering and achieve comprehension do not trend in this direction, both recognize that happiness is an inextricable part of the ethical considerations that motivate them, and both make this point more or less explicitly. (So does Camus, as he informs his "German friend" in the quotation that opens this chapter that instead of succumbing to despair, he seeks to "create happiness in order to protest against the universe of unhappiness.") The impetus for Rieux's and Tarrou's ruminations on happiness is the plight of Rambert, a journalist from another city who had been investigating the living conditions of the Arab population in Oran, only to find himself trapped once the city is quarantined. Separated from the woman he loves, Rambert is desperate to escape the city by any means necessary "for the sake of happiness," and neither Rieux nor Tarrou deem it appropriate to stop him. Rieux tells Rambert that "for nothing in the world" would he try to dissuade him from leaving the city, for he is not wrong "to put love first" (P, p. 163), and, more directly, that there is nothing shameful in preferring happiness (to which Rambert replies, as we have seen, that "it may be shameful to be happy by oneself.") Following up on Rieux's point, Tarrou tells Rambert that if he commits himself to rectifying other people's unhappiness, he will have no time left for his own happiness (P, p. 209), and when speaking to Rieux, he declares that "a man should fight for the victims, but if he ceases caring for anything outside that, what's the use of fighting." (At this point, Tarrou persuades Rieux to break the law and take a swim with him on the beach "for friendship's sake," which gives both a moment of happiness, P, p. 256.) In short, then, through Rambert not only is the right to happiness vindicated but it is vindicated in the face of what duty would seem to otherwise command, and Rambert's first "justification" for leaving, that "public welfare is merely the sum total of the private welfares of each of us" (P, p. 88), while seemingly weak, has enough truth to persuade both Rieux and Tarrou.

Understanding, happiness, and the diminution of suffering – these are the three primary components of Camus's emerging ethical constellation, and to conclude our consideration of *The Plague*, it is important to make some sense of the ethics that he is offering in it, for there is much in this novel that betokens his later positions, both theoretical (*The Rebel*) and practical (the Cold War and the Algerian War). Although anything like a thorough summary of contemporary moral theories is well beyond what can be undertaken here, to make sense of Camus's emerging ethics, we must at least frame it in terms of such theories. To start, then, we must ask whether he is a utilitarian, for there is much in *The Plague* to suggest that he is.[8] A type of consequentialism (i.e., the view that the morality of an act is determined by the consequences it will produce), utilitarianism says that an act is "right" if, among the acts open to an individual, it is the one that maximizes social welfare, which is understood in terms of maximizing the collective pleasure (and minimizing the collective pain) of those who are to be affected by the act. Speaking for Camus, both Rieux and Tarrou argue that the reduction of suffering is that which is morally paramount – as we have seen Rieux assert, "the essential thing [is] to save the greatest possible number of persons from dying and being doomed to unending separation" (P, p. 133) – which clearly articulates one side of the utilitarian equation. And, while maximizing happiness (rather than minimizing suffering) is not dealt with in *The Plague* (for obvious reasons, given the situation) the concern with fostering happiness, as is represented by Rambert, clearly gestures at the other side of the equation.

What's more, the arguments that Camus makes in *The Plague* sound quite similar to those made by a leading contemporary utilitarian, Peter Singer. In an article addressing what he takes to be our duties to those who do not have adequate food, shelter, or medical care, "Famine, Affluence, and Morality," Singer begins "with the assumption that suffering and death from lack of food, shelter, and medical care are bad . . . [and that] if it is in our power to prevent something bad from happening, without thereby sacrificing something of comparable moral importance, we ought, morally, to do it."[9] ("Comparable moral importance," in the context of this article, means necessary food, shelter, or medical care.) For Singer, the recognition that this kind of privation is bad and that, as an initial matter, we are morally obliged to render aid, is simply a matter of "two and two makes four," which, of course, is exactly the way that Rieux characterizes the decision-making process concerning the choice to join the sanitation squad. (This is why Singer says that "those who disagree need read no further": if a person cannot do the moral analogue of "two and two makes four," what more can be said.) Furthermore, according to Singer, his understanding of our duty redraws (if not obliterates) our conventional duty/charity distinction. Much the same is suggested in *The Plague.* For Rieux, those who joined the sanitation squad showed "no great merit in doing as they did . . . and the unthinkable thing would then have been not to have brought themselves to do it." And, after stating that "the essential thing was to save the greatest possible number of persons from dying," and that the only way to do this is "to fight the plague," he says that "there was nothing admirable about this attitude; it was merely logical" (P, pp. 132–3).

Despite these similarities, however, Camus is not a utilitarian. At bottom, utilitarians are "calculators," in the sense that (at least in theory) it is morally incumbent on them to total up, as best they can, the aggregate amounts of pleasure and pain that will emanate from the actions open to them and then choose the one that maximizes pleasure, and this is not Camus. (Indeed, no utilitarian would let Rambert escape the city "for the sake of happiness," for one man's happiness does not stack up to the potential misery that this could engender.) Like deontology, which is rule based (see note 8), utilitarianism is predicated on a "method" for determining the right thing to do, and when Clamence declares that "when one has no character one has to apply a method" (F, p. 11), he speaks for Camus. Now, it could be argued that one must have the right sort of character to be open to the utilitarian calculus in the first place, but this is not dispositive. What is dispositive for Camus in all forms of decision-making, as Clamence implies, is character, and in this way he is more of a piece with the modern return to "virtue ethics." Indeed, in the passage that begins this section, Camus says that human beings "are more or less ignorant, and it is this that we call vice or virtue," which is the language of virtue ethics. What this means is that the person who "comprehends" (to use Tarrou's dictum in the broadest sense), and is otherwise of fine character, will be virtuous and thus act virtuously, which, for the time being, leads to one final qualification.

Within contemporary virtue ethics itself, there is a debate between what are described as "agent-based" and "agent-focused" accounts, which, essentially, revolves around the question of what is prior, the virtuous agent or the virtuous act. The agent-based account, which is deemed more radical, holds that what makes an act virtuous is that persons of virtuous character will do it, while the agent-focused account holds that a person is virtuous if, with the right disposition of character, he or she does virtuous acts. Camus's "virtue ethics" is of the second category, for he believes that there are certain acts that are *basically* virtuous or vicious. Thus, killing is *basically* vicious, and a person that refuses to kill because of his or her character is virtuous. With agent-focused accounts, what is dispositive is neither a rule nor a calculus but, rather, a certain kind of "seeing" or "perceiving" (as Aristotle, the father of virtue ethics, puts it), as well as a certain kind of decision-making process, which is anchored in both our reason and our emotions.[10] This need to see or perceive results from the fact that every situation (even if only in the nuances, which are often ethically dispositive) is different, and without a method for making ethical decisions, it takes a person of highly refined character to see or perceive the right thing to do. Even in ancient times, when there was a relatively elaborate background comprised of norms that signified what constituted virtuousness (whether in the person or in the act) and ultimately "the good," a person of fine character was one who could see or perceive the right thing to do when the particulars of the situation fell in the ethical cracks. In modern times, however, this ability to see or perceive might be all that is left of virtue ethics, and while a contemporary virtue ethicist would not put it in this way, what this implies, at least for Camus, is a phenomenological ethics of sorts. In other words, for Camus, as we shall see, modernity (in its communistic, fascistic, and bourgeois forms) has all but destroyed the background of norms that signify what constitutes virtuousness, and all that we are left with is seeing or perceiving. If one does not "see" that it is wrong to put a person to death, if one is not nauseated by the sheer experience of taking a person's life, there is nothing to be achieved by argument (which is why Camus does not give reasons for joining a sanitation squad). In sum, virtue ethics becomes phenomenological ethics in an epoch in which social life has broken down and the individual is thrown back onto his or her own ethical resources.

I stated above that Camus believes that killing is *basically* vicious because even one who operates in the agent-focused lineage of virtue ethics, which means one who views acts as either virtuous or vicious, must leave room for character to·deliberate, since there are times when virtue demands the performance of what is normally a vicious act. (If an act is deemed vicious in itself, such that it is categorically prohibited, then it is a rule, and the one who so holds is a deontologist, not a virtue ethicist.) Camus's injunction against killing, I believe, is actually of this nature, and, so understood, a basic problem is skirted. Tarrou, who most closely resembles Camus, refuses to kill under any circumstance, and he came to this position because he concluded that it was wrong to kill for the revolutionary organizations of which he was a member, which is fair enough. Still, the person of fine character could conclude that killing for the sake of an ideal, such as "the just society," is wrong, but that killing to save victims who are more or less directly confronting death at the hands of executioners is not, which would permit Tarrou to join the resistance movement for which his sanitation squads serve as a metaphor.

From a Natural to a Social Siege

> [In] *State of Siege*, I wanted to attack a kind of political society that set itself up, or is setting itself up, on a totalitarian model, both on the Right and on the Left. No one in good faith can fail to see that my play defends the individual, the flesh in its noblest aspects . . .
>
> Albert Camus, "Why Spain?" (Reply to Gabriel Marcel)[11]

If *The Plague* takes up a natural phenomenon that serves as a metaphor for a social one, *State of Siege*, a play that was first performed in 1948, takes up a social phenomenon that assumes, in no small part, the metaphors of a natural one. According to Camus, *State of Siege* is most akin to a medieval morality play, and its characters are essentially "symbolical" (CTOP, p. ix). The more nefarious lead characters are a dictator named "The Plague"; his book-keeping accomplice, "The Secretary"; and a variety of collaborators, most prominent among them a nihilist named "Nada" ("Nothing") and a small-minded judge named "Casado" ("Married"). To overthrow this tyranny a "wind from the sea" is needed, and the instigator of this wind is the hero of the play, Diego (a medical student), who is buoyed up by his fiancé Victoria (Casado's daughter). Building on the moral of *The Plague*, *State of Siege* implies that totalitarianism results from a bourgeois vapidity that fails to foster solidarity, and, in turn, that it is only through the cultivation of solidarity that a totalitarian regime can be overthrown.

The play begins with a comet crisscrossing the sky over the Spanish town of Cadiz, and while the residents basically see it as a bad omen, the lead characters exhibit their characters with respect to it. Nada sees in the comet the sign of devastation for which he hopes, Casado sees in it the occasion to instruct the populace to fall to its knees and beseech God to pardon their sins, and Diego, perhaps tacitly recognizing the comet's social significance, tells his compatriots to "keep stout hearts and all will be well." The Governor's Herald arrives shortly thereafter, declares that "good governments are governments under which nothing happens," and warns that anyone who speaks of the comet as anything but a "natural phenomenon" will be rigorously punished (CTOP, pp. 137–42). The citizens comply, and the Governor eventually shows up to reiterate his order, proclaiming that he detests change and, above all, "stands for immobility," which prompts a poor man to sarcastically feign relief that his lot has not been improved (CTOP, pp. 151–2). At this point, the plague breaks out among the citizenry, which the buffoonish Governor ignores, but the plague itself is merely an omen, and The Plague and The Secretary arrive shortly thereafter. The Governor is swiftly dispatched, and a totalitarian regime is installed.

On taking power, The Plague and The Secretary close off the city and regiment daily life. Declaring that he rules in fact and, therefore, by right, The Plague promulgates rules that are both obscure and arbitrary, one of which is that citizens must always keep pads soaked with vinegar in their mouths, ostensibly to fight the plague but actually to teach "the art of silence," as the aim is to destroy communication. Moreover, all persons are instructed to get "certificates of existence," which requires each person to justify his or her existence, and "useless public works" projects are established (CTOP, pp. 166–81). Parroting the logic of The Plague, Judge Casado supports his rule on legal grounds, asserting that the law must be obeyed simply because it is the law (CTOP, pp. 189–90), and Nada's only concern, as he expresses it to The Plague, is that "we don't go far enough" (CTOP, p. 211). Only Diego stands up to The Plague and The Secretary, and, by virtue of his courage, he emboldens others, which causes the tide to turn against the dictatorship. Still, The Plague has one last card to play. Victoria is infected with the plague, and he can either spare her life or quickly end it, which leads him to make Diego an offer: although he is obliged to take Diego's life rather than Victoria's if Diego offers it, he will spare both of them if Diego sells out the revolt. Diego refuses, stating that the freedom of his compatriots is not something that is his to sell (CTOP, p. 221), and he gives up his life to save both Victoria's life and Cadiz's freedom. The play ends with The Plague's departure and Nada's suicide.

Although the play's symbolism is crystal clear, and, as Camus rightly asserts, "no one in good faith can fail to see that [the] play defends the individual," there are still a few matters that need to be raised. First, although Camus vehemently denies that *State of Siege* is an adaption of *The Plague*, he uses the imagery of the plague again. In light of the complaint most often leveled against *The Plague*, that a plague is an inapt metaphor for political oppression because struggling against microbes is a far different matter than struggling against other human beings, why, then, does he go back to it, especially when *State of Siege* explicitly (rather than only implicitly) deals with political oppression? Without giving short shrift to the critics' objections, which, I already suggested, have some merit, Camus's return to the plague metaphor must be seen as a deliberate refusal to give credence to the types of distinctions that his critics desire to make on the grounds that such distinctions can frequently be used to obfuscate rather than to clarify. Although Camus stages *State of Siege* in Spain as an implicit retort to Franco's fascism, since "the first weapons of totalitarian war were bathed in Spanish blood," he is ultimately attacking totalitarianism as such, which, whether from the right or the left, is the modern political plague: "All this together must be denounced at one and the same time" (RRD, p. 79). In this sense, his use of the "The Plague" to represent a dictator can be better defended than his use of a plague to make sense of either the historical preconditions of totalitarianism or the weapons that can be used to fight it. Indeed, this refusal to make ideological distinctions is made good in the play, as Nada and Judge Casado (the nihilist and the law-and-order judge), who stand opposed in bourgeois society, smoothly coalesce around The Plague, each happily buying into the notion of "absolute power for absolute power's sake" that he instantiates. As the Chorus appropriately puts it at the end of the play, "those who stand for no rules at all, no less than those who want to impose a rule for everything, overstep the limit" (CTOP, p. 231).

Second, although the character of Diego is not especially well developed, in broad outline he seems to transcend both Rieux and Tarrou in the direction of the sort of virtue ethics of which I spoke in the last section. Like Rieux, when the plague (small "p") hits Cadiz, Diego, a medical student, sets himself to the job of alleviating human suffering as best he can, and, like Tarrou, he not only ceaselessly reflects on both the limits and requirements of honor but also plainly rejects "the old argument that to do away with murder we must kill, and to prevent injustice we must do violence" (CTOP, p. 231). Nevertheless, Diego also recognizes that he is a man of his time and place, that he is not pure (CTOP, p. 222), and, indeed, that the armed struggle against The Plague is, in some sense, taking place under his auspices. With Diego, accordingly, there is a movement away from Tarrou's refusal to kill under *any* circumstances to a general refusal to kill that can be overridden when judged absolutely necessary by a person who comprehends the dangers that are inherent in this breach and, therefore, the absolute necessity to strictly limit it.

Third, the importance of happiness to ethics is made clearer in *State of Siege* than in *The Plague*. Of course, Rieux and Tarrou not only acknowledge the legitimacy of Rambert's bid for happiness but actually encourage it, as they see that it is the ultimate goal of their labors (as does Camus himself in *Letters to a German Friend*), but how happiness factors into our ethical stance is not made clear, for Rambert's "happiness" is remote, and thus it is abstract. Through Victoria, this is partly redressed. Following in the one-dimensional footsteps of Caesonia (*Caligula*) and Maria (*The Misunderstanding*), Victoria represents the moment of happiness, but while Caesonia and Maria are ineffectual, Victoria is not. When Diego's spirit wavers in the face of The Plague, Victoria tells him that if he masters the anguish within himself, the rest will follow, and when he replies that he is alone, she emphasizes, through her love for him, that he is not, and this reminds him of his reasons for struggling (CTOP, p. 199). Similarly, when Casado refuses to give Diego asylum in his home, Victoria's criticism of him is directly on point: "Always you have judged in terms of hatred, though you masked it with the name of the law. Thus even the best laws took on a bad taste in your mouth, the sour mouth of those who have never loved anything in their lives" (CTOP, p. 193). And, finally, even when Diego declares right before his death that he had loved Victoria with his "whole soul," Victoria rejects this ethereal love, crying that "you loved me with your soul, perhaps, but I wanted more than that, much more" (CTOP, p. 229). With this cry, she speaks for the concrete happiness that history has denied for the nominal sake of its realization.

Ultimately, the moral of *State of Siege* is well captured by the "Chorus of Women," who, right after Victoria's cry here, declare at the end of the play: "Our curse on him! Our curse on all who forsake our bodies. . . . Men go whoring after ideas . . . and make [their] way from solitude to solitude, toward the final isolation, a death in the desert" (CTOP, p. 229). What Victoria (and, indeed, women, in general) represents in the play, as Camus says in the quotation that begins this section, is "the flesh in its noblest aspects," and, for Camus, this is where any ethics worth its salt must begin. Ethical ideas that lose the body turn against the very impulse that motivated them in the first place, and, in a very real sense, this is the cause of the quandaries that Camus will tackle in *The Rebel*.

notes

1 RRD ("Fourth Letter"), pp. 27–8.
2 CTOP, p. 83.
3 Albert Camus, *Notebooks: 1942–1951*, trans. Justin O'Brien (New York: Harcourt Brace Jovanovich, 1965), pp. 83 and 86, respectively.
4 Martin Heidegger, *Being and Time*, trans. John Macquarrie and Edward Robinson (New York: Harper-Collins, 1962), pp. 193 and 303–7, respectively (all emphases in original).
5 Hannah Arendt, *Eichmann in Jerusalem*, in *The Portable Hannah Arendt*, ed. Peter Baehr (New York: Penguin Putnam, 2000), p. 365.
6 P, p. 131.
7 Thomas Nagel, *Mortal Questions* (Cambridge: Cambridge University Press, 1979), p. 23.
8 The other major contemporary moral theory, deontology, says that there are certain acts that are right or wrong in themselves, and that it is our duty to perform or refrain from performing these acts regardless of the consequences. Camus is surely not a deontologist, as any moral theory that abstracts from time, place, person, situation, and, especially, consequences is not one that he would embrace.

9   Peter Singer, "Famine, Affluence, and Morality," in *Philosophy and Public Affairs*, 1, no. 3 (Spring 1972), p. 231.
10   See Michael Slote, "Agent-Based Virtue Ethics," in *Virtue Ethics*, ed. Roger Crisp and Michael Slote (Oxford: Oxford University Press, 1997).
11   RRD, p. 78.

further reading

Kellman, Steven G., *The Plague: Fiction and Resistance* (New York: Twayne, 1993).
Sprintzen, David, *Camus: A Critical Examination* (Philadelphia: Temple University Press, 1988).
Tarrow, Susan, *Exile from the Kingdom: A Political Rereading of Albert Camus* (Tuscaloosa: University of Alabama Press, 1985).

rebellion

Having lived for a long time without morality, like many men of my generation, and having actually advocated nihilism, although not always knowingly, I then understood that ideas were not only emotionally moving or pleasant-sounding games, and that, on certain occasions, to accept certain thoughts amounted to accepting murder without limits. It was then that I began to reflect upon this contradiction that was consuming us. . . . It appeared to me, lacking sufficient knowledge or better guidance, I had to try to draw a rule of conduct and perhaps an initial value from the only experience with which I was in agreement, namely, our revolt. Since nothing that was then proposed to us could teach us, [given the nihilism of] our entire political society . . . it was therefore precisely at the level of our negation and of our barest and most impoverished revolt that we had to find within ourselves and with others the reasons to survive and struggle against murder.

Albert Camus, "In Defense of *The Rebel*"[1]

Although *The Rebel* was published a scant four years after *The Plague*, the post-War world rapidly polarized between 1947 and 1951, and, due to this polarization, the political space within which the French left could potentially forge socioeconomic arrangements more desirable than either Soviet-style communism or American-style capitalism all but vanished. During this time period, the Soviet Union increasingly swallowed up Eastern Europe and blockaded West Berlin, which led to the American airlift, while the United States intervened in the Korean conflict and sought to extend its influence throughout Western Europe. What's more, both sides ratcheted up their domestic repression: the Soviet Union conducted its political show trials, banishing political rivals to work camps, while the United States came under the influence of Senator Joseph McCarthy's House Un-American Activities Committee, whose witch hunts ruined many lives and discouraged political dissent of every leftist stripe. Invariably, this polarization came to be mirrored in France, which, in a politically weakened condition, found itself precariously perched between the two emerging superpowers. Not only did the French left and right polarize, but each was internally wracked by dissent, as the trade union movement split between communists and the non-communist left, and the more extreme factions of de Gaulle's rightist coalition attempted to rehabilitate both Nazi collaborators and former members of the Vichy government. Already beginning to loom on the political horizon, moreover, was the Algerian War, as anti-colonial sentiment in Algeria had already begun to stir.

In this polarized context, in which all were forced to stake out their positions in relation to the overarching Cold War, relatively minor political differences could produce major political fallouts, and this is precisely what occurred with Camus's publication of *The Rebel*, which was a political lightening rod. Although in the larger scheme of things Camus's politico-philosophical positions were not considerably different than those of other leading French philosophers on the left (such as Sartre, de Beauvoir, and Merleau-Ponty), he was one of the first to unequivocally break with Soviet communism, and it cost him. I shall consider the strictly political implications of *The Rebel* (philosophically, sociohistorically, and personally) in the following chapter. In the meantime, however, I shall, in addition to explicating the book, consider its ethical implications. Although it might be deemed somewhat arbitrary to differentiate the ethical and political in this way, this division of labor is not one with which Camus would be unsympathetic, given that *The Rebel* itself was motivated, in no small part, by what he took to be the improper subordination of ethics to politics. Moreover, it also gives me the chance to further expand on what I have called Camus's phenomenological ethics, which he saw as a necessary precondition of political action.

This theme comes across quite clearly in the passage that opens this chapter. Drawn from "In Defense of *The Rebel*" – which Camus composed some time after his highly public battle over the book with Sartre's periodical *Les Temps Modernes* but chose never to publish – it implies that we have lost our way politically precisely because we have lost our way morally. For Aristotle, the first virtue ethicist, the task of moral education belongs to society, and, finally, to the political class, which by promulgating the right laws properly teaches us in ethical matters, but Camus's problem is that "political society" is no longer up to this task. It is not by accident that in the opening paragraphs of *The Rebel* he calls the law itself into question, declaring that in modern times crime is "as universal as science," and that if "yesterday it was put on trial, today it determines the law" (R, p. 3). Beyond the law, however, when Camus admits that he is "lacking sufficient knowledge or better guidance," and declares that "nothing that was then proposed to us could teach us," he is lamenting that society no longer has the ethical resources to confront this institutionalized illegality, which is far more problematical. In other words, not only has crime usurped political power but, what is worse, it has reoriented civil society's ethics, as even the historical memory of socioethical traditions that might confront this usurpation has all but faded away. This is basically what Camus means when he states elsewhere in this article that "we were almost completely devoid of reason drawn from a *living* morality."[2] (By "living" here, he surely means to differentiate the full-blooded ethics of which he speaks from both deontology and utilitarianism, abstract moralities that he sees as part of the problem.) Thus, as I suggested in the last chapter, with the breakdown of modern social life (and, concomitantly, the background of shared commitments and practices that could delineate virtuousness), virtue ethics reduces to a phenomenological ethics of sorts, and what we are left with, at least as an initial matter, is a bare seeing or perceiving. And, indeed, Camus suggests as much in the first paragraph of "In Defense of *The Rebel*," stating that "a profound and simple emotion" had motivated the book, the failure to understand how "men could torture others while looking them straight in the face."[3]

Before proceeding to consider the book itself, a final preliminary point needs to be made, a point that concerns its title. The actual title of the book, *L'Homme Révolté*, is not particularly well captured by the translation "The Rebel," which more directly corresponds to *Le Rebelle*, a title that Camus clearly chose not to use. Two better translations (and, ostensibly, Camus's point was to play off the ambiguity) are "Man in Revolt" and "Revolted Man." As Ronald Aronson indicates, a rebel's identity is inextricably intertwined with the authority against which he or she rebels, and, as we shall see, it is this sort of unqualified identification with sociohistorical forces that Camus is railing against. Both a "man in revolt" and a "revolted man," in contrast, humanistically imply some degree of independence in regard to these sociohistorical forces. "Man in revolt" suggests that the impulse of revolt arises within the individual, and, beyond this, it implies a metaphysical revolt against the human condition (which was also surely Camus's aim), while "revolted man" suggests a man who is revolted by the cynical misappropriation of this impulse by sociohistorical forces that would turn it against its noble impetus.[4] With this stipulation, I shall continue to use the title *The Rebel*, which will not preclude me from using "rebel" and "revolt" interchangeably.

From Absurdity to Revolt

I rebel – therefore we exist.

Albert Camus, *The Rebel*[5]

Although *The Rebel* is, in no small part, motivated by Camus's gut response to institutionalized political violence, and, in particular, institutionalized political violence that has the imprimatur of that "perfect

rebellion

alibi, philosophy, which can be used for any purpose" (R, p. 3), the book is anything but an anti-philosophical political pamphlet. Camus views *The Rebel* both as a philosophical diagnosis of the modern age and as a philosophical sequel to *The Myth of Sisyphus*, as he aims to philosophically link up his growing commitment to solidarity (evidenced in *Letters to a German Friend*, *State of Siege*, and *The Plague*) with his past philosophical commitments. This promises to be no easy task, however, for the philosophical problematic that gave rise to the Absurd in the first place, the Cartesian separation between consciousness and the world, would appear to be at odds with the communitarian impulse that underlies Camus's commitment to solidarity. Indeed, most exponents of the ideal of community, which includes most virtue ethicists, take it as a given that all forms of Cartesianism are utterly incompatible with any project of social reconstruction, as they take the community to be prior to the individual, not to mention abstract "consciousness," and in this respect Camus seems to be even more recalcitrant than Descartes. Even if Descartes did seek to make subjectivity the ground of indubitable knowledge, he estranged consciousness from the world only for methodological reasons, as his aim was to better ground our (epistemic) relationship to it (through his reconciling proofs of God's existence), while Camus already finds consciousness, with its feeling of the Absurd, existentially estranged from the world, and there is nothing to bridge the gap. Of course, Camus's Cartesianism brings to the table a healthy concern for the individual's prerogatives, which is lacking in many communitarian accounts, but this only points to the overly ambitious character of his philosophical project. The gap between Camus's Cartesianism, which begins from consciousness, and the community based on *genuine* solidarity (rather than an expedient social contract or a galvanizing *ressentiment*) may be unbridgeable.

According to Camus, even if the Absurd "is an experience [that must] be lived through," it is only "a point of departure, the equivalent, in existence, of Descartes's methodical doubt" (R, p. 8): it "has wiped the slate clean" (R, p. 10). Camus's "in existence" here is crucial, for while Descartes's methodological doubt, which is motivated by epistemological concerns, is a ladder of sorts that can be kicked away once it has been demonstrated that we can basically trust our sense perceptions, the Absurd, which is "in existence," is not something that can be kicked away, and, indeed, as we shall see momentarily, Camus thinks that for ethical reasons it ought not to be kicked away. What this reflects is the difference between the theoretical and practical perspectives, and it reveals the fact that Camus has completed the practical turn whose beginnings were discussed in the previous chapter. "The important thing," he now asserts, is not "to go to the root of things, but, the world being what it is, to know how to live in it" (R, p. 4), and once the issue becomes one of knowing how to live in the world, different considerations come into play: "The absurdist position, translated into action, is inconceivable, [and] it is equally inconceivable when translated into expression. Simply by being expressed, it gives a minimum coherence to incoherence, and introduces consequence where, according to its own tenets, there is none" (R, p. 8).

Camus believes that with this turn from the theoretical to the practical, the question of the Absurd turns into a question of rebellion, and, concomitantly, the question of suicide turns into a question of murder. He reasons as follows: The Absurd arises from our encounter with a silent, meaningless universe, and in the face of this universe the question of suicide is not unreasonable. If "confronted with [this] unjust and incomprehensible condition" we choose to act, however, we are tacitly revolting against this "spectacle of irrationality," and our action must be understood as a "demand [for] order in the midst of chaos, and unity in the very heart of the ephemeral" (R, p. 10). For Camus, the crucial question then becomes what this demand justifies, and, in particular, whether it justifies murder. On his first consideration of the problem, he argues that because the question of murder is yoked to revolt in the same way that the question of suicide is yoked to the idea of the Absurd, the two pairs are "inextricably bound together," and because suicide was not considered to be a coherent response to the Absurd in *The Myth of Sisyphus*, murder cannot now be considered as a coherent response to revolt: "If we deny that there are reasons for suicide, we cannot claim that there are grounds for murder" (R, p. 7). This argument is a particularly weak one, however. It will be recalled that Camus deemed suicide incoherent in *The Myth of Sisyphus* because he believed that reason requires us to maintain the hopeless encounter between human inquiry and the silence of the universe. Reason demands no such thing, and if Camus's argument against murder wholly derives from his argument against suicide it is in serious trouble. Camus readily acknowledges that an "awareness of the Absurd, when we first claim to deduce a rule of behavior from it, makes murder seem a matter of indifference" (R, p. 5), and if piggybacking on his argument against suicide in the face of the Absurd is his only argument against murder, the Absurd will be not only our "point of departure" but also our destination point, and it will justify "wiping the slate clean" in ways that go well beyond the purely methodological.

Crucially, it is one thing to say that an *awareness* of the Absurd is sufficient for an ethics, which, in some sense, this first argument implies, and it is another thing to say that it is necessary for an ethics. I take it to be the case that, for Camus, the Absurd is only a necessary condition for an ethics, and for two interrelated reasons. First, as Camus says, the slate must be "wiped clean," given that the modern ethico-political enterprise has broken down, and the Absurd, which is not only "in existence" but underlies human existence, justifies this move. To put it in the language of phenomenology, we ought to "bracket" the "natural attitude" that we have with respect to our prevailing ethico-political systems, as the content of these institutions is generated within history, and, therefore, they do not begin from non-negotiable first principles, as their partisans generally claim. (As we shall see, what Camus rejects most in *The Rebel* is what he sees as the deification of sociohistorically engendered values.) In other words, the Absurd is the basis for "methodical doubt" with respect to all sociopolitical arrangements, and not only for methodological reasons, as was the case for Descartes, but, more substantially, for metaphysical reasons. To use a recent philosophical phrase, in the face of the Absurd, the self-justifying premises of all sociopolitical arrangements can be "deconstructed." Second, given that this is the case, once the sociopolitical slate is wiped clean and the project of social reconstruction (theoretical or practical) commences, the Absurd counsels a perpetual questioning with respect to our new arrangements. Ultimately, there can never be a genuine sociopolitical closure because, in the face of the Absurd, there can never be a genuine metaphysical closure, and this indicates that our sociopolitical arrangements, ungrounded and ever fallible, should be approached in the spirit of moderation. As Camus sums it up in the concluding pages of *The Rebel*, "the irrational imposes limits on the rational, which, in its turn, gives it its moderation. Something has a meaning, finally, which we must obtain from meaninglessness" (R, p. 296).

It is thus the immoderate compulsion toward sociopolitical closure that *The Rebel* attacks, and while Camus takes after the particulars of our existing sociopolitical institutions, the deeper problem, as this passage from *The Rebel* intimates, is with our conception of "the rational" itself, particularly as it manifests itself in our ethico-political reasoning. As stated above, sociopolitical institutions frequently take themselves to be justified by non-negotiable first principles, but this "indubitability" is just what Camus rejects, as he makes clear on the very first page of *The Rebel*: "As soon as a man, through lack of character, takes refuge in a doctrine, as soon as crime reasons about itself, it multiplies like reason and assumes all the aspects of the syllogism" (R, p. 3). The basic problem with a syllogism is that while the reasoning is valid, the conclusion might be false because one or more of the premises are false, and what Camus is suggesting here is that there is a problem with the very *form* of our modern ethico-political reasoning. Thus, the modern age is, in no small part, defined by "crimes of logic" that have the appearance not only of rightness but, indeed, of necessity, which reveals the fact that an overly rationalized form of ethical reasoning can yield the most unethical (not to mention irrational) results. Aristotle himself had cautioned against just such an approach in the *Nicomachean Ethics*, stating that ethics cannot have as high a degree of exactness as other disciplines, and that we should only pursue exactness to the extent that the subject matter allows. Moreover, he had cautioned, we must be sure that we are arguing toward our first principles rather than (unreflectively) from them.[6] By Camus's lights, however, the modern form of ethico-political reasoning makes both of these mistakes, as it seeks necessity in a discipline not amenable to it and syllogistically argues from sociohistorically generated first principles (that it takes to be "indubitable") rather than (haltingly) toward them. Ironically, then, although Camus's starting point is undeniably Cartesian, by virtue of the Absurd, which reflects that chasm between consciousness and the world not bridged by Descartes's reconciling God (or, for that matter, anything else), his "final" results, ever provisional, are most un-Cartesian.

What this suggests is that Camus's non-negotiable Cartesian "first principle," unearthed phenomenologically, must be minimal, as anything more will illicitly smuggle in particulars that are sociohistorically generated, which would effectively deify sociohistorically generated values, the very thing that Camus is railing against. For this reason, as Camus tells us, he is only looking for a "guiding principle" (R, p. 10), a "common value, recognized by all as existing in each one" (R, p. 23). Such a value, in the words of David Sprintzen, would merely provide "the boundary conditions of any ethical inquiry,"[7] but, beyond that, would not run roughshod over the kinds of dialogically established sociopolitical arrangements that a particular community might reach. (As philosophers might put it, such a value should "underdetermine," not "overdetermine," the forms that sociopolitical life might assume.) Since, as we have seen, Camus's "argument by analogy" (i.e., because suicide is not a coherent response to the Absurd, murder does not coherently follow from revolt) is a weak one, Camus must look elsewhere for his "guiding principle," and the place to which he looks is the very notion of revolt itself: "It is absolutely necessary that rebellion find its reasons within itself, since it cannot find them elsewhere. It must consent to examine itself in order to learn how to act" (R, p. 10).

According to Camus, the rebel is "a man who says no, but whose refusal does not imply a renunciation." Indeed, when the rebel says no, he is also saying "yes," for his refusal affirms the "existence of a borderline" that preserves a space for his personal integrity. Camus contends that this no, in and of itself, constitutes a transition from facts to rights, and thus the rebel "implicitly brings into play a standard of values" (R, pp. 13–14). What's more, and this is Camus's essential point, although the rebel explicitly raises these values on his own behalf, simply by raising them he is necessarily committed to the idea that they are universal in scope: "He is acting in the name of certain values which are still indeterminate, but which he feels are common to himself and to all men" (R, p. 16). Now, to be sure, people often stand up for themselves without "feeling" that their claims are "common" to all other people, but there is more to Camus's position than would appear at first blush, for when asserting one's rights, one cannot *ultimately* be making a claim on behalf of oneself alone: at some point in one's chain of justification, even if only implicitly (as is generally the case), a universal value is necessarily invoked. For instance, if I assert a particular right that only I have under a contract to which I am a party, I am implicitly asserting that rights created by contracts must be universally enforced whether they involve me or not, since claiming that only I have a right to have my contractual rights enforced is not especially compelling. This argument, moreover, is even more direct when rights that concern one's basic personal integrity are involved, and this, of course, is what chiefly concerns Camus. The fundamental point, then, is that what ultimately gives every assertion of a right (irrespective of how particular it might seem to be) its normative oomph is its claim to universality. Accordingly, Camus declares, "when he rebels, a man identifies himself with other men and so surpasses himself, and from this point of view human solidarity is metaphysical" (R, p. 17).

Camus's reference to the metaphysical here is problematical, and when mentioning it in the context of universality it calls to mind Kant's "metaphysics of morals," which is unfortunate. As we shall see, Camus's continuing emphasis on the metaphysical in *The Rebel* engenders more than a few problems, but, in the meantime, it is necessary to make clear the precise nature of this universality. For Kant, all genuine moral decision-making, purged of a person's drives, desires, and inclinations (which he takes to be the stuff of empirical anthropology), derives from a single, fundamental principle, the categorical imperative, which imposes the same moral obligations on all rational beings regardless of time, place, person, or consequences. What's more, by engaging in this sort of moral decision-making, which reduces the decision-maker down to his rational core, and thus to the status of a universal subject of sorts, the moral decision-maker intends to legislate universal law and (at least as a regulative ideal) to bring about the universal "kingdom of ends." Kant's moral philosophy is thus universalist from top to bottom, which is precisely why Camus rejects it. As we saw in chapter 2, when Camus says in *The Fall* that "when one has no character one has to apply a method," he is basically rejecting a universalist approach to ethics, and he also seems to be doing this on the opening page of *The Rebel* when he says that "man, through lack of character, takes refuge in doctrine," although the rejection here is somewhat more ambiguous, as he probably has in mind determinate sociohistorical doctrines rather than formal moral doctrines. (Still, it should be noticed that both Kant's formal morality and material sociohistorical doctrines share the same kind of top-down reasoning that Camus finds so disturbing.[8]) Camus's emphasis on character is an emphasis on having the right kinds of drives, desires, and inclinations, and this is needed because he thinks that genuine moral decision-making is highly sensitive to its context, which is just another way of saying that time, place, person, and consequences are precisely what do matter. For this reason, there should not be a "fundamental principle" that streamlines (or, to use Kant's words, "schematizes") moral decision-making, and Camus's "guiding principle," that the defense of one's own personal integrity implies its defense on behalf of all human beings, is not such a principle. Aside from the fact that it is irreducibly minimal, this principle of solidarity is only *guiding*, and, therefore, not even inviolable, although, as we shall see, Camus evinces some ambivalence here. Moreover, while the claim that "human solidarity is metaphysical" appears to suggest it, there are no "universal ends" on Camus's account, because he would take such ends to be totalitarian. To put it colloquially, the universal moment stems from our shared starting point, which Camus calls our "first piece of evidence," the fact that "we're all in the soup together":

> In absurdist experience, suffering is individual. But from the moment when a movement of rebellion begins, suffering is seen as a collective experience. Therefore the first progressive step for a mind overwhelmed by the strangeness of things is to realize that this feeling of strangeness is shared with all men and that human reality, in its entirety, suffers from the distance which separates it from the rest of the universe. (R, p. 22)

The metaphysical moment in Camus's thought thus refers to the old Cartesian divide, but with essential modifications. First, as this passage indicates, the logic that is indigenous to revolt brings all other (human) consciousnesses back to this side of the consciousness-world divide, and it is aptly captured by Camus's modified *cogito*. If, for Descartes, "I think, therefore I am" serves as an epistemological Archimedean point, the linchpin for enabling us to build back to the world of our sense perceptions, "I rebel – therefore we exist" is a moral Archimedean point for Camus. Since it "founds its first value on the whole human race" (R, p. 22), "I rebel – therefore we exist" is the linchpin for enabling us to construct an ethical world, if not truly build back to the world itself (given the ultimate unbridgeability of the divide and, consequently, the ultimate persistence of the Absurd). Second, not only are other (human) consciousnesses brought back to this side of the divide, but so is nature, which, as we shall see, performs an essential ethical role for Camus. "Analysis of rebellion," according to Camus, "leads at least to the suspicion that, contrary to the postulates of contemporary thought, a human nature does exist," and this raises the specter of a "natural community" (R, p. 16). These notions of "human nature" and a "natural community" in and of themselves do not necessarily imply a resurrection of the role of nature itself in our ethical thought, but Camus does make very clear that he thinks that one of the main problems of modern thought, whether bourgeois or Marxist, is the belief that "nature must be subdued," and in this respect, too, he lauds the Greeks, who were "of the opinion that it is better to obey it" (R, p. 190). Indeed, for Camus, nature is not only one of our consolations but, in no small part, the fount of our happiness, as he had suggested in his early works. This means that "nature," which refers to both our internal natures and external nature, is also brought back to this side of the Cartesian divide, and, therefore, we must "reject injustice without ceasing to acclaim the nature of man and the beauty of the world" (R, p. 276). Thus, what the Cartesian divide separates for Camus is the fullness of our world, which has been mistakenly renounced, and a silent universe, which, in the final analysis, is tantamount to a Godless one.

According to Camus, with the death of God we moderns have not only excised this divide but have also (metaphorically) assumed God's vacant throne. This means that not only have we delegated the task of generating our values to the movement of our own history, but, through our modern philosophies, which (though nominally secular) have tended toward utopian messianism, we have deified history itself and, therefore, the values that it has produced. Although Camus is contemptuous of the formal moralities of capitalist societies, he sees Russian communism as the fruition of this movement: "Russian communism . . . has appropriated the metaphysical ambition that this book describes, the erection, after the death of God, of a city of man finally deified" (R, p. 186). Camus's examination of revolt thus aims to overcome what, in effect, is a deification of the history that is engendered by revolt, a history that has run off the rails because revolt has not been faithful to its own motivating impulse. When one acts in the name of the value implicit in rebellion, Camus contends, one has a "concept of values as preexistent to any kind of action, [and] this contradicts the purely historical philosophies, in which values are acquired (if they ever are acquired) after the action has been completed" (R, p. 16). Camus thus aims to walk an extremely fine line in *The Rebel*: On the one hand, as against formal moralities, he contends that values are worked out in concrete contexts, and thus they are constructed in history, ideally by way of "the free exchange of conversation" (R, p. 283). On the other hand, as against historically generated moralities, he contends that there is (at least) one preexistent value, a (meta-)value of sorts, that is predicated on the commitment to solidarity implicit in revolt: "We have, then, the right to say that *any* rebellion which claims the right to deny or destroy this solidarity loses simultaneously its right to be called rebellion and becomes in reality an acquiescence to murder" (R, p. 22).

In the final analysis, in accord with the "historical philosophies," Camus is committed to a concrete universality (as opposed to the abstract universality of bourgeois philosophies), but he is opposed to what he takes to be their totalitarian impulse, and this leads to what is arguably his essential distinction, the distinction between "totality" and "unity." According to Camus, revolt is a "perpetual demand for unity" (R, p. 101), but it is a perpetual demand whose ideas originate in (and remain tethered to) concrete individual experience, while the demand for totality, which originates in the demand for unity, twists away from its experiential source and abstractly seeks "to fit the world into a theoretic frame" (R, p. 106). As Camus puts it, totality is "nothing other than the ancient dream of unity . . . but projected horizontally on to an earth deprived of God" (R, p. 233), and its aim "to fit the world into a theoretic frame" succeeds what was previously called "the God's eye view." Camus nicely captures the dangers of this viewpoint in his *Notebooks*:

> The airplane as one of the elements of modern negation and abstraction. There is no more nature; the deep gorge, true relief, the impassable mountain stream, everything disappears. There remains *a diagram* – a map. Man, in short, looks through the eyes of God. And he perceives then that God can have but an abstract view. This is not a good thing.[9]

As God's viewpoint, not to mention His perfection, is unattainable by mere mortals (and given that even He did not establish the kingdom of ends on earth), Camus believes that revolt's "perpetual demand" metamorphoses into a "limitless metaphysical crusade" (R, p. 108) when the disciples of the historical philosophies climb to the throne. Motivated by a utopian messianism that is not unlike the religions that have been supplanted, they justify on the basis of reason rather than the divine all actions that are putatively in the service of bringing about the kingdom of ends.

Metaphysical Revolt

> The nihilistic question "for what?" is rooted in the old habit of supposing that the goal must be put up, given, demanded *from outside* – by some *superhuman authority*. Having unlearned faith in that, one still follows the old habit and seeks *another* authority that can speak *unconditionally* and *command* goals and tasks.
>
> Friedrich Nietzsche, *The Will to Power*[10]

As should now be clear, Camus's position with respect to metaphysics, and, in particular, Judeo-Christian metaphysics, is nothing if not complicated. On the one hand, Camus views history's appropriation of

Judeo-Christian metaphysics as a disaster, for in assuming its teleological form, history gracelessly takes from God what was God's: it deifies its own ends, which human beings cannot even glimpse, much less attain, and, even worse, it deifies the most reprehensible actions to the extent that they purport to be in the service of these unforeseeable ends, which, in actuality, are only the (often cynical) ends of fallible human beings rather than an infallible history. On the other hand, it is Judeo-Christian metaphysics that engenders the metaphysics of the Absurd, and, as we have seen, Camus surely does not renounce *this* residuum of the Judeo-Christian tradition. Indeed, as I asserted earlier, by hanging on to the Cartesian divide, which, for Camus, ultimately amounts to little more than the fact that we live in a Godless universe, he emphasizes our lack of metaphysical foundations, or the impossibility of metaphysical closure, in order to emphasize the impossibility of sociopolitical closure, and, therefore (to put it rather strangely), the metaphysical *necessity* for approaching the sociopolitical contingently (i.e., in the spirit of moderation). As we have seen Camus maintain, the irrational imposes moderating limits on the rational, and thus the meaning that we wrench from meaninglessness (see R, p. 296), and he reaffirms this point in the context of the distinction between "totality" and "unity":

Totality can demand the submission of the irrational, if rationalism suffices to conquer the world. But the desire for unity is more demanding. It does not suffice that everything should be rational. It wants, above all, the rational and the irrational to be reconciled on the same level. There is no unity that supposes any form of mutilation. (R, p. 97)

Camus's critique of totality makes good sense, as does his desire to carve out a space for unity. What makes less sense, and what opened him up to attack (some of which was justified), was his desire to hang on to this metaphysical residuum. Is the concept of the Absurd necessary for the purpose of justifying sociopolitical moderation? In other words, along the lines that I just put it, must sociopolitical moderation be metaphysically justified to preclude the manufacture of totalities? Why not reject Judeo-Christian metaphysics across the board, which would not in the least undermine his ability to attack the ways in which the historical philosophies have smuggled in a utopian messianism? And, most of all, given that Camus has hung on to this metaphysical residuum, what is the relationship between metaphysical and historical revolt? Although Camus equivocates on this, the answer in *The Rebel* appears to be that historical revolt largely plays out our metaphysical revolt: "Revolution is only the logical consequence of metaphysical rebellion." "The revolutionary spirit," he goes on to declare, "tries to assure [man] his crown in the realm of time and, rejecting God, it chooses history with an apparently inevitable logic" (R, pp. 105–6). Thus, "even revolution . . . which claims to be materialist is only a limitless metaphysical crusade" (R, p. 108), and, as we saw earlier, even "Russian communism has appropriated the metaphysical ambition that [*The Rebel*] describes, the erection, after the death of God, of a city of man finally deified" (R, p. 186). I shall return to this matter, which raises the issue of political praxis, in the next chapter. In the meantime, following Camus's own division of labor, I shall consider what I take to be the more important elements of his discussion of metaphysical rebellion and historical rebellion in the rest of this section and the following one, respectively. I shall then conclude this chapter with a section that attempts to tease out what I take to be the ethical implications of *The Rebel*.[11]

Camus characterizes "metaphysical rebellion" as "a claim, motivated by the concept of a complete unity, against the suffering of life and death, and a protest against the human condition both for its incompleteness, thanks to death, and its wastefulness, thanks to evil" (R, p. 24). As he points out, such concerns were undeniably a part of the fabric of the ancient Greek world, as is evidenced in the Greek myths, but he says that theirs was not a metaphysical rebellion because they did not rebel against creation. To rebel against nature would have been seen as tantamount to "butting one's head against a wall," according to Camus, and while Prometheus and Sisyphus rebelled against the gods, there was not a hard and fast divide between mortals and gods but just a "series of stages." Camus contends that what was ultimately lacking was a personal god from whom the rebel could demand a "personal accounting," and thus it was only with the God of the Old Testament that the phenomenon of metaphysical rebellion came into its own. Christianity, he says, repaired this breach, as Christ, mediating between mortals and God, solved the problems of death and evil (and otherwise gave meaning to suffering), but once "the critical eye of reason" was brought to bear on Christianity, "the abyss" opens again, and "the ground is prepared for the great offensive against a hostile heaven" (R, pp. 26–35). Metaphysical rebellion thus comes into its own with the enlightenment project.

At this point, Camus proceeds to offer a narrative of metaphysical rebellion that roughly corresponds with the narrative of historical rebellion that he will subsequently offer. One could surely quibble with his two-track approach, as it becomes extremely problematical to disentangle the conceptual unfolding of metaphysical rebellion from its sociohistorical context, but if Camus is, in some sense, arguing for the logical priority of metaphysical rebellion, then this is what he is committed to doing. Thus, as Camus notes in passing, it is no mere coincidence that the Marquis de Sade, whose rebellion reflects "the first coherent [metaphysical] offensive," is writing at the time of the French Revolution, and that one of the major figures of the French Revolution, St Just, who was the prosecutor that demanded the death of Louis XVI and a major instigator of the ensuing Terror, parallels Sade in crucial respects. According to Camus, while Sade was a frenzied immoralist and St Just a tedious moral prig, both were driven by a relentless passion, which, among other things, is directed toward the denial of God (in favor of our natural instincts and our natural virtue, respectively) and both "justify terrorism – the libertine justifies individual terrorism, the high priest of virtue State terrorism" (R, p. 125). Indeed, with the death of God (which is played out literally with the execution of his earthly representative, Louis XVI), both careen between the poles of absolute affirmation and absolute negation, of absolute freedom and absolute destruction. Sade's libertinism entails the absolute freedom of our natural instincts, which, as Camus points out, actually anathematizes liberty, for the "unlimited freedom of desire implies the negation of others and the suppression of pity." Not merely content with an anarchic libertinism, however, "Sade, as was the custom of his period, constructed ideal societies" so as to "codify the natural wickedness of mankind," and, in so doing, he established a rule structure not unlike religious communities. Thus, the greatest of libertines ends up recapitulating "an unhappy form of asceticism," absolute destruction based on a cold, calculated dehumanization (R, pp. 36–47). If Sade rejects "the presumptuous alliance of freedom with virtue," St Just does not simply accept it but seeks to embody it. Nevertheless, his demand for absolute virtue cannot be sated, as all human beings fall short of it and, thereby, "the republic of forgiveness leads, with implacable logic, to the republic of the guillotine." In the end, Camus argues, not only St Just but also Sade manifest the limited bourgeois nature of the French Revolution, the penchant for formality, and, as Camus puts it, "morality, when it is formal, devours" (R, p. 124). This penchant, for Camus, is "one of the alternatives of the twentieth century," the bad result that transpires when "rebellion cuts itself off from its roots and abstains from any *concrete* morality" (R, pp. 131–2).

Camus's condemnation of bourgeois morality will be further considered in the context of his analysis of historical rebellion, but now, exclusively following his "metaphysical line," I shall briefly discuss his view of metaphysical rebellion when it exhibits itself aesthetically. According to Camus, romanticism is Sade's early-nineteenth-century heir, for like Sade it opts for "evil and the individual" in response to its nostalgic desire for an all but unrealizable good, and, like Sade, it places "its emphasis on its powers of defiance and refusal," thus causing rebellion to "forget its positive content." The self-defeating logic intrinsic to this position pushes the romantic rebel to ever more extreme acts, as the boredom that marks the life of bourgeois complacency is rejected in favor of an orgiastic frenzy fuelled by its defiance of both moral and divine law. Ultimately, then, according to Camus, romanticism is marked by a puerile narcissism, a cult of individuality that, as was the case with Sade, reveals a "degraded form of asceticism" (R, pp. 47–54). In much the same way, Camus also attacks what he calls the "poets' rebellion" of the late nineteenth and early twentieth centuries, which, once again, careened between the extremes of absolute negation and absolute affirmation, absolute rebellion and absolute conformity, absolute irrationality and absolute rationality. According to Camus, like the romantics, Count Lautréamont, the author of *The Songs of Maldoror* (a story about an evil character who rejects Creation *writ large*), bounces between a privileging of the instincts that refuses to recognize rational consciousness and a push toward unqualified banality, which would drown out the initial impulse to rebel. Lautréamont, in turn, spurs the surrealists, who also start by privileging "absolute rebellion, total insubordination, sabotage on principle, [and] the humor and cult of the absurd," which led André Breton to declare that "the simplest surreal act consisted in going out into the street, revolver in hand, and shooting at random into the crowd." Deifying the unconscious, the surrealists called for the destruction of society, which necessarily limits untrammeled desire, but they joined forces with revolutionary Marxism, which, in overthrowing the state, demanded the submission of the irrational every bit as much as the surrealists demanded its liberation. In the end, Camus asserts, those who cashed out with orthodox Marxism were really motivated by its nihilistic core, and those who did not, such as Breton, felt constrained "to return to traditional morality." What should be recognized here is that Camus is rejecting that with which he is all too quickly associated, an aesthetic immoralism. Like the surrealists, Camus mistrusts enlightenment rationality, and he is surely concerned with the existential implications of the Absurd, but unlike those aesthetes whom he critiques here, he never throws out the baby with the bathwater, which, in this case, is a form of critical reason that is to be distinguished from the enlightenment's more rationalistic premises (R, pp. 88–99).

Camus believes that Dostoyevsky and Nietzsche both plumb the depths and tease out the existential implications of metaphysical rebellion in a much more nuanced way than either their predecessors (the romantics) or their followers (the surrealists), and thus they comprise the conceptual core of his discussion. What's more, because Dostoyevsky lays the groundwork for God's death through his famed character Ivan Karamazov and Nietzsche analyzes the existential implications of this event (which, among other things, demands that we confront the nihilistic underpinnings of contemporary life), they are also the major transitional figures in the history of metaphysical rebellion. Thus, according to Camus, Ivan Karamazov was unlike any prior metaphysical rebel because he did not extol "evil and the individual," which constitutes an infantile "flirtation" with God, but, instead, siding with humankind (and emphasizing its innocence), he forthrightly calls God out: "His first impulse . . . is to plead for justice, which he ranks above the divinity. Thus he does not absolutely deny the existence of God, [but] refutes Him in the name of a moral value" (R, p. 55). In effect, then, God "is put on trial," and He is found wanting from the standpoint of His own criteria, which, among other things, would not seem to justify the Christian belief in the internal relationship between suffering and truth, and this is particularly so with children, whose suffering torments Ivan most of all (as it does Rieux in *The Plague*, who, it will be recalled, had attacked Father Paneloux for just this reason). Of course, Christianity promises an ending that is both happy and eternal, but Ivan declares that not even eternal life could justify human suffering, and thus he rejects the Christian bargain, for he will "accept grace only unconditionally." In this way, Camus asserts, Ivan embodies what is best in metaphysical rebellion: he not only demands truth and justice unequivocally but he demands it for everyone.

As such things are not forthcoming, however, Ivan is thrown into a dilemma: how should he live in the face of this mutilated world? Even Kant had implied that it might be necessary to believe in such things as God and the immortality of the soul to make sense of why we should be moral, and it could be argued that without believing in these "regulative ideas," his moral system cannot get off the ground. As Ivan has already submitted God to moral judgment and found Him wanting because human suffering cannot be justified under any condition, God no longer plays a meaningful role for him, virtue is no longer justified, and consequently he utters the words with which "the history of contemporary nihilism really begins": "Everything is permitted" (R, p. 57). With this utterance, Ivan does not embrace immoralism: he is no more an immoralist than he is a moralist. Rather, "caught between unjustifiable virtue and unacceptable crime," he is torn by the contradictions and ends up going mad. Philosophically, however, the consequence of his view is that we must make good what God has not, and thus, Camus asserts, rebellion undertakes action:

> His plot to usurp the throne . . . remains completely moral. He does not want to reform anything in creation. But creation being what it is, he claims the right to free himself morally and to free all the rest of mankind with him. On the other hand, from the moment when the spirit of rebellion, having accepted the concept of "everything is permitted" and "everyone or no one," aims at reconstructing creation in order to assert the sovereignty and divinity of man, *and from the moment when metaphysical rebellion extends itself from ethics to politics*, a new undertaking, of incalculable import, begins, which also springs, we must note, from the same nihilism. (R, pp. 59–60; emphasis added)

It must be emphasized that Dostoyevsky himself does not identify with Ivan's existential outlook, which he sees as the quintessence of the enlightenment position, but, rather, uses Ivan to illustrate what he takes to be the fundamental limitations of this very position. For Dostoyevsky, ideals such as freedom, justice, and happiness are not brought to fruition by the enlightenment's push toward an abstract perfectionism but are corrupted by it. As an initial matter, he thinks that the enlightenment's commitment to "human perfectibility" fails to acknowledge the intractability of humanity's darker side and, therefore, gives expression to it all the more, if only surreptitiously. Moreover, by virtue of their universality, these ideals, which originally grew out of the religious worldview, fail to connect up with a viable form of concrete communal life that could give them genuine meaning, and, untethered, become not only unrealizable but also destructive (of self and other). Now, what should be noted in passing with respect to Camus here is that he is essentially torn between Dostoyevsky and his character. In many ways, Camus is like Ivan Karamazov (and it is fitting that he liked to play this character in the theater). Both Camus's absurdist sensibility (which is based on the God's eye view without God) and his austere humanism grow out of the religious worldview, and, like Ivan, he is frequently torn by the contradictions. Yet, Camus also reflects Dostoyevsky's position: he rejects the enlightenment pretensions that would appropriate God's empty throne, which manifests, more generally, his unremitting demand for human limits, and he is unambiguous in his rejection of abstract enlightenment morality, whether it manifests itself in the formal morality of bourgeois society or in the never-realized *telos* of communism's "concrete" morality. What Camus lacks, I shall argue later, is a secular humanist variation on Dostoyevsky's more spiritualized concrete community.

On the other side of Ivan Karamazov's ambivalences, according to Camus, is Nietzsche, for it is only with Nietzsche that "rebellion begins with 'God is dead,' which is assumed as an established fact." As was discussed in chapter 2, if Nietzsche is the first to diagnose nihilism, it is surely not to endorse it but, instead, to reveal it as *the* problem to be overcome. And, although Nietzsche was no fan of Christianity, as he believed that it is innately nihilistic, the "established fact" to which Camus refers is not that God was dead for Nietzsche but, rather, that He was dead for Nietzsche's contemporaries, who nevertheless continued to pay lip service to Christianity and its values. Yet, Camus goes on to assert that Nietzsche's aim was "to transform passive nihilism into active nihilism," and this claim is far more problematical. If by "active nihilism" he means that Nietzsche aims to destroy "everything that still hides nihilism from itself, [such as] the idols that camouflage God's death," this is true but only to a point: Nietzsche believed that unshackled by conventional morality the masses would perpetuate the most horrendous crimes (such as later took place in Nazi Germany), and this was something that frightened him. As for the remainder, "the few" (i.e., the elite) for whom he actually wrote, Nietzsche was mostly concerned with the *reconstruction* of values, which would largely transcend rather than merely destroy conventional moral precepts, many of which Nietzsche just took for granted. Camus's claim that Nietzsche's attack on morality as he finds it reflects his support for the "absolute negation" of the putatively nihilistic "ought" that makes up morality as such is thus overdone (R, pp. 65–70).

Much as he did with the practitioners of aesthetic rebellion, Camus goes on to claim that Nietzsche ultimately careens from absolute negation to absolute affirmation, for if nihilism is the "inability to believe in what is," then what would appear to be called for is not a rejection but an acceptance of "what is." Thus, Camus claims, Nietzsche "ends in a deification of fate," which is reflected in three of his "doctrines": eternal recurrence, *amor fati* ("love your fate"), and the will to power. This claim is also rather overdone. While Nietzsche was quite mindful of the fact that an unnuanced rejection of "what is" has a nihilistic element, when confronted by the increasingly hollowed out Judeo-Christian world, the nihilistic "what is" of his time, he did not simply affirm it but, rather, through *Thus Spake Zarathustra*, offered a competing narrative. Indeed, although, as Camus rightly contends, Nietzsche largely rejects all teleological narratives, and the circular account of time offered by the doctrine of eternal recurrence is meant to reject such endpoints in favor of an emphasis on the present moment, in a certain sense what he is offering in *Thus Spake Zarathustra* is a qualified one of his own. Moreover, Nietzsche's doctrines are not as quietistic as Camus claims. Without belaboring the point, eternal recurrence is not a cosmological thesis but, rather, a psychological litmus test, and if one will not will the recurrence of one's own life in the way that it has played out, one should change one's life, which is hardly a continuing affirmation of "what is." (Similarly, the ability to say *amor fati* does not reflect a passive resignation but an active achievement.) Thus, when Camus declares that "the Nietzschean affirmative, forgetful of the original negative, disavows rebellion at the same time that it disavows the ethic that refuses to accept the world as it is," he misses the mark, since Nietzsche does not careen toward absolute affirmation any more than he begins from absolute negation. What Nietzsche does do, and this is the nub of truth in Camus's position, is walk a perilously thin tightrope, a tightrope from which he occasionally falls to one of these sides or the other (R, pp. 70–77).

Still, given that Nietzsche does walk this tightrope, and, indeed, not only speaks of truths that his contemporaries are not ready to hear but does so in a way that can appear to support their own worst proclivities, Camus is not wrong to say that (while history "shall never finish making reparation for the injustice done to him") Nietzsche nevertheless bears a certain responsibility for what was made of him. Camus is also not wrong to say that Nietzsche "confused freedom and solitude," and, for this reason, if Nietzsche was a social or political philosopher (which, contrary to certain trends in Nietzsche scholarship, I seriously doubt), he was not a particularly good one. In the final analysis, then, although Camus might be somewhat hyperbolic in depicting Nietzsche as the one who lays the ground for the manifestation of nihilism in history by the "secularization of [revolt's] ideal" (R, p. 77), and although this position manifests a certain limit in Camus's own position (which includes the very idea of "metaphysical revolt," not to mention the primacy that he affords it), from Camus's post-War standpoint there was good reason to fear any philosophy that might end in "biological or historical Caesarism" (R, p. 79), especially when it is much too easy for power to stress the letter instead of the spirit of that philosophy and otherwise ignore the virtues that it simply takes for granted. In any case, according to Camus, in this way "the spirit of metaphysical rebellion openly joins forces with revolutionary movements" (R, p. 103).

Historical Revolt

> Rights can never be higher than the economic form of society and the cultural development which is conditioned by it. In a higher phase of communist society, after the subjection of individuals to the division of labor, and thereby the antithesis between mental and physical labor, has disappeared . . . only then can the limited horizon of bourgeois right be wholly transcended, and society can inscribe on its banner: from each according to his abilities, to each according to his needs!
>
> Karl Marx, *Critique of the Gotha Program*[12]

As I discussed at the start of the last section, Camus is often inclined to say that historical revolt merely stems from the more basic impulse of metaphysical revolt, and, as we saw at the start of the last chapter, he first signals what I have called his practical turn by stating in *Letters to a German Friend* that "I merely wanted men to rediscover their solidarity in order to wage war against their revolting fate." While Camus will qualify this position toward the end of *The Rebel*, in his move from metaphysical revolt to historical revolt he reinforces the distinction between them along moral lines, suggesting, for the most part, that following God's symbolic murder with the execution of Louis XVI, revolution is what rebellion becomes when it does *anything* to kill another, and the revolutionary who kills is morally culpable unless he pays for his victim's death with his own life: "the period of rebellions comes to an end in 1793 and revolutionary times begin – on a scaffold" (R, pp. 110–11). Thus, after he offers up Spartacus's slave rebellion as a model of sorts, given his commitment to the principle of equality, his refusal to lay siege to Rome ("the city of the gods"), and his willingness to die for his actions, Camus only speaks approvingly of one group of modern rebels, the Russian terrorists of the early twentieth century: "For them, as for all rebels before them, murder is identified with suicide. A life is paid for by another life, and from these two sacrifices springs the promise of a value" (R, p. 169).

Camus is no doubt right that modern revolutions have often lost their moral bearings and, in so doing, have turned on their better impulses. Yet, he asks for too much here, and the reason is his ongoing commitment to metaphysical revolt, which, tied up with his lingering commitment to what he sees as God's non-negotiable injunctions, appears to preclude even the most defensive forms of killing (except, that is, when the person who kills defensively then atones for it with his own life). Now, Camus is surely right to suggest that modern political doctrines (and not merely revolutionary ones, as recent events have borne out) have expanded the definition of "defensive" in a grotesque way, and that ruling regimes have thereby justified killing their opponents with a syllogistic form of reasoning. Nevertheless, we must still answer the question that was raised by Roland Barthes in his critical review of *The Plague*: "What would the fighters against the plague do confronted with the all-too-human face of the scourge?" As so many human beings have, in fact, been confronted by unabashedly murderous regimes, Camus must provide some conceptual space for a political revolution that collapses neither into nihilism nor fecklessness, lest Barthes's assertion that he "lays the foundation for an ahistorical ethic and an attitude of political solitude" ring true in terms of *The Rebel*. Camus can provide such a space, and it can be grounded in the commitment to solidarity that he finds implicit in the concept of revolt, which, in itself, harbors no metaphysical commitments. I shall pursue this position in the next section. In the meantime, I shall consider his analysis of historical revolt, with special emphasis on its conceptual grounds.

According to Camus, the conceptual foundations of the French Revolution, and, indeed, the Terror that ensued, were laid by Jean-Jacques Rousseau's *The Social Contract*, which was then "introduced into the pages of history" by St Just. What is especially revolutionary about *The Social Contract* is not its claim that political power ought to derive from the will of the people rather than the will of the king, although this was certainly a monumental shift in terms of the grounding of political legitimacy, but its claim that what is politically relevant is "the general will" rather than "the will of all." Transcending the will of all, which, in some sense, would be the sum of the private wills of each person that makes up the political body (somehow adjusting, of course, for conflicts), the general will is the product of a collective will formation in which each person is compelled to put aside all private interests in favor of the public interest. Rousseau believed that the general will is the ultimate manifestation of our reason, and thus, given the way in which the relationship was conceived at the time, totally in accord with our basic human nature. As long as factionalism is avoided and all people individually bring their reason to bear in the right way, the general will is always in the right, according to Rousseau, for it always inclines toward the public good. In this way, as Camus puts it, the general will "is primarily the expression of universal reason, which is categorical, [and thus] the new God is born." Indeed, so as to ground the general will as securely as the king's sovereignty, which was based on God, the general will had to be viewed as a divine entity in its own right, which is why Rousseau often refers to it as "absolute, sacred, inviolable," and in this way it becomes a civil faith (R, pp. 114–17).

The problem with this approach, as we have seen Camus rightly maintain, is that formal morality "devours," and the general will is nothing if not absolutely formal. As Camus indicates, this is reflected in the fate of Louis XVI himself, as St Just relied on the logic of the general will to justify his execution: while all might will to pardon the king, St Just asserted, the general will could not because the very personage of the king directly threatened the general will's sovereign authority, and thus the king was the very embodiment of crime itself. Even more ominous, what Rousseau took to be a troubling factionalism that could disrupt the uniformity of the general will reflects nothing other than the particulars that, while distinguishing us, also make up the concrete stuff of our lives, both individually and collectively. In other words, although factions invariably exist by virtue of nothing more than the free expression of individual viewpoints (and, therefore, the existence of concrete individuals themselves), the general will cannot tolerate them, and thus "at the logical conclusion of this morality of virtue, the scaffold represents freedom, as it assures rational unity and harmony in the ideal city" (R, p. 126). What this reveals, according to Camus, is that civil virtue itself cannot exist abstractly but needs concrete justification, lest it careen into a deadly abstraction that, impelled by what Hegel calls the "fury of destruction," seeks to destroy all who do not conform to its abstract strictures, which, of course, ultimately means everyone. In the end, however, the law never actually does reflect universal reason but, rather, reflects the will of the legislators, who trumpet its nominally universal principles so as to give the imprimatur of universal reason to what are really their own particular interests. Camus thus declares:

The bourgeoisie succeeded in reigning during the entire nineteenth century only by referring itself to abstract principles. Less worthy than Saint-Just, it simply made use of this frame of reference as an alibi, while employing, on all occasions, the opposite values. By its essential corruption and disheartening hypocrisy, it helped to discredit, for good and all, the principles it proclaimed. Its culpability in this regard is infinite. (R, p. 132)

More than any other theorist of his time, it was Hegel who diagnosed the destructive core of abstract universal reason and, moreover, recognized that the modern individual was alienated from a (bourgeois) social world that was no longer bound together by God and Church. Although Hegel remained completely committed to universal reason, which he thought would perform the function of reconciling the modern individual to his social world, his repudiation of abstraction was no less complete. As a result, Camus claims, Hegel aims to make good "concrete universal reason" by incorporating reason into the "the stream of historical events, which it explains while deriving its substance from them" (R, p. 133). Camus is alluding here to Hegel's notorious but little understood "dialectic," which, for present purposes, can be understood as the movement of consciousness and, consequently, history on the basis of the rational resolution of social conflict. Put more simply, Hegel thinks that every society necessarily understands both itself and its world in concrete, particular ways, and that when a breakdown in the ways a society understands itself or its world comes about, it attempts to rationally resolve the problem, which then leads to newer, truer ways of understanding itself and its world. Values are thus taken to be generated *within* the movement of history, and this "definitive destruction of all vertical transcendence – particularly the transcendence of principles" (R, p. 142) is the essential problem with which *The Rebel* deals. If "truth, reason, and justice [are] . . . incarnated in the progress of the world" (R, p. 134), Camus believes, then history is deified, and, in essence, "what is" becomes what ought to be.

Camus's argument here is somewhat problematical. As a general matter, his discussion of Hegel has a canned sort of feel, and he is not always true to Hegel's meaning, although some of his criticisms are right on the mark. First, Camus analyzes Hegel's contention that "the real is rational," and he states that this justifies not only "every ideological encroachment of reality" but "the condition of fact" itself (R, p. 135). This is simply not correct. The appropriate translation of Hegel's claim is that "the actual is rational," and what is "actual" is only what realizes its true nature, as it is delineated by its own concept. For example, while both capitalist and communist societies contended that they had realized freedom, both actually had truncated notions of it, and thus "freedom" was neither "actual" nor "rational" in either society. "Actuality," in short, is the overly rationalized yardstick by which reality is measured rather than simply the equivalent of it. Second, Camus spends a fair bit of time rehearsing what is called Hegel's master-slave dialectic, and he states that, for Hegel, "the entire history of mankind is . . . nothing but a prolonged fight to the death for the conquest of universal prestige and absolute power" (R, p. 139). This, too, is just not correct. The master-slave dialectic, which is a parable, refers to an early but crucial moment in Hegel's *Phenomenology of Spirit*, one in which two primordial human beings come across one another in the state of nature, engage in a fight to the death, and ultimately end up in the master-slave relationship. The parable is not, as it would seem, about social relationships, but, instead, about the process of self or ego formation, and it is designed to illustrate a number of important points, two of which are worth emphasis here. As against state of nature theorists like Rousseau, it is designed to show that in the state of nature we are barely human, not fully developed selves prepared to enter into a social contract. And, as against the liberal tradition, more generally, it is designed to show that our self-conceptions are bound up with recognizing and being recognized by other human beings in the right sort of way. Even if history has never stopped playing out the dynamics of this relationship, Camus's implicit claim that the master-slave relation is established by Hegel as an interpersonal ideal has it the wrong way around. As the incarnation of a complete recognitive breakdown, it is, rather, the antithesis of the ideal. Third, Camus charges Hegel with relinquishing "to history alone the task of producing both values and truth" (R, p. 146). In some sense, this is right, but it must be recalled that *we* produce history, and that it is in its production that values are engendered. Ideals such as liberty, equality, and fraternity, even if nowhere near being realized, are hard-won historical achievements, and, for Hegel, they do not just fall by the wayside in the ideal movement of history but are enriched in its unfolding. And, lastly, he does hold out the prospect that history could have gone irreparably wrong, reflecting a "bad infinite."

Now, having said this, Hegel does purport to be speaking from "the end of history," and, at least with regard to this point, Camus is not wrong to say that his claims are "intellectually and forever suspect" (R, p. 147). Hegel believed that with the advent of the modern bourgeois liberal state, humanity had realized its *telos*, or, to put it simply, had the right philosophical template for making sense of itself and its world, which means that while events would, of course, continue to transpire, there would not be any real change in our conceptual categories. Camus rightly asserts later in *The Rebel* that "the dialectic correctly applied cannot and must not come to an end" (R, p. 223), and, as we shall see in the context of his discussion of Marxism, this is arguably even more important to realize when those in power hold that the end of history is not yet here but that they know what it looks like and that we are compelled to make sacrifices to facilitate it. As Camus puts it: "There is in this universe no reason to imagine the end of history . . . which introduces into history a value foreign to history. Since that value is, at the same time, foreign to ethics, it is not, properly speaking, a value on which one can base one's conduct" (R, p. 224). I think that Camus is basically right here, and his belief that "end of history" theses are the very stuff of totalitarian justifications is surely not unreasonable.

Although both conceptually and historically Marx follows Hegel, in *The Rebel* there is a two-chapter gap between Camus's discussions of Hegel and Marx. In Camus's schema, Hegel's dialectic concretizes the French Revolution's abstract universal morality, at which point he shifts to consider the phenomena of individual terrorism and irrational state terrorism. (He then links back up with Marx before considering the regime that allegedly draws on him, the Soviet regime, which he sees as representative of rational state terrorism.) Although the particulars of Camus's expositions of individual terrorism and irrational state terrorism are interesting, there are only a few conceptual points that need to be made with respect to them. As I previously indicated, what is particularly interesting about Camus's discussion of individual terrorism, as it manifested itself in Russia between, roughly, 1878 and 1905, is his sympathy for certain variants of it. To be sure, in his exposition of the unfolding dialectic of Russian terrorism, Camus repudiates a good deal of it out of hand, as much of it lapsed into nihilism (Nechaiev, Chigalev). Yet, some terrorists, like Ivan Kaliayev and Dora Brilliant, garner only respect for both their motivations and their tactics. Indeed, Camus had already written a play about Kaliayev and Brilliant titled *The Just Assassins*, and the play, first performed in 1949 (two years before *The Rebel* was published), had received good reviews. Tellingly, in his own review, Camus later asserts: "My admiration for my heroes, Kaliayev and Dora, is complete. I merely wanted to show that action itself had limits. There is no good and just action but what recognizes those limits and, if it must go beyond them, at least accepts death" (CTOP, p. x). Conversely, for the German and Italian fascists of the 1940s, there were neither limits nor reason, and Camus has relatively little to say about these "psychopathic dandies," who "chose to deify the irrational, and the irrational alone, instead of deifying reason, and in this way renounced their claim to universality" (R, pp. 177–8). By renouncing its claim to universality, fascism does not even pretend to do justice to revolt's motivating impulse, and if Camus does not otherwise spend much time on fascism, it is because he thinks (perhaps a bit too optimistically) that its evils should be readily apparent: in contrast to rationalized terror, it has no confusing sophistical arguments, as it encourages "the destruction, not only of the individual, but of the universal possibilities of the individual, of reflection, of solidarity, and the urge to absolute love." As a result, fascism does not even bother paying lip service to ethical concerns, as its aim is to establish a "mystique beyond the bounds of any ethical considerations" (R, pp. 183–4).

Conversely, communism, which Camus takes to be the primary form of rationalized state terror in his own day, was premised on the aim of realizing all of these goods, and for this reason he believes that diagnosing its underlying nihilistic impulse is that much more imperative. And, in turn, as communism was nominally based on Marx, Camus spends a fair bit of time examining Marx's thought itself. I say "nominally" here because Camus believes that Marx's thought had been appropriated by Soviet communism in much the same way that Nietzsche's philosophy had been appropriated by the Nazis, which is to say that while there were elements of Marx's thought that could be seized on to support Soviet ideology, those who were doing the seizing violated the spirit, if not always the letter, of it. Accordingly, Camus contends, Marx's thought blended "the most valid critical method with a Utopian Messianism of highly dubious value" (R, p. 188). As to the former, he has nothing but admiration, declaring that Marx's "most profitable undertaking has been to reveal the reality that is hidden behind the formal values of which the bourgeois of his time made a great show, [and that] his theory of mystification is still valid, because it is, in fact, universally true, and is equally applicable to revolutionary mystifications" (R, p. 200). The revolutionary mystifications relate back to the latter, the Utopian Messianism, and while Camus is surely right to level this charge against Soviet ideology and many, if not all, of its apologists, it is less clear that it can be leveled against Marx.

What Camus is arguing here is that Marx himself (and not only the Soviet Marxists) has bought into Hegel's philosophy of history, and, more specifically, his "end of history" thesis, the key difference being, as was already suggested, that for Marx (and not only the Soviet Marxists), the end of history has not yet been realized. Beyond the fact that this thesis provides no basis for conduct, Camus is also right to say that, "paradoxically, [it] can be used to justify conservatism," for the unjustified assumption that "tomorrow, in the natural order of events, will be better than today" encourages a quietistic outlook (R, p. 194). Still, in regard to Marx, in particular, Camus draws at least two conclusions much too quickly. First, although Marx might have been unduly optimistic in his belief that technological advancement and increased industrial production would bring about human progress (by way of increasingly severe socioeconomic crises and, ultimately, revolution), he never gave the sorts of guarantees that Camus implies he did. Marx often spoke in terms of capitalism's innate "tendencies," and his analyses of capital were intended to be used by the working classes strategically, as he clearly recognized that human emancipation would not effortlessly emerge from these tendencies. It was precisely because Marx was a deeply historical thinker, as Camus claims, that he did not preclude the sorts of counter-tendencies to which Camus appropriately points (i.e., planned production, the rise of the "Moloch" State, increasing numbers of small industrialists and small shareholders, and shifts in the make up of the working classes, to name a few). Thus, even if Marx's "crisis theory" in regard to capitalism was overly optimistic, to tab him "the prophet of production" who "ignored reality in favor of the system" is excessive in turn (R, p. 204).

Second, given what Camus takes to be Marx's unwarranted optimism with respect to the unfolding of capitalism, and, more broadly, history, he alleges that Marx's "scientific socialism" is a "messianism of Christian and bourgeois origin" (R, p. 189). Expanding on this point, Camus goes on to say that Marx's atheism only "reinstates the supreme being on the level of humanity. Criticism of religion leads to this doctrine that man is for man the supreme being, [and] from this angle, socialism is therefore an enterprise for the deification of man and has assumed some of the characteristics of traditional religions" (R, p. 192). While some of what Camus states here is not inappropriate with respect to Soviet Marxism, his claims are rather troubling. Does "criticism of religion" in and of itself necessarily lead to the "doctrine that man is for man the supreme being" and, ultimately, "the deification of man"? This smacks of the "absent God" problem in Camus's own dubious absurdist metaphysics, for why must the criticism of religion entail the deification of humanity, unless it is assumed not just that this space exists but that, like a vacuum, it must be filled. Moreover, does this charge apply to all varieties of socialism? It is Camus's claim that it does:

> But every kind of socialism is Utopian, most of all scientific socialism. Utopia replaces God by the future. Then it proceeds to identify the future with ethics; the only values are those which serve this particular future. For that reason Utopias have almost always been coercive and authoritarian. Marx, in so far as he is a Utopian, does not differ from his frightening predecessors, and one part of his teaching more than justifies his successors. (R, p. 208)

It is surely not the case that "every kind of socialism is Utopian," or otherwise "deifies man," if by this we mean that history is conceived teleologically, and ends that will never be achieved are forever used to justify the most reprehensible means. There are variants of democratic socialism, indeed, that appear to be on all fours with one of Camus's privileged social forms, "revolutionary trade unionism," whose "syndicalist and libertarian spirit" springs from and "relies primarily on the most concrete realities" (R, pp. 297–8). In the end, what Camus objects to is not socialism as such but what he occasionally calls "authoritarian socialism," which unjustifiably "confiscates living freedom for the benefit of an ideal freedom [that] is yet to come" (R, p. 217).

Now, even if Marx does not go so far as to "identify the future with ethics," he is undeniably reticent to speak about ethics, as is reflected in his refusal to ethically condemn even the most avaricious members of the bourgeois class, and Camus is absolutely right to call him on it: "The demand for justice ends in injustice if it is not primarily based on an ethical justification of justice; without this, crime itself one day becomes a duty" (R, p. 209). Although it is hard to imagine that Marx was not spurred by the deepest ethical considerations, his refusal to explicitly articulate these ethical considerations and how they would pertain to the task of achieving social justice no doubt gave ideological support to Soviet communism, which was guilty of many of the charges that Camus levels against Marx. Camus was not wrong to be as contemptuous of Soviet "historical cynicism" as he was of bourgeois "formal virtue," and he was not wrong to claim that, economically, bourgeois and Soviet ideologies are "subject to identical laws, the accumulation of capital and rationalized and continually increasing production" (R, p. 218). In short, what I hope to make clear is that Camus was not an "anti-Communist" (as that term came to be used), and if at times his criticisms of the Hegelian-Marxist tradition were not sufficiently nuanced, it was not due to a limited ideological mindset. Indeed, while I shall not consider Camus's study of Lenin, which in this context would serve no useful purpose, it should be indicated that even here he was not wholly unsympathetic, referring, for instance, to Lenin's commitment to justice, which "can still be opposed to the Stalinist regime" (R, p. 232).

In the final analysis, Camus does not object to history, if by this rather strange sounding claim we mean that he does not object to an historical approach for the purpose of making sense of both ourselves and our world. He surely does not deny that we are, in large part, the stuff of our history, which concretizes the excessively formal concepts of "freedom" and "virtue" found in bourgeois society (which, in any event, tends to smuggle its own substantial commitments into these concepts). Indeed, it is history that engenders what Camus calls "vital traditions," and he rejects their "renunciation" by historical groups that seek "to deny or to silence the things in the history of the world which cannot be assimilated by [their] doctrines" (R, p. 236). In this sense, he would argue, it is those whom he attacks that object to history. What Camus does object to is a *totalizing* conception of history, one in which freedom is "suppressed" and there is a "sacrifice of ethics and virtue" for the purpose of making good an end that history itself promises to deliver but, in fact, will never be realized, if for no other reason than the fact that an utter indifference to means will all but preclude it. As Camus rightly states, such a conception, which is totalitarian at its core, does not even evince the "historical objectivity" to which its pays lip service but, rather, "an interminable subjectivity which is imposed on others as objectivity": this "objectivity has no definable meaning, but power will give it a content by decreeing that everything of which it does not approve is guilty" (R, p. 243). What Camus also objects to is the outright rejection of human nature that is innate in this *totalizing* conception of history, or, as he puts it, "the certainty of the infinite malleability of man and the negation of human nature" (R, p. 237). In sum, then, history is "necessary but not sufficient" for engendering value (R, pp. 249–50), and what Camus objects to is making it sufficient by fiat, which he sees as nihilistic. To order human behavior from some distant point in the future or to order it from an eternal present both of which constitute an all-encompassing historical "ought," is to do violence to the normative impulse no less than to oder human behavior with ahistorical, formal principles, and it is Camus's aim to sidestep these bad alternatives.

It is here that Camus's essential value, rebellion, comes into play. Camus believes that to adopt history, either prospectively or retro-spectively, is to defy "the teachings of rebellion" (R, p. 246), which innately generates the "ought" that impels toward unity instead of total-ity within history. Included in this impulse, for Camus, are such value couplings as freedom and justice, and community and nature (internal "human nature" and the natural world), and mindful of these values, I shall try to make sense of what I see as his desire to build back to a full-blooded virtue ethics from the bare bones phenomenological ethics that is his starting point.

From Phenomenological Ethics to Virtue Ethics

Revolution . . . cannot do without either a moral or metaphysical rule to balance the insanity of history. Undoubtedly, it has nothing but scorn for the formal and mystifying morality found in bourgeois society. But its folly has been to extend this scorn to every moral demand. At [revolution's] very source . . . is to be found a rule that is not formal but that can nevertheless serve as a guide. Rebellion, in fact, says . . . revolution must try to act, not to come into existence at some future date in the eyes of a world reduced to acquiescence but in terms of the obscure existence that is already made manifest in the act of insurrection. This rule is neither formal nor subject to history. . . . To the "I rebel, therefore we exist" and the "We are alone" of metaphysical rebellion, rebellion at grips with history adds that instead of killing and dying in order to produce the being that we are not, we have to live and let live in order to create what we are.

Albert Camus, *The Rebel*[13]

I have suggested that virtue ethics becomes phenomenological ethics in an epoch in which social life has broken down and the individual is thrown back on to his or her own ethical resources. In this last section, I shall outline what I take to be the scaffolding with which Camus hopes to build back to a thicker virtue ethics from this thin phenomenological one. Many of the considerations that will inform this ethics are contained, either implicitly or explicitly, in this passage, and I will return to it often. Before proceeding, however, I must emphasize that because Camus was not a systematic philosopher, the outline that I shall offer is somewhat reconstructive in nature, which is to say that it follows from what Camus argued but was not articulated by him in just this way.

In the closing pages of his discussion of historical rebellion, Camus distinguishes what he calls "atheist existentialism" (i.e., Sartre's existentialism) from communism, stating that "atheist existentialism *at least* wishes to create a morality . . . but [that] the real difficulty lies in creating it without reintroducing into historical existence a value foreign to history." In other words, while Camus lauds atheist existentialism's refusal to depict morality as nothing more than a bourgeois pretense (and thus, contrary to communism, it refuses to dispense with morality), he rejects what he takes to be its goal of fashioning morality solely from the materials generated by history itself: it is only by avoiding a wholesale collapse into the logic of history that we might be able to avoid its "insanity." For Camus, as we saw, history is "necessary but not sufficient" for the purpose of generating values, as it does not furnish a "value that allows [humanity] to judge history" in turn (R, p. 250). Crucially, however, as history *is* necessary (although not sufficient) for the purpose of generating values, Camus is surely not recommending a wholesale withdrawal from it, for he also rejects disincarnated values, which are innate to "the formal and mystifying morality found in bourgeois society." As he will later say when defending *The Rebel*, he rejects values that are either "placed above history" or "absolutely identified with it": "The truth that I must reiterate . . . is that my book does not deny history (a denial that would make no sense) but only criticizes the attitude that aims to make history into an absolute."[14] However, all of this gives rise to a pivotal question: what conceptual space remains for the purpose of grounding values, which is obviously something that Camus aims to do? To make sense of Camus's ethical framework, it is necessary to begin by making sense of how he can reject both ahistorical and historicized values.

In effect, Camus does not reject either ahistorical or historicized values but, rather, splits the difference between them, and thereby qualifies both, by offering a two-tiered approach. The first tier, the primary one, is, *in some sense*, transcendental, which is to say that it is comprised of relatively non-negotiable ahistorical meta-values that are meant to delineate the nature and scope of those historical values that comprise the second tier. When Camus states that we need "either a moral or metaphysical rule to balance the insanity of history," he is referring to the values that comprise the first-tier – I hesitate to call them "rules" for reasons to be considered shortly – and, as we saw in the first section of this chapter, as well as in the passage that begins this section, he gives us two such values (one moral and one metaphysical): "the 'I rebel, therefore we exist' and the 'We are alone' of metaphysical rebellion." The moral value, "I rebel, therefore we exist," is what "allows [humanity] to judge history" (R, p. 250), while the metaphysical value, the Absurd, precludes sociopolitical closure. As both of these values were rather extensively discussed in the first section, I shall only summarize them here, emphasizing no more than what is crucial for our present purposes.

As I have asserted throughout, Camus's metaphysics of the Absurd must be distinguished from his (phenomenological) experience of the Absurd, and discarding the former in favor of the latter is essential for making sense of his ethical framework. Understood metaphysically (i.e., in terms of the Cartesian divide, with consciousness on one side and the indifferent universe on the other), the Absurd cannot counter "the insanity of history," and if Camus believes otherwise, it is because he tacitly presupposes an older scheme, one that obtained soon after "the throne of God [was] overturned." Camus's metaphysical approach, in other words, remains a vivid example of philosophizing in the "shadow of God," and he does not deny this. To the contrary, he contends that "the history of metaphysical rebellion," of which he is a part, "cannot be confused with that of atheism," and that the goal is to create "justice, order and unity . . . to justify the fall of God" (R, p. 25). Thus, though an anti-theist of sorts, Camus folds into an older humanist problematic, one not unlike Kant's. As we saw, Kant, a devout Christian, realizes that God's moral rules must be grounded differently, and he turns to pure practical reason to provide the metaphysical sanction, all the while clinging to God, freedom, and the soul's immortality as regulative ideals. And, as we saw, Camus rejects this move, for he sees Kant's abstract deontological approach as "nothing but a semblance of God, relegated to the heaven of principles" (R, p. 120). Nevertheless, this is just what Camus is offering insofar as he appeals to the absent God, and when he speaks in *these* terms, he tends to speak as a deontologist, such as when he declares that the moral acceptability of taking a life, *irrespective* of the situation, depends on your willingness to then sacrifice your own. This internalized variation on the biblical rule of "an eye for an eye" is part and parcel of "the heaven of principles," and it is the basis for Barthes's concerns in his review of *The Plague*.

What I am arguing here, in sum, is that Camus's *metaphysics* of the Absurd is not helpful for the purpose of making good his ethical concerns – indeed, it cuts against them – and it is not required, for what is best in his ethical thought gets off the mark better without the metaphysical baggage. Yet, as I asserted at the start of this chapter, this does not mean that Camus was wrong not to discard the Absurd altogether. As he says in an essay titled "Pessimism and Courage":

> It is essential for us to know whether man, without the help either of the eternal or of rationalistic thought, can unaided create his own values. . . . If the epoch has suffered from nihilism, we cannot remain ignorant of nihilism and still achieve the moral code that we need. No, everything is not summed up in negation and absurdity. We know this. But we must first posit negation and absurdity because they are what our generation has encountered and what we must take into account. (RRD, pp. 58–9)

Because "negation and absurdity" *is* what Camus's generation encountered, as the enlightenment project ran aground in Nazism's rationalized concentration camps, it is this *experience* (historical and phenomenological) that is the point from which the attempt to "create its own values" must start. The *experience* of absurdity reflects this ethico-political collapse, and, in this way, it works like Descartes's methodical doubt, as everything must be called into question: the slate, as Camus says, must be "wiped clean." Moreover, as I argued at the start of this chapter, to the extent that the Absurd is seen as a rejection of foundations, an ultimate groundlessness (without importing the nostalgic Judeo-Christian metaphysics, as Camus is prone to do), it precludes sociopolitical closure, and thus counsels moderation in the project of ethico-political reconstruction, which is in accord with Camus's tastes. The essential point, then, is that Camus's justifiable rejection of metaphysical closure should not be grounded in metaphysics but, rather, must reflect a rejection of metaphysics, which obscures the fact that we are fallible human beings for whom "certainty" is a misnomer. *This* is why we must perpetually question our ethico-political arrangements.

What is best in Camus's ethical thought is, indeed, its fine-grained recognition of limits. This is reflected not only in this rejection of ethico-political closure, which runs against the grain of all metaphysical tendencies (including his own), but also in his moral value, "I rebel, therefore we exist," for this idea analytically presupposes solidarity, and solidarity puts limits on what can be done. (As we saw, Camus thinks that rebellion analytically presupposes solidarity because to rebel is to demand one's rights, and for this demand to carry normative weight it must ultimately be universal in nature.) Thus, in response to the idea that "the end justifies the means," which is not an uncommon position among those whose politics are metaphysically underwritten, Camus asks what justifies the end, to which "rebellion replies: the means" (R, p. 292). In this way, all tendencies toward absolutism are rejected, including the absolutist tendencies inherent in our highest values, freedom and justice: "Absolute freedom mocks at justice. Absolute justice denies freedom. To be fruitful, the two ideas must find their limits in each other" (R, p. 291). Camus is right here, and, indeed, Hegel and Marx, if not their epigones, would agree. As Camus concedes, Hegel offers a devastating critique of absolute freedom in the *Phenomenology of Spirit*, in which he argues that the desire for such freedom demands the destruction of everything that stands over and against it (which, ultimately, *is* everything), and Marx (like Nietzsche) rejects a base leveling in the *Economic and Philosophic Manuscripts*. For Camus, there is a clash between freedom and justice only when they are considered in absolute terms, which is just what rebellion will not do: Rebellion "can only promise an assured dignity coupled with relative justice. It supposes a limit at which the community of man is established. Its universe is the universe of relative values. . . . [This] expresses fidelity to the human condition" (R, p. 290).

Having purged the metaphysical, thus relativizing freedom and justice, and having been informed that rebellion "supposes a limit at which the community of man is established," an idea to which we will return, we can now look at the remainder of the excerpt that begins this section. Camus speaks of the need to produce "a rule that is not formal but that can nevertheless serve as a guide," which, as we have seen, he finds in "I rebel, therefore we exist," and he goes on to say that rebellion reveals itself "in terms of the obscure existence that is already made manifest in the act of insurrection," which means "that instead of killing and dying in order to produce the being that we are not, we have to live and let live in order to create what we are." Beyond again saying that the commitment to solidarity inherent in rebellion cannot be renounced without renouncing rebellion itself, Camus is emphasizing that rebellion inevitably occurs on a fluid but determinate landscape, one whose particulars cannot simply be ignored in the pursuit of ends, and this means that it is incumbent on us to ceaselessly recontextualize both ends and means, lest there be a fall into the sort of nihilism that arises when we orient ourselves toward abstract, absolute ends that are untethered by the particulars of the given situation. Moreover, with his emphasis on creation, Camus is implying that both collectively and individually we are like an artwork in progress, and that, ideally, rebellion respects this moment of aesthetic creation, a notion that hearkens back to his earlier works and, ultimately, to Nietzsche. (Along these lines, he states that by emphasizing economic production, both bourgeois and communist societies do violence, as "the society based on production is only productive, not creative," R, p. 273.)

Now, I stated earlier that "I rebel, therefore we exist" is, "*in some sense*, transcendental," a "meta-value" that delineates the nature and scope of those historical values that comprise what I called the second tier of Camus's ethical model. Yet what, precisely, is the status of this "rule" that "is neither formal nor subject to history" but can still "serve as a guide"? The most fruitful way to make sense of this "rule," as I have been suggesting, is within the context of virtue ethics. In the last chapter, it will be recalled, I contended that Camus's virtue ethics was agent-focused instead of agent-based, which means that the virtuous agent is one that, with the right disposition of character, does virtuous acts (instead of it being the case that a virtuous act is simply what the virtuous person does). For Camus, as we know, there are some acts, regardless of the agent, that are *basically* virtuous or vicious. What makes "I rebel, therefore we exist" the basis for virtuous acts? Why is it the proper "guide" for a person with the right disposition of character? To make sense of this question another basic distinction within virtue ethics must be made: the distinction between a virtue ethics grounded in the community or *polis* and one grounded in nature. Both of these approaches are expressed in Aristotle's classical account, but in the contemporary literature it is usually the case that one or the other is emphasized, as the convergence purportedly found in Aristotle's less than egalitarian times is no longer viable, much less desirable. For Camus, it is the nature-based approach that is dispositive.

Of course, Camus himself speaks in terms of a "natural community" (R, p. 16), and this alone leaves the matter in doubt, but on closer inspection it becomes clear that he is attempting to build back to community based on some prior concept of "natural goodness." As we have seen, he often contends that with the breakdown of political society there are no viable ethico-political traditions on which to draw, and this means that to revitalize the community it is necessary to get normative traction somewhere outside of it. This is why Camus thinks we need a "guide," and if "I rebel, therefore we exist" can perform this role it is because the moment of solidarity built into it ultimately derives from the fact that by nature we are social beings who, in turn, live in and are nourished by the natural world. The rebel thus "demands respect for himself . . . only insofar as he identifies himself with a natural community" (R, p. 16), whether real or imagined. Or, put rather differently, it is only when we are faithful to this (relatively) non-negotiable first-tier "rule" that we can forge a community that will produce the sorts of substantive (second-tier) virtues that are worth having (i.e., that are "naturally good"). Thus, for Camus, not only is it "*possible* eternally to reject injustice without ceasing to acclaim the nature of man and the beauty of the world" (R, p. 276), but it is necessary, as the failure to do justice to human nature and the natural world only reinforces the prisonhouse of historical absolutism: "Historical absolutism, despite its triumphs, has never ceased to come into collision with an irrepressible demand of human nature," and "in the common condition of misery, the eternal demand is heard again: nature once more takes up the fight against history" (R, p. 300).

Camus's belief that a nature-based approach to ethics is a necessary condition for having the right sorts of socially engendered virtues, rather than the belief that the virtues begin with the community, is also evinced by the fact that the community-based approach to ethics, which often comes under the rubric of "communitarianism," is inherently conservative in nature, and this cuts against Camus's fundamental inclinations. For example, Alasdair MacIntyre, one of the leading exponents of a community-based virtue ethics, believes that ethics effectively breaks down with the enlightenment, arguing that when stripped from the traditional communal practices that gave rise to them, terms like "good" and "bad" no longer have any real meaning. For MacIntyre, the problem is the enlightenment's emphasis on "individualism," and, in particular, the notion of the individual as a chooser of his own good in the absence of a background of traditional communal practices that might furnish the grounds for making this choice. When Camus speaks in terms of "vital traditions," conversely, he is speaking of *enlightenment* traditions, and, in particular, their emphasis on individualism. Camus thus says that what needs to be revitalized is the "libertarian tradition" (R, p. 300), and that the "we are" that is innate to "I rebel, therefore we exist" actually "defines a new form of individualism" (R, p. 297). In sum, then, while Camus is sympathetic to the idea that any rebellion worthy of the name "relies primarily on the most concrete realities, on occupation [and] on the village, where the living heart of things and of men is to be found" (R, p. 298), his brand of republicanism, grounded in the idea of a rebellion informed by "untrammeled dialogue" (R, p. 283), is much too energetic to be straitjacketed by traditionalist conceptions. He never ceases to be guided by the enlightenment ideal of the free, self-determining individual, and with his "I rebel, therefore we exist" he attempts to strike a balance between the ambitions of the individual and the community that is the condition of its possibility.

Understood within the context of a nature-based virtue ethics, then, Camus's "guide," "I rebel, therefore we exist," must be seen not so much as a "rule" (which suggests a deontological approach) or a "transcendental value" (which suggests that it abstracts from concrete realities or, as Husserl would put it, "the natural attitude"), but, rather, as a "principle" or "meta-value" that is a necessary condition for human beings to thrive. Although projecting contemporary theories on to earlier thinkers is surely at least somewhat problematical, Camus seems to come closest to those current virtue ethicists who take a nature-based approached to virtue ethics that is informed by the Greek idea of *eudaimonia*, which is perhaps best translated as "flourishing." Philosophers such as Philippa Foot and Rosalind Hursthouse are particularly noteworthy in this regard, as both approach virtue ethics from an agent-focused, nature-based perspective that judges actions to be right or wrong on the basis of whether they promote or hinder human flourishing. Foot contends, for example, that practical rationality must be understood in terms of virtuous action (and, in the final analysis, human flourishing), which runs contrary to the general philosophical inclination to ask virtuous action to justify itself in the court of practical rationality. In an important sense, this seems to be right, and I believe that Camus is gesturing at this position in *The Rebel* and, for that matter, *The Plague*. Moreover, when Foot states that *"life* is at the center of her discussion," and that "the grounding of a moral argument is ultimately in facts about human life,"[15] she says very little with which Camus would disagree. In (at least) one crucial respect, however, Camus would disagree with the agent-focused, nature-based account that a virtue ethicist like Foot offers, and this disagreement is highly instructive for making sense of Camus's own position. To set up this argument, however, it shall be necessary to first briefly consider Foot's critique of Nietzsche.

In the last chapter of *Natural Goodness*, Foot attacks Nietzsche's "immoralism," arguing against what was essentially his agent-based virtue ethics, which maintained that "the true nature of an action depended . . . on the nature of the individual who did it."[16] In other words, according to Foot, there were no inherently right or wrong actions for Nietzsche, and this, coupled with his highly individualistic aristocratic elitism, seemed to sanction patently immoral actions, provided that they were done by "higher types" pursuant to such Nietzschean virtues as creativity, daring, and self-overcoming. "But given the horrors of the past century," she opines, "I think that today it would be especially strange not to see the 'what' of actions as even more important [than who does them],"[17] and, in no small part, she is right. Nevertheless, when Foot states that "telling the truth, keeping promises, or helping a neighbour is *on a par* with the rationality of self-preserving action,"[18] she arguably evinces an intention to bring back a full-fledged deontological approach under the rubric of human flourishing, which would lead Nietzsche to argue, in turn, that such a virtue ethics is actually nothing more than a Trojan horse for the kind of "shopkeeper's morality" that he found so enervating. (And, indeed, such a move is also open to the argument that Marx leveled against the classical economists, that authoritative statements about what human nature requires do nothing more than smuggle in the ideological prejudices engendered by the dominant socioeconomic paradigm.)

Now, Camus would basically agree with Foot's critique of Nietzsche, and, indeed, as we saw, he is somewhat less favorably disposed toward Nietzsche in *The Rebel* than in his previous works because he experienced first-hand at least some of what Foot calls "the horrors of the past century." And yet, Camus would also agree with the Nietzschean critique of Foot that I sketched out above. Camus thus recognizes the shortcomings in both positions, and, as was the case with the interrelated question of whether values are ahistorical or historicized, he effectively splits the difference. In opposition to Nietzsche, he agrees with Foot's demands for limits on the kinds of actions we can take and for a commitment to social solidarity. Both demands, as we have seen, are inherent in "I rebel, therefore we exist," his first-tier "guide." In opposition to Foot, he still emphasizes Nietzschean virtues like creativity, daring, and self-overcoming, and he also rejects attributing too many rules to human nature. Rather, limiting himself to the boundary conditions established by "I rebel, therefore we exist," he entrusts the generation of a community's (second-tier) substantive virtues to interpersonal dialogue, which reflects both his dislike of disincarnated values (even when they purportedly derive from human nature) and his commitment to a vibrant republicanism. "The mutual understanding and communication discovered by rebellion can only survive in the free exchange of conversation" (R, p. 283), he asserts, and this necessary condition of any value structure worth its salt is "no farther above life and history than history and life are above it" (R, p. 296). Simply put, to do justice to *all* individuals, values must reflect the concrete particularities of life, and they must be generated in a collective fashion.

In the final analysis, then, for Camus, it is only by keeping open our substantive (second-tier) virtues, subject to the limits imposed by rebellion, that we can do justice to the life-affirming impulse manifested in the act of rebellion. What nature gives us, Camus thinks, are imagination, creativity, and a drive to unity that gives meaning to our lives, and this assemblage is reflected in art, which is why he views "artistic creation" as rebellion "in its pure state" (R, p. 252). Whether evinced in a two-year-old's "no," teenage rebellion, the midlife crisis, or the crusty independence of the elderly, rebellion is part of our nature and a basic condition of our growth, and it is only if we respect this individuating, meaning-conferring impulse in others that we can rightly demand that they respect it in us. And, in this way, "if, after all, men cannot always make history have a meaning, they can always act so that their own lives have one" (RRD, p. 106).

notes

1 Albert Camus, "In Defense of *The Rebel*," in *Sartre and Camus: A Historic Confrontation*, ed. and trans. David Sprintzen and Adrian van den Hoven (Amherst, NY: Humanity Books, 2004), pp. 207–8.
2 Ibid., p. 206 (emphasis added).
3 Ibid., p. 205.
4 See Ronald Aronson, *Camus and Sartre* (Chicago: University of Chicago Press, 2005), p. 116.

5 R, p. 22.
6 Aristotle, *Nicomachean Ethics*, trans. Terence Irwin (Indianapolis: Hackett Publishing Co., 1985), book 1, chapters 3–4.
7 David Sprintzen, *Camus: A Critical Examination* (Philadelphia: Temple University Press, 1988), p. 131.
8 Provocatively, although probably unintentionally, the section in which Camus treats Lenin's version of Bolshevism is titled "The Kingdom of Ends."
9 Albert Camus, *Notebooks: 1942–1951*, trans. Justin O'Brien (New York: Harcourt Brace Jovanovich, 1965), p. 182.
10 Friedrich Nietzsche, *The Will to Power*, trans. Walter Kaufmann and R. J. Hollingdale (New York: Random House, 1967), pp. 16–17 (emphasis in original).
11 Camus's analyses of metaphysical and historical revolt make up the lion's share of the book. Coming after the introduction and part 1 ("The Rebel"), which, combined, total roughly 19 pages, parts 2 and 3, "Metaphysical Rebellion" and "Historical Rebellion," total roughly 230 pages combined, and account for about 80 percent of the remainder of the book. Parts 4 and 5, "Rebellion and Art" and "Thought at the Meridian," which total roughly 53 pages combined, are the most suggestive with respect to the ethical implications that can be gleaned from the book.
12 Karl Marx, "The Critique of the Gotha Program," in *Marx: Later Political Writings*, ed. Terrell Carver (Cambridge: Cambridge University Press, 1996), pp. 214–15.
13 R, pp. 251–2.
14 Albert Camus, "A Letter to the Editor of *Les Temps Modernes*," in David Sprintzen and Adrian van den Hoven, eds. and trans., *Sartre and Camus: A Historic Confrontation* (Amherst, NY: Humanity Books, 2004), p. 115.
15 Philippa Foot, *Natural Goodness* (Oxford: Oxford University Press, 2001), pp. 5 and 24, respectively.
16 Ibid., p. 110.
17 Ibid., p. 113.
18 Ibid., p. 11.

further reading

Aronson, Ronald, *Camus and Sartre* (Chicago: University of Chicago Press, 2005).
Sprintzen, David, *Camus: A Critical Examination* (Philadelphia: Temple University Press, 1988).

realpolitik

A free man would only be one who need not bow to any alternatives, and under existing circumstances there is a touch of freedom in refusing to accept the alternatives. Freedom means to criticize and change situations, not to confirm them by deciding within their coercive structure.

Theodor W. Adorno, *Negative Dialectics*[1]

In the last chapter, I tentatively offered a Camusian ethics, maintaining, in essence, that Camus's ethical orientation harks back (and, with its recent resurgence, forward) to a virtue ethics of sorts, and what I called his phenomenological ethics was his starting point for this reclamation project, as this is what is left of virtue ethics when social life has all but broken down. Even if Camus's approach is more of a piece with Aristotle's naturalism than with his communitarianism (which, as in the case of MacIntyre, frequently exhibits itself in anti-liberal ways that Camus would have repudiated), it is still necessary to take up the virtues within the framework of *some* community-based ethical perspective, and with this notion Camus would agree. Without a social framework that can make them determinate, the virtues of "natural goodness" are much too abstract for the purpose of offering ethical guidance, but it was just the lack of this grounding social perspective that Camus and his compatriots confronted, as Camus himself lamented. Under these conditions, it can be unclear what criteria are relevant for adjudicating between the bad choices offered by a riven social reality. Or, to put the matter somewhat differently, under extraordinary conditions, ethical theories can take us only so far, and then we must decide what to do, if only on the basis of character alone (at least in the case of the virtue ethicist). Of course, reposited in the person of good character are the remains of what we saw Camus refer to as "vital traditions," and, in some sense, these inform a bare bones phenomenological ethics, but how the remains of these traditions can be applied within the context of bleak sociopolitical realities in which every choice is a bad one can turn out to be anyone's guess. (Although not in this global way, Hursthouse admits that virtue ethics can and does confront "irresolvable and tragic dilemmas."[2]) This quandary refs to what is called the "theory-practice problem," and, harking all the way back to Aristotle's idea of praxis (i.e., the application of theory to practice), it is one of the most nettlesome in philosophy.

Adorno famously remarks that "wrong life cannot be lived rightly,"[3] which points to the limits of even the best ethical theories in bad socio-political times, and the fact that even the best choice, however it is ultimately determined, might still be a particularly odious one. Sartre puts the complexities of this dilemma rather well: "There is a morality in politics – a difficult subject, and never clearly treated – and when politics must betray its morality, to choose morality is to betray politics. Now, find your way out of that one! Particularly when the politics has taken as its goal the reign of the human."[4] Sartre's contention is that a politics committed to "the reign of humanity" and, therefore, to making good a genuine morality, has its own intrinsic morality – the facilitation of the political ends considered necessary to bring about the "genuine morality" – and that to betray this political morality, even in the name of the more intuitively compelling aspects of conventional morality, is to betray the genuine morality at which it aims, and thus reinstantiate Adorno's "wrong life." What does one do under these circumstances, in which the conventional morality would reinstantiate the bad status quo and efficacious political action would require the violation of even that which the "genuine morality" would proscribe (particularly when there are no guarantees that this action actually is in the service of "genuine morality" rather than "wrong life" made even worse)? There are, crudely, two possible ways to go. One can refuse to cede the moral high ground, as best one can discern it, and thus either withdraw from the political sphere or pursue politically untenable options, or one can choose between the bad alternatives offered, and then (preferably without compromising one's critical capacities, and, therefore, the prospect of changing one's commitments) throw oneself into the political sphere on the most promising, if still fundamentally unsatisfactory, side. The first approach, reflected in the opening excerpt from Adorno's *Negative Dialectics*, was Camus's, while the second approach was Sartre's. It is in this way that individuals who, politically, have far more in common than not, can end up on opposing sides, as was the case with Camus and Sartre.[5]

The Confrontation with Sartre and the French Intellectual Left

Politics is never the encounter between conscience and individual happenings, nor is it ever the simple application of a philosophy of history. Politics is never able to see the whole directly. It is always aiming at the incomplete synthesis, a given cycle of time, or a group of problems. It is not pure morality nor is it a chapter in a universal history which has already been written. Rather it is an action in the process of self-invention.

Maurice Merleau-Ponty, *Adventures of the Dialectic*[6]

Although Camus had always bristled at the idea that he was an "existentialist," there were surely affinities between his earlier philosophy and Sartre's existentialism, and if he rejected the term's relevance to his own work, as will be recalled, it was because he believed it implied a systematic approach, as in its Sartrean or Heideggerian expressions. Following Nietzsche, Camus believed that the will to systematize was a dishonesty of sorts, and he surely thought that to commit to any political system without both monitoring and responding to its ever changing positions was most dishonest of all. Ironically, it was Sartre rather than Camus who had previously been accused of lacking political commitment, as he was much less active than Camus during the Resistance, but in the face of much more ambiguous moral realities, Camus hesitated, while Sartre unrepentantly committed himself to supporting communism, both in France and in Stalin's Soviet Union.

In 1951, the year *The Rebel* was published, *Les Temps Modernes* was a highly influential periodical in France, and Sartre was the periodical's editor-in-chief. Sartre and Camus were already moving in different directions, both personally and politically, but ostensibly out of concern for their lingering friendship, Sartre hesitated to assign Camus's book for review. For the most part, the periodical's editorial board did not like the book, but after a fair number of months had passed, Francis Jeanson volunteered to review it, and his review appeared in May 1952, approximately nine months after the book was published. Although Sartre subsequently contended that he had wanted the review to be handled delicately, Jeanson's review functioned like a sledgehammer, and because Sartre was not in Paris at the time it was published, he was not in a position to ask Jeanson to tone it down. (Of course, whether he would have is an open question.) As the periodical's temporary editor-in-chief, Merleau-Ponty, whose *Phenomenology of Perception* had made him almost as famous as Camus and Sartre, did ask Jeanson to tone his review down, and when Jeanson refused to comply a quarrel broke out.[7] Merleau-Ponty had, ironically, fought with Camus in 1946 over Merleau-Ponty's own views on communism, which he set forth the following year in *Humanism and Terror*. Despite Merleau-Ponty's recognition of the Soviet Union's severe shortcomings, he had then claimed that it must continue to be supported because, in essence, it was the only humanist alternative to the ravages of capitalism, and it still could not be said that it would not ultimately bring its purported aims to fruition. Nevertheless, Merleau-Ponty progressively came to the view that the Soviet Union was, in fact, incorrigible, and for reasons similar to Camus's, which might be why he intervened with Jeanson in 1952. Indeed, he resigned from *Les Temps Modernes* the following year, and in 1955 he published *Adventures of the Dialectic*, which rejected his earlier "wait-and-see Marxism" and Sartre's continuing "ultra-Bolshevism" in favor of more democratic commitments.

Jeanson himself was a formidable intellectual. His previously published book on Sartre's existential phenomenology, *Sartre and the Problem of Morality*, offered a penetrating analysis of the ethico-political consequences of Sartre's thought, prompting Sartre to declare in a foreword to the book that Jeanson had discovered tendencies in his work that he himself had not. What's more, Jeanson had also moved to Marxism more quickly than Sartre, and he was less inclined to indulge what he took to be Camus's moralizing tendencies. In any case, his review appeared as it was first written, and his attack on Camus begins with the title itself. In French, *l'homme* and *l'âme* ("man" and "soul," respectively) sound more or less the same, and when Jeanson titles his essay "Albert Camus, or the Soul in Revolt" ("Albert Camus *ou l'âme révoltée*"),[8] he is not only punning with respect to the French title of *The Rebel* (*L'homme révolté*) but is making a stinging philosophical point. In Hegel's *Phenomenology of Spirit*, there is a form of consciousness called "the Beautiful Soul," and Hegel's contention is that this type of consciousness, which is tacitly motivated by a sense of moral superiority, gets twisted up in existential knots when it attempts to flee the profane world in the service of what it alleges to be a higher moral calling. For Jeanson, Camus's positions in *The Rebel* reflect just such a consciousness.

The body of Jeanson's review is no less unrelenting. He starts by pointing out that many prominent right-wing newspapers and periodicals have praised the book, thus tacitly calling into question Camus's claim that he remains a man of the left. Then, adverting to the fact that there are also various right-wing newspapers and periodicals that do not like the book, as well as many left-wing newspapers and periodicals that do, Jeanson reconciles the apparent inconsistencies by pointing to what he calls Camus's "vague humanism," which "renders [his thought] indefinitely plastic and malleable, capable of assuming many diverse forms." Jeanson then attacks Camus's style, saying that it is "too beautiful, too sovereign, [and] too sure of itself," all of which is made possible by the fact that it avoids "any smudge of existence," and in this way it is able to reduce to neat formulas, and, ultimately, to the "transcendental." It is here that Jeanson gets to the heart of his complaint. Aside from the fact that he is (justifiably) put off by Camus's interpretations of both Hegel and Marx, Jeanson believes that Camus's absurdism reflects a metaphysical view of history that ends up "rejecting any role for history and economics in the genesis of revolutions," and thereby reduces the concept of revolution to the "divinization of man." Having thus stripped the content from both history and revolution, what Camus is left with, Jeanson claims, is "a pure dialogue of ideas" in which rebellion is tantamount to "the metaphysical protest against suffering and death," while revolution is tantamount to the violation of rebellion's principles in the service of "omnipotence." Ultimately, according to Jeanson, Camus has driven the historical actor into a corner, such that virtually any attempt to change the prevailing state of affairs that might actually be efficacious runs the risk of hubris, and thus runs afoul of the spirit of rebellion by capitulating to the revolutionary impulse to deify man: "Efficacy thus appears acceptable [to Camus] only to the extent that it becomes inconceivable." Camus is thus left with the notion of "pure rebellion," which sanctions little more than a "Red Cross morality" (and, in this way, Jeanson picks up the thread of Barthes' concerns with respect to *The Plague*).

Camus's reply to Jeanson's review appeared in *Les Temps Modernes* three months later. His article, which opens with the salutation "Dear Editor," makes clear that he takes Sartre to be responsible for the poor review, and at no point in the article does he directly address Jeanson, at most referring to him as Sartre's "collaborator." After mentioning the review's "ironic title," and declaring that "if the truth seemed to be on the Right, I would be there," Camus says that Sartre's "collaborator can't help thinking that there is no precise border between the man of the Right and the critic of dogmatic Marxism." He then declares that, aside from the distorted personal attacks, the review has deliberately mischaracterized his views. Contending that *The Rebel* did not forget about historical and economic causes but intentionally chose not to add to this literature, and that its stated goal was instead to examine the ideological underpinnings of revolution, Camus claims that the book's central arguments have not been dealt with. Clearly addressing himself to Sartre, Camus states that "instead of trying to ridicule an imaginary thesis, a loyal and wise critic would have dealt with my true thesis: namely, that whoever seeks to serve history for its own sake ends in nihilism." Whatever the limits of his more general expositions of Hegel and Marx, Camus is (rightly) pointing to the nettlesome orthodox Marxist "end of history" hypothesis, which appears to justify virtually any action, including the Soviet Union's forced labor camps, which exemplify this very principle. Pointing out that the "end of history" hypothesis conflicts with Sartre's own existentialism, Camus rejects the position that there "is no alternative to either the status quo or Caesarian socialism," which, he thinks, is the consideration that underlies Sartre's unwillingness to attack the Soviet camps. Lastly, taking a swipe at Sartre's own commitments during the Nazi occupation, Camus states that "I am beginning to become a little tired of seeing myself . . . receive endless lessons in effectiveness from critics who have never done anything more than turn their armchair in history's direction."

Sartre's reaction to Camus, published under the title "Reply to Albert Camus," was quick in coming, and it ratcheted up the nastiness of the polemics. Sartre opens by personally attacking Camus in no uncertain terms: he contends that Camus's response to Jeanson has the "nasty smell of wounded vanity," evidencing his "mixture of dreary complacency and vulnerability"; he calls into question Camus's style, which, with the help of a "portable pedestal," enables him to preach from above the fray; he criticizes Camus's refusal to directly address his reviewer, Jeanson, who is thus transformed into an "object," such as a "soup tureen"; and, finally, he questions Camus's philosophical competence, stating, for example, that he (Sartre) has "at least this in common with Hegel, you have not read either of us." In response to the question of his political commitments during the Nazi occupation, Sartre implicitly admits that Camus's involvement, which was "not far from being exemplary," had outstripped his own, but he goes on to claim that while the world has changed, Camus has not. Conversely, Sartre asserts, pursuant to the concepts of freedom and responsibility inherent in his existentialism, he has come to see the necessity of making "the free choice to fight in order to become free," and by virtue of this, he is implicitly suggesting, he has now left Camus behind. Along more substantive lines, Sartre indicates that *Les Temps Modernes* has criticized the Soviet forced labor camps and, turning on Camus, says that Camus has become an "anti-Communist." Sartre is implying here (rather unfairly) that Camus is not just opposed to the Soviet camps but, rather, that like many cynical politicians and journalists, he is using their existence to discredit (Soviet) Marxism's loftier (if unrealized) ambitions in an unnuanced way, thus serving the interests of the bourgeois classes.

In the second half of his response, Sartre goes on to consider Camus's political positions within the broader framework of Camus's thought, and it is here that he goes to the heart of some of the theory-practice problems with which we are especially concerned. Starting with Camus's general refusal to commit, Sartre maintains that, despite the desperate nature of the times, "when a man can only see in present struggles the idiotic duel of two equally abject monsters," he does not transcend this situation but is determined by it: "Far from dominating, as an arbiter, an era on which he deliberately turns his back, I see him as wholly conditioned by this era, and stymied by the rejection that a very historical resentment inspires in him." As a result, he claims, Camus is relegated to the politically impotent position of unnuanced condemnation. Then, converging on the peculiarly metaphysical nature of Camus's thought, Sartre contends that "since, on your own terms, injustice is *eternal* – that is, since the absence of God is a constant throughout the changes of history – the immediate and continually reaffirmed relation of a man who insists on having a meaning . . . to this God who maintains an eternal silence is itself transcendent to history." In this way, according to Sartre, there is no place for historical progress, and with the exception of those situations in which one side represents the veritable bane of humanity itself (such as the Nazis or a plague), virtually every qualitative distinction is leveled down by the acid bath of metaphysical absurdity. Sartre thus claims that Camus ends up "comparing a world without justice to a Justice without content." Lastly, Sartre directly attacks the normative role that nature plays in Camus's thought, declaring that "even Nature has changed meaning, because man's relationship with her has changed, [and] you are left with memories and an increasingly abstract language."

The Confrontation and the Theory-Practice Problem

> Why should a difference which is apparently one of nuance arouse so much passion? Sartre and Camus are neither Communists nor "Atlanticists"; both of them recognize the existence of iniquities in either camp. Camus would denounce those of the East as well as those of the West; Sartre would denounce only those of the West, without denying the existence of the others.
>
> Raymond Aron, *The Opium of the Intellectuals*[9]

Raymond Aron, a well-known French philosopher in his own right and a former friend of Sartre's who had moved to the right after the War, is right when he says that the differences that separated Camus and Sartre were only a matter of "nuance." And, indeed, Sartre himself agrees, as he states in the first paragraph of his reply to Camus that "many things drew us together, few separated us, but these few were still too many." I do not start in this way so as to belabor the peculiarly personal dimensions of this confrontation but, rather, to make clear that it raises elemental questions about political praxis, questions that come to the fore precisely because the differences between Camus and Sartre were not all that substantial and the bleak sociopolitical choices with which they were confronted were nothing short of epochal. As a preliminary reply to Aron's rhetorical question, then, the reason that "the duel" gave rise to "so much passion" was that it reflected the dreadfully limited choices that remained for a French left that, only a few years earlier, had thought that it would vigorously chart its own sociopolitical destiny in a far more compelling fashion.

To put the questions of praxis here in perspective, two initial points must be made: first, there is more than a quantum of truth in the varied criticisms that both Camus and his adversaries direct against one another, and, second, Camus and his adversaries are basically talking past one another. Viewed from the broadest possible angle, Jeanson and Sartre are not wrong to question Camus's style of argumentation in *The Rebel*, which often assumes the form of bare conclusions largely unsupported by rigorous conceptual or sociohistorical analyses, and they are not wrong to question Camus's relatively reductive approach to the Hegelian-Marxist tradition, which tends to obscure the fact that this tradition gave rise to many thinkers that rejected Soviet communism but did not take its problems to be inevitable by virtue of Hegelian-Marxism's alleged "divinization of man." For his part, Camus is not wrong to repeatedly emphasize the moral unacceptability of the Soviet Union's forced labor camps, which is not mitigated by the fact that dyed-in-the-wool "anti-Communists" employ their existence to further their own baneful political ends, and, more generally, he is not wrong to reject the idea that political ends, even in the service of a "genuine morality," do not justify every means (which, when unsavory enough, will preclude these ends in any case). In what follows, I shall focus on three issues of political praxis that are raised by the confrontation, the three raised by Sartre and set forth at the end of the last section: the refusal to commit in the face of bad political options (which I shall look at last), the effects of metaphysics on praxis, and the importation of nature into the political calculus.

As I suggested in the last chapter, Camus gives us good reason to think that metaphysical considerations continue to trump historical ones in *The Rebel*, and when Jeanson and Sartre state that matters of historical injustice can appear less stark when viewed through the refractory lens of metaphysical injustice (i.e., the inevitability of "suffering and death"), they are right. And, in fact, they are also right when they argue that "the absence of *God*" in Camus's thought continues to be morally dispositive, as it restricts the forms that political praxis can assume. (It is for these reasons that I tried to show that a Camusian ethics can get off the mark without the metaphysical baggage). Although Camus does equivocate somewhat with respect to the relationship between violence and praxis, this limitation is certainly evidenced in his claim that killing even "a single master" undermines the justification for rebellion, which is to build "the community of men," and that the only way the rebel can make amends for the act of killing is "to accept his own death and sacrifice" to demonstrate that "murder is impossible" (R, pp. 281–2). Yet, such a position, Jeanson and Sartre can reasonably argue, tacitly gives support to the masters, as violence is taken off the table before the ways in which it is institutionalized by the masters are even considered. It is for reasons such as these that, in the final analysis, Camus's reply to Barthes's criticisms of *The Plague* and Jeanson's and Sartre's criticisms of *The Rebel* never actually gets to the core of their concerns. Conversely, the "political realism" that Jeanson and Sartre allegedly evidence, which justifies all actions in the service of a politics that purports to work for "the genuine morality," is arguably no less idealistic than Camus's metaphysically laden political position, since the Soviet Union had already made it abundantly clear that its commitments to a just, classless society were only nominal. Jeanson and Sartre were, in essence, "willing to stake the lives of the masses on a teleological gamble,"[10] and while this "teleological gamble" was not grounded in a metaphysical conception of history, which Jeanson and Sartre clearly rejected, it was undertaken on the basis of shaky evidence. Even if one rejects Camus's categorical claim that the end never justifies the means (which are limited by the commitment to solidarity that he takes to be inherent in "I rebel, therefore we exist"), arguing instead that such a claim is only a rebuttable presumption, Jeanson and Sartre have not rebutted it.

Sartre's rejection of the normative role that nature plays in Camus's thought is much less compelling than his rejection of the normative role that metaphysics plays in it. Although Sartre is right to suggest that nature "changes meaning" as humankind's relationship to it changes, his outright dismissal of nature in Camus's thought is way too precipitous, and while there is much truth in his claim that Camus's idea of nature is based on "memories and an increasingly abstract language," this in and of itself is not a bad thing. Camus himself reemphasizes the importance of these memories (if not an abstract language) in a collection of essays that he published in 1954, a scant two years after the dispute with *Les Temps Modernes*. Titled *Summer*, which is intended to convey the difference between his own Mediterranean sensibility (based on the notion of natural happiness and natural limits) and the cold rationalism of the north European sensibility, Camus tacitly makes a plea for the remembrance of nature. Lamenting the fact that we have "turned our back on nature [and] we are ashamed of beauty," Camus says in "Helen's Exile" that "our reason has swept everything away," and, "alone at last, we build our empire on a desert" (LCE, p. 150). (Helen here refers to Helen of Troy, whose beauty allegedly launched a thousand ships.) So, too, in "The Enigma," an essay that looks at the peculiarities of being a well-known writer, he speaks of "an instinctive fidelity to a light in which I was born, and in which for thousands of years men have learned to welcome life even in suffering" (LCE, p. 160). And, perhaps most famously, in "Return to Tipasa," Camus speaks of fleeing from "the night of Europe, from a winter of faces," for the beaches that he frequented as a boy, stating that "in the depths of winter, I finally learned that within me there lay an invincible summer" (LCE, pp. 163, 169). More than just a memory, although it is clearly that, this "invincible summer" is also a promise of happiness, even if such a promise can only be articulated in "abstract language," as

Sartre puts it. Perhaps most important of all, however, it is also the source on which we ought to be drawing when we act politically:

> [T]he long demand for justice exhausts even the love that gave it birth. In the clamor we live in, love is impossible and justice not enough. That is why Europe hates the daylight and can do nothing but confront one injustice with another. In order to prevent justice from shriveling up . . . one must keep a freshness and a source of joy intact within, loving the daylight that injustice leaves unscathed, and returning to the fray with this light as a trophy. (LCE, p. 168)

Camus's contention here is vitally important. Without returning to nature (both internal human nature and the external natural world) to "keep a freshness and a joy intact," the promise of happiness, which motivates every impulse to justice that is worth its salt, is extinguished, and the impulse to justice can thereby tend to metamorphose into an impulse to injustice. Nietzsche, arguably the greatest psychologist of all, captures this insight well when he states that "whoever fights monsters should see to it that in the process he does not become a monster, [for] when you look into an abyss, the abyss also looks into you."[11] For Camus, as the quotations from *Summer* suggest, the working metaphorical juxtaposition is between "heat and light" and "cold and dark," and when he speaks of the coldness and darkness of Europe, he is speaking, as we have seen, of reason run amuck, such that the worst kinds of injustices are syllogistically justified in the name of overcoming injustice. Yet, crucially, Camus is *not* recommending that we simply assume our social sufferings, alleviating them with the consolations of nature as well as we can. When in a biography of Sartre the French philosopher Bernard-Henri Lévy says that Camus "defends man's submission to nature," and asks "is a moral scheme that talks about happiness more than justice still a moral scheme, and can a politics content with adoring the world, and thus contemplating and consenting to it, blessing it, still be a politics?"[12] he is badly misrepresenting Camus's position. Camus does not advocate a collapse into nature, which, in effect, would make the existing social injustices akin to second nature. Rather, he is contending that we must not forget that happiness is the goal toward which justice strives and, as such, must be factored into all questions of praxis. When Camus states in "Return to Tipasa" that "in the days of innocence I did not know morality existed" (LCE, p. 165), and that what he is now seeking to convey is "something that transcends ethics" (LCE, p. 170), he is not recommending that we unreflectively attempt to "go back home" (as is portrayed in his first two collections of Algerian essays, *The Wrong Side and the Right Side* and *Nuptials*) but is only reminding us that what we truly seek is on the other side of a reflective ethics, and that this ideal must function regulatively in all matters of political praxis. And, lastly, while Sartre is right when he contends that there is something abstract about this, it also could be argued that all ideals transcend the given situation, while the most concrete language, evidencing a brute realism, only reinforces it. It is the ability to at least minimally abstract from the present situation that is the condition of possibility for ethics itself.

Finally, when Sartre asserts that Camus is relegated to unnuanced condemnation because he can only see a battle of "equally abject monsters," and that such a perspective (motivated by a deep "historical resentment") enables the sociohistorical situation to "wholly condition" him, his charge goes to the very heart of the theory-practice problem. As is invariably the case in matters of theory and practice, to make sense of this sort of claim it is necessary to consider not only the particulars of the sociohistorical context but also the role that the individual plays in it, lest this complex problem degenerate into an a priori endorsement of either actionism or quietism. When this is done with regard to Camus and Sartre, the theory-practice problem reduces to the question of what *they* should have done (i.e., what form praxis should have taken for *these* leading French intellectuals) when confronted by the fact that their more or less shared ethico-political principles could not find genuine expression in the predominant practices of French society, which were as polarized as the world that they mirrored. Of course, the answer to this question is as convoluted as its statement is simple, as their divergent positions amply suggest. Yet, to begin with, even if there is a grain of truth in the charges that Sartre levels against Camus, it could be contended that they can just as easily be leveled against Sartre himself. The importance of Sartre's and Camus's political engagements resided in the fact that they were leading intellectuals, and the question of praxis in their specific cases had to take into account this primary role, as it is the function of the intellectual to hold open those values theoretically that a world of corrupted practices conspires to close down practically. For a certain period of time, however, Sartre did not do this. His book *The Communists and the Peace* is probably his worst, and thus, even if he did assume the part of "the loyal opposition," his political commitments not only caused him to engage in some dubious practices but, more importantly, disfigured his theoretical work. They reflected, in other words, an intellectual "wholly conditioned" by the sociohistorical situation.

For Marx, there was no conflict between theory and practice, as the movement toward a more humane socialist society seemed to be built into the unfolding dynamic of capitalist society itself, which would establish the material preconditions for such a society while (unintentionally) unleashing the social forces that would bring it about. By the early 1950s, however, it was clear that this convergence could no longer be assumed, and that intellectuals had to theorize against the grain of existing social practices, thus creating a division of labor that placed a heavy burden on the intellectual. To assert that it is incumbent on the intellectual to hold open the (theoretical) space for those social practices that might make good the earlier promise under these conditions, as I suggested above, does not mean that the intellectual must refrain from practice, which might cultivate the very "historical resentment" to which Sartre refers. Rather, it means throwing one's lot in with those oppositional practices that bear some reasonable relationship to the higher ideals (which necessarily precludes the use of certain means to achieve them) even if such practices are not especially viable at the time, provided that this does not exacerbate the underlying conditions in such a way as to make the actualization of these ideals even less likely. As we shall now see, Camus did, in some sense, attempt to do this, and if he failed, it is because oppositional practices meeting these criteria had been largely squeezed out.

Camus's Politics, The Cold War, and the Algerian War

> We do not believe in ready-made principles or theoretical plans. In the days to come we will define, through our actions as well as in a series of articles, the content of the word "revolution." . . . We want without delay to institute a true people's and workers' democracy. In this alliance democracy will contribute the principles of freedom and the people will contribute the faith and courage without which freedom is nothing. We believe that any politics that cuts itself off from the working class is futile. . . . That is why we want immediate implementation of a Constitution that will restore full guarantees of freedom and justice; serious structural reforms, without which any politics of freedom would be a sham; merciless destruction of the trusts and the moneyed interests; and a foreign policy based on honor and loyalty . . . In the present state of affairs, such a program goes by the name "Revolution."
>
> We are determined to replace politics with morality. That is what we call a revolution.
>
> Albert Camus, Combat (1944)[13]

These political principles, which Camus sets forth in *Combat* even before the liberation of Paris, are ones to which he essentially adhered for the remainder of his life. When Sartre charges in his "Reply to Camus" that Camus had failed to change with the times, he is right, and it is likely that Camus agreed. In the final analysis, perhaps the basic point of disagreement between Camus and Sartre pertained to the underlying status of ethico-political principles – that is, whether they are a function of the specific sociohistorical situation or a yardstick against which the course of history ought to be measured – and Camus's ongoing *moral* commitment to the same political principles is in keeping with the latter view. When Camus contends that politics should be replaced by morality, therefore, he is saying that morality must serve as politics' (ahistorical) foundation, and when he contends in *The Rebel* that politics should start with "revolutionary trade-unionism" because this is a "concrete basis . . . the living cell on which the organization builds itself" (R, pp. 297–8), he is saying that any "top down" political form (such as the Soviet Union's bureaucratic centralism) is *morally* suspect. For Camus, this claim is ultimately grounded in human nature itself, which, among other things, is characterized by a strong impulse toward both spontaneity and creativity, and his commitment to a radically democratic ("bottom up") form of political organization, as manifested in revolutionary trade-unionism or the Paris Commune of 1871, is, arguably, most in keeping with this fundamental condition of human flourishing. Politically, therefore, whether in 1944 or 1954, Camus is best understood as a libertarian socialist or, more exactly, an anarcho-syndicalist (anarcho-syndicalism being the theory that politics should begin with voluntary associations of cooperative, labor-based groups rather than the state).

After the liberation of Paris, Camus made clear his own political commitments in a 1946 series of articles published in *Combat* under the general title *Neither Victims nor Executioners*. In the eight articles that constitute the series, Camus builds on his earlier, more generic, positions to make clear his hostility toward any politics that would transgress fundamental democratic norms, and the pivot around which the series revolves is, arguably, the necessity of dialogue. In the first article, "Century of Fear," he speaks of his fear that "the long dialogue among human beings has now come to an end"; in "A New Social Contract," he speaks of the need to put together "a clear statement of principles necessary for any civilization based on dialogue"; and in the final article, "Toward Dialogue," he concludes with the assertion that there is "only one honorable choice: to wager everything on the belief that in the end words will prove stronger than bullets." Camus's concern for dialogue relates to two basic fears. First, he fears that a "conspiracy of silence" has come to mark the politics of the nascent Cold War, such that an honest discussion of the flaws of the Soviet Union or the United States is merely deemed support for the other side (which reflects the *modus operandi* of internal repression). Given his own commitment to libertarian socialism, Camus desires to make good concepts such as "liberalism" and "socialism" through dialogue, for he contends that they are distorted by a United States that is not liberal and a Soviet Union that is not socialist. Second, he fears that without some sort of dialogue that would at least rule out "the legitimacy of murder," the world itself could be annihilated, as the then recent use of the atomic bomb over Hiroshima and Nagasaki evidenced. In the end, Camus contends, any real revolution must be international, but in a polarized age with atomic weapons this would be nothing short of suicidal. What Camus calls for, then, is an international democracy of sorts, and while he admits that this, too, is utopian, he denies that it is more utopian than the Soviet alternative, and he holds that it is different in kind. He thus says in "Saving Bodies" that "the refusal to legitimate murder forces us to reconsider our notion of utopia," which means that it must be relativized to conform to a "modest political philosophy" based on a "provisional accord among those of us willing to be neither victims nor executioners."

To his credit, the commitment to dialogue that Camus counsels in *Neither Victims nor Executioners* is one that he himself evidenced. Shortly after the liberation of France, many Nazi collaborators were put on trial, and Camus not only supported these trials but advocated the death penalty for the most egregious collaborators. François Mauriac, a committed Catholic who had been active in the Resistance, argued against the trials, urging, instead, a policy of clemency. After a number of very public battles, Camus saw not only that the most egregious collaborators were going free while lesser collaborators were being put to death, but also that the very process of meting out justice in this way was innately corrupting. Thus, in a speech to an order of monks in 1948 he forthrightly declares that "I have come to admit to myself, and now to publicly admit here, that for the fundamentals and on the precise point of our controversy François Mauriac got the better of me" (RRD, p. 70). Camus's change of heart here reflects why he is so committed to democratic dialogue: no one is immune to being wrong. As he says in a 1947 article for *Combat*, "Democracy and Modesty," a "democrat is a person who admits that his adversary may be right, who therefore allows him to speak, and who agrees to consider his arguments."

Ultimately, in *Neither Victims nor Executioners* we see Camus already balancing himself on a tightrope that he will attempt to walk for the remainder of his life: on the one hand, he rejects the forced either/or choice that is offered by the Cold War ideologies of Marxism and capitalism in favor of "a third way," while, on the other hand, he chiefly sets himself to the task of attacking the underpinnings of Soviet ideology. These concerns are reflected in at least two of Camus's political commitments during the late 1940s. In 1948, he supports (along with Sartre) a new French organization called the Revolutionary Democratic Union, which is committed to the "third way" that many French leftists are seeking: a truly free, democratic socialism. Under the pressures of the Cold War, however, the organization quickly polarized, and it thus ceased to be a viable alternative. So, too, in 1948 he co-founded the Group for International Liaisons in the Revolutionary Union Movement. Foreshadowing

Amnesty International, the organization gave political and economic aid to dissidents who were the victims of political oppression, irrespective of their specific ideologies. This kind of concrete action on behalf of individuals was especially favored by Camus, who did not like humanitarian groups that were long on ideology but short on action.

Although undermined both personally and professionally by the 1952 confrontation with Jeanson and Sartre over *The Rebel*, Camus does not stop speaking out both for his third way and against Soviet communism. In what might be his most significant article, "Bread and Freedom" (based on a 1953 speech to French workers), he asserts that the dichotomy between freedom and justice is false, and that the two concepts are internally related: "We cannot choose one without the other. If someone takes away your bread, he suppresses your freedom at the same time. But if someone takes away your freedom, you may be sure your bread is threatened, for it depends no longer on you and your struggle but on the whim of a master" (RRD, p. 94). Camus's first claim belies the bourgeois notion that one is free without those basic necessities required to genuinely exercise one's freedom, while his second claim belies the communist notion that one's basic necessities are secure when administered by another. Yet, Camus finds an asymmetry here, for he contends that justice is only done to people who first have their rights recognized, which is why, historically, those who have fought hardest for freedom have been the oppressed classes. According to Camus, then, "the great event of the twentieth century was the forsaking of the values of freedom by the revolutionary movement," and the great mistake along these lines was equating "bourgeois freedom" with freedom itself: "For it should have been said merely that bourgeois freedom was a hoax, and not all freedom. It should have been said simply that bourgeois freedom was not freedom or, in the best of cases, was not yet freedom, but that there were liberties to be won and never to be relinquished again" (RRD, p. 90). In the wake of this mistake, there is now a "double-hoax, bourgeois and pseudo-revolutionary," and thus the intellectuals that support state socialism are "separated from their sole source of authenticity, the work and suffering of all, cutting them off from their natural allies, the workers" (RRD, p. 94). Ultimately, albeit in different ways, the problem with both bourgeois freedom and pseudo-revolutionary freedom is that they are abstract. Bourgeois freedom privileges an already existing abstract freedom at the expense of concrete freedom, whereas communism privileges a merely potential (and thus abstract) concrete freedom while it rejects the abstract freedom that is its condition of possibility.

Camus makes this point most forcefully in his pointed attacks on communism. After the Soviet Union crushed the Hungarian uprising of 1956, Camus declares in "Kadar had his Day of Fear" that "the untiring insistence upon freedom and truth . . . and, finally, political democracy as a necessary and indispensable (although surely not sufficient) condition of economic democracy is what Budapest was defending" (RRD, p. 162). And, in an interview dealing with the Hungarian uprising, "Socialism of the Gallows," he states that "the indispensable conditions for intellectual creation and historical justice are liberty and the free confronting of differences" (RRD, p. 171). In the final analysis, as Camus contends in a speech titled "Homage to an Exile" (made on behalf of an exiled Columbian journalist), it is the breakdown of dialogue, which must be underwritten by freedom, that sustains totalitarianism, as "only the word fed by blood and heart can unite men, whereas the silence of tyrants separates them. Tyrants indulge in monologues over millions of solitudes" (RRD, p. 104). Of course, the problem is that dialogue might not always be possible, and this seemed to be the case in Algeria, where the opposing sides were locked into escalating cycles of terror and repression.

The Algerian uprising, which began in 1954, pressed Camus's political priorities in a way that surpassed the discouraging political dynamics of the Cold War, and not simply because of its destructiveness. For Camus, the conflict itself was profoundly personal. Although a *pied-noir* (a descendant of French colonists), he saw Algeria as his homeland, and he rigorously distinguished between working-class *pieds-noirs* (such as his own family), who continued to live hardscrabble existences, and the *colons*, the monied classes that had reaped, and were continuing to reap, large benefits from French colonial repression. Camus's position on the conflict, which was largely in keeping with his general political commitments, was one that was doomed to failure, but before considering it, what must be made clear is that he had always been an outspoken critic of French colonial oppression. While working as a journalist for the newspaper *Alger-Républicain* in 1939, he reported on the terrible living conditions of Arabs in Kabylia, for which he principally blamed French colonialism. And in 1945, after thousands of Arabs were killed by the French authorities in response to Arab nationalist violence that had caused a number of French Algerian deaths, he wrote a series of articles for *Combat* in which he maintained that the Arab movement away from assimilationism toward nationalism was entirely understandable, if not desirable, and that it was incumbent on the French to do full justice to the Arabs, both economically and politically, stating that the age of imperialism was over. By 1954, however, the time in which assimilation could have been a viable option had long since passed, as the widespread support among Arabs for the Front for National Liberation (FLN) amply attested. The FLN, which used terrorist tactics against the civilian population, was absolutely committed to independence, and the French options appeared to be limited to increasingly violent repression or withdrawal.

Camus rejected both of these options, siding neither with the Gaullists, who supported the use of whatever force was required to maintain colonial control over Algeria, or the French left, who backed the FLN and its demand for complete withdrawal. Instead, Camus supported Pierre Mendès-France, who briefly served as French prime minister from mid-1954 to early 1955 and was responsible in this short time both for the French withdrawal from Vietnam (in the wake of Dien Bien Phu) and for the policies that would put Tunisia on the road to independence. In the face of the Algerian uprising, however, Mendès-France, an ardent anticolonialist, supported dialogue and some fashion of reconciliation instead of absolute withdrawal, given the longstanding French population, and this was essentially Camus's own position. When Mendès-France's government fell in early 1955, this possibility was all but ruled out – its lack of political viability is no doubt one of the reasons that the government fell – and from this point forward Camus's own position was without any real political representation. Still, he persisted. In 1955, Camus supported the Algerian militant, Aziz Kessous, who also sought some form of reconciliation, and while Camus acknowledged that both were "taking [a] stand in the no man's land," he stated that each is doing the right thing by "preaching pacification to his people," for the "essential thing is to leave room, however limited it may be, for the exchange of views that is still possible" (RRD, p. 128). By 1956, however, the situation had considerably worsened, as terrorist activities against the civilian population had dramatically increased, and the possibility of such an exchange no longer seemed possible. When Camus delivered a lecture in Algiers to an audience made up of FLN supporters and *pieds-noirs*, therefore, he explicitly refused to offer substantive views, declaring, instead, that the "exchange of views" he believed was still possible stemmed from "simple humanity," which would best be expressed by a civilian truce: "It is possible today, on [this] single definitive point, to agree first and then save human lives. In this way we may prepare a climate more favorable to a discussion that will at last be reasonable" (RRD, p. 134). Camus's non-negotiable bottom line here, as he put it in *Neither Victims nor Executioners*, is with "saving bodies," which he did not take to be the answer to Algeria's political problems but, instead, a necessary condition for justly answering them. And, finally, even as Camus asserts in 1958 that he will no longer comment on Algeria, as any further intervention on his part would be counterproductive in light of the terribly polarized political realities, he implicitly reaffirms the position that he had taken all along, seeing it as nothing less than his duty as an intellectual: "The intellectual has the role of distinguishing in each camp the respective limits of force and justice. That role is to clarify definitions in order to disintoxicate minds and to calm fanaticisms, even when this is against the current tendency" (RRD, p. 121).

The theoretical commitments hanging behind Camus's middle-ground position on Algeria are a portent of more contemporary political sensibilities. For example, when he says in his 1956 lecture in Algiers that "I believe only in differences and not uniformity . . . because differences are the roots without which the tree of liberty, the sap of creation and civilization, dries up" (RRD, p. 136), he anticipates the more contemporary concern with fostering a robust pluralism, and, more generally, a multicultural sensibility. His emphasis on the role of "difference" in the democratic enterprise is, indeed, of a piece with the more contemporary lexicon, although, it must quickly be added, he would not have been especially enamored of "identity politics," as such a politics tends to have an anti-humanistic flavor and frequently breaks down into differences that are deemed to be non-negotiable. Along these lines, his emphasis on meeting the conditions for dialogue, and, more generally, dialogue itself, is a portent of another contemporary political sensibility, which is usually depicted in terms of the notion of "communicative rationality." When Camus eschews any substantive position in his 1956 lecture but harps on the need to meet the minimal conditions required for a dialogue that might address the substantive issues, he is pointing in this direction, although he certainly does not elaborate on (much less systematize) this commitment, as certain contemporary philosophers have done. For Camus, such a commitment does not run roughshod over republican concerns, as is the case with certain liberal notions, but, rather, seeks a minimal framework in which they might be expressed. In this way, he attempts to mediate the liberal and republican moments, universal norms and concrete forms of life, which is wholly in keeping with his position in *The Rebel*. And, indeed, Camus's ultimate commitment in terms of Algeria aimed to do just this. He backed a loose federalism – a "union of differences" based "not [on] different territories but communities with different personalities" (RRD, p. 149) – in which Algeria would be integrated into France but would be largely autonomous. Under such a scheme, Arabs would receive full economic and political rights, reparations for the damage done by colonialism would be made to them, the Algerian French would remain in Algeria, and the politics of Algeria would be based on "a regime of free association" (see RRD, pp. 143–9).

Camus's position was severely attacked from both ends of the political spectrum. When he spoke in Algeria in 1956, many *pieds-noirs* viewed him as a traitor, and some chanted "Camus to the gallows," while the supporters of the FLN viewed him as uncomprehending (at best) or an apologist for colonialism (at worst). From a more philosophical vantage point, he was viewed by some as an abstract universalist, a moralist whose values could find no traction in the politics of the Algerian crisis, while others viewed him as someone who was unable to rise above his own particularities, which were informed by the fact that he was a *pied-noir*. This latter position was bolstered by Camus's (in)famous remark in Sweden when, in connection with his acceptance of the Nobel Prize for Literature in 1957, he responded to an Algerian critic by stating that "I have always condemned terrorism, and I must condemn a terrorism that works blindly in the streets of Algiers and one day might strike at my mother and family. I believe in justice, but I will defend my mother before justice."[14] Although there is no doubt some truth in the view that this remark, as well as others like it, demonstrates that Camus could not transcend his particular viewpoint – a position that some take to be a virtue (Michael Walzer) and some do not (Edward Said)[15] – it seems to me that such a view misses a crucial point. The basic issue is not Camus's mother but, instead, terrorism, and his concern with his own mother is one that he would have been ready to universalize. Indeed, for Camus, who did not put it all that well, the opposition between justice and his mother is a false one, as the murder of the innocent could not be just and an ultimate condition of justice could not emanate from it, which is merely in keeping with his discussion of the relationship between means and ends in *The Rebel*.

Camus's political failing, if it could be called that, might well be found just where Sartre had indicated, namely, in his inability to adequately deal with the exigencies of history. Even if, in opposition to Sartre, Camus was right to hold open a conceptual space for a moral framework that would not be washed away by the (relativizing) movement of history, it does not necessarily follow that history will transpire in such a way that the possibility of actually making good this moral framework will always be a viable option. Indeed, it might well be that the movement of history precludes certain possibilities (such as the ones Camus favored for resolving the Algerian crisis), and, under such circumstances, the overarching imperative might involve little more than ending the violence, which is in accord with Camus's aim of "saving bodies." Since dialogically reconciling differences is not always a possibility, Stephen Eric Bronner might be right to assert that Camus's "*primary ethical aim* should have led him to embrace the side with the best chance of ending the bloodshed, [which] was the only concrete position for a humanist ethically opposed to terror to take."[16] Yet, generally speaking, I would not want to press this point too hard, nor, in fact, would Camus: although no doubt far less than is claimed by demagogues, there are values worth risking not only one's own life for but (if only derivatively) other people's lives as well. In any case, wedged between the particular parties to the crisis, for whom he sought what he took to be a just solution, and the universal imperatives that he thought applied, were minds not amenable to "disintoxication" by virtue of a long history of violence, and Camus was relegated to silence.

notes

1 Theodor W. Adorno, *Negative Dialectics*, trans. E. B. Ashton (New York: Continuum, 1973), p. 226.
2 Rosalind Hursthouse, *On Virtue Ethics* (New York: Oxford University Press, 1999), chapter 3.
3 Theodor W. Adorno, *Minima Moralia: Reflections from Damaged Life*, trans. E. F. N. Jephcott (New York: Verso Books, 1974), p. 39.
4 Ronald Aronson, *Camus and Sartre* (Chicago: University of Chicago Press, 2005), p. 172.
5 It has always seemed to me that a variant of the Camus-Sartre battle later played out, albeit in a different context, between what were then the chief philosophers of Critical Theory, Adorno and Marcuse. Adorno and Marcuse had similar views on most theoretical issues, as a comparison of *Dialectic of Enlightenment* and *One-Dimensional Man* (not to mention their writings on aesthetics) suggests. Yet, Adorno eschewed all political commitments, even as he privately sympathized with many of the criticisms and goals of the New Left, while Marcuse threw himself into politics, becoming one of the New Left's intellectual gurus, along with the now-deceased Camus himself. It was Adorno's position that any involvement in political movements compromised theory, and, in response to Sartre's idea of commitment, he produced an essay titled "Resignation." Camus, it should be clear, was nowhere near as opposed to political engagement as Adorno, and, had he lived, it is not hard to imagine that he would have unreservedly thrown himself into the politics surrounding the student and worker movements of the late 1960s.
6 Maurice Merleau-Ponty, *Adventures of the Dialectic*, trans. Joseph Bien (Evanston, IL: Northwestern University Press, 1973), p. 4.
7 Ronald Aronson, *Camus and Sartre*, p. 139.
8 Jeanson's "Albert Camus, or the Soul in Revolt," Camus's reply, "A Letter to the Editor of *Les Temps Modernes*," and Sartre's comeback, "Reply to Albert Camus," appear in David Sprintzen and Adrian van den Hoven, eds. and trans., *Sartre and Camus: A Historic Confrontation* (Amherst, NY: Humanity Books, 2004), pp. 79–105, 107–29, and 131–61, respectively. I have not referenced the passages that I quote from any of these pieces, all of which are contained therein.
9 Raymond Aron, *The Opium of the Intellectuals* (New Brunswick, NJ: Transaction Publishers, 2001), p. 53.
10 Stephen Eric Bronner, *Camus: Portrait of a Moralist* (Minneapolis: University of Minnesota Press, 1999), pp. 97–8.
11 Friedrich Nietzsche, *Beyond Good and Evil*, trans. Walter Kaufmann (New York: Random House, 1966), p. 89.
12 Bernard-Henri Lévy, *Sartre: The Philosopher of the Twentieth Century*, trans. Andrew Brown (Cambridge: Polity Press, 2003), p. 317.
13 Albert Camus, *Camus at Combat*, ed. Jacqueline Levi-Valenski, trans. Arthur Goldhammer (Princeton: Princeton University Press, 2006), pp. 13 ("From Resistance to Revolution," August 21, 1944) and 27 ("Morality and Politics," September 4, 1944), respectively.

14 Olivier Todd, *Albert Camus: A Life,* trans. Benjamin Ivry (New York: Alfred A. Knopf, 1997), p. 378.

15 Michael Walzer, *The Company of Critics: Social Criticism and Political Commitment in the Twentieth Century* (New York: Basic Books, 1988), chapter 8 ("Albert Camus's Algerian War"); and Edward Said, *Culture and Imperialism* (New York: Alfred A. Knopf, 1993), chapter 7 ("Camus and the French Imperial Experience").

16 Stephen Eric Bronner, *Camus,* p. 114 (emphasis in original).

further reading

Aronson, Ronald, *Camus and Sartre* (Chicago: University of Chicago Press, 2005).

Bronner, Stephen Eric, *Camus: Portrait of a Moralist* (Minneapolis: University of Minnesota Press, 1999).

Isaac, Jeffrey, *Arendt, Camus, and Modern Rebellion* (New Haven, CT: Yale University Press, 1992).

Sprintzen, David, and Adrian van den Hoven (eds. and trans.), *Sartre and Camus: A Historic Confrontation* (Amherst, NY: Humanity Books, 2004).

chapter 8

exile and rebirth

I cannot live as a person without my art. And yet I have never set that art above everything else. It is essential to me, on the contrary, because it excludes no one and allows me to live, just as I am, on a footing with all. To me art is not a solitary delight. It is a means of stirring the greatest number of men by providing them with a privileged image of our common joys and woes. . . . And the man who, as often happens, chose the path of art because he was aware of his difference soon learns that he cannot nourish his art, and his difference, solely by admitting his resemblance to all. The artist fashions himself in that ceaseless oscillation from himself to others, mid-way between the beauty he cannot do without and the community from which he cannot tear himself.

Albert Camus, Nobel Prize Address[1]

On awarding Camus the 1957 Nobel Prize for Literature, the Nobel Academy discussed, among other things, his "authentic moral commitment." Predictably, this justification did not play well among the Paris intellectual elite (both on the Communist left and the Gaullist right), who took Camus's selection to be politically motivated, as well as an implicit confirmation of the fact that, although he was only 44, his best work was behind him. In fact, this was the case but for reasons that could not then be known: less than three years later Camus would be dead. Earlier that year, Camus's final book, a collection of short stories titled *Exile and the Kingdom*, was published, as was an essay titled "Reflections on the Guillotine." Both works, albeit in different ways, reflect what is, perhaps, Camus's deepest and most abiding concern, the untenable plight of the modern individual.

In "Reflections on the Guillotine," Camus reaffirms his steadfast opposition to the death penalty, a position that he held (it will be recalled) since he came to see the unjust ways in which it had been applied to those who were charged with being Nazi collaborators. To begin with, he competently ticks off the standard abolitionist arguments. He contends that statistics do not bear out that the death penalty is truly a deterrent; that the death penalty is not justified on retributive grounds because there is no equivalence between the experience of the condemned murderer that awaits death and the experience of his (generally) unsuspecting victim; that the administration of justice is flawed, and the execution of the innocent cannot be rectified; and, finally, that there are very few human beings who are beyond rehabilitation. However, it is when Camus goes beyond the standard fare that his deepest concerns come to the foreground. He contends not only that the death penalty dehumanizes society in general, but that the state, in particular, does not have the standing to prosecute it, as the state is often responsible for the conditions that breed murderers. For Camus, it is not that the murderer lacks responsibility, irrespective of the circumstances, but, rather, that because the state also lacks clean hands it is not in a position to demand this ultimate penalty. Indeed, in the final analysis, it is the modern state – Hobbes's Leviathan having clearly become the Behemoth it always already was – that is Camus's most profound concern, and from this standpoint, all individual actions pale in contrast. "The number of individuals killed directly by the State has assumed astronomical proportions and infinitely outnumbers private murders," Camus maintains, and "our self-defense must be aimed at the State first and foremost" (RRD, p. 227). Thus, "we must call a spectacular halt and proclaim, in our principles and institutions, that the individual is above the State" (RRD, p. 229).

Accordingly, even in the context of the murderer, Camus's commitment to the dignity of the individual does not waver, as is revealed not just by "Reflections on the Guillotine" but, even more importantly, by the fact that he actively sought reprieves for every kind of criminal defendant, including Algerian Arabs sentenced to death for terrorist acts. Still, of greater interest to Camus, at least from an artistic vantage point, is the plight of the more or less ordinary individual, and it is the exploration of this theme that ties together the six short stories that constitute *Exile and the Kingdom*.

Exile

> It was late in the evening when K. arrived. The village was deep in snow. The Castle was hidden, veiled in mist and darkness, nor was there even a glimmer of light to show that a castle was there. On the wooden bridge leading from the main road to the village, K. stood for a long time gazing into the illusory emptiness above him.
>
> Franz Kafka, *The Castle*[2]

Before it grew to the size of a novel, *The Fall*, published in 1956, was meant to be a part of *Exile and the Kingdom*. Clamence's life-denying scorn, which Camus took to be one of the dominant inclinations of those intellectuals who were attacking him, vividly reflects (I argued in chapter 4) one of the two ways in which, according to *The Myth of Sisyphus*, the Absurd can be overcome. Along with Meursault, whose equally life-denying commitment to "life" exhibited the other way, Clamence is a purified phenomenological portrait, one designed to explore the immanent logic of a distilled existential position. In *Exile and the Kingdom*, by way of contrast, the characters are, for the most part, much more concrete. With the exception of the first-person storyteller in "The Renegade," who is the essence of Nietzschean *ressentiment*, they are ones with whom we can far more easily identify. The major characters in "The Adulterous Woman," "The Silent Men," "The Guest," "The Artist at Work," and "The Growing Stone" are a middle-class housewife, a worker, a schoolteacher, a painter, and an engineer, respectively. In a number of these stories, moreover, the question of colonialism comes very much to the fore and heavily impacts the major character. More generally, much as Camus describes it in the portion of his Nobel Prize address set forth at the start of this chapter, in these stories the major character is wedged, in one fashion or another, between his or her own dreams and aspirations and the social world of which they are ineluctably a part. In some sense, they are like Kafka's K., seeking access to a castle (grace, in some form or other) that is not only inaccessible but, perhaps, also inadvisable, and the problem then becomes what is to be done with "the remains of the day." In a certain way, this is simply a follow up to the problem that was considered in the last chapter: if "wrong life cannot be lived rightly," how, then, can it be lived?

As was the case with *The Fall*, "The Renegade" is a monologue, which, for Camus, is the tyrant's ideal communicative form, for it precludes the kind of genuine dialogue that might call into question its prerogatives. (As we saw Camus declare in the last chapter, "tyrants indulge in monologues over millions of solitudes.") Like Clamence, the renegade (whose name we are not given) has deeply rooted totalitarian tendencies, but his *modus operandi* is diametrically opposed to Clamence's. The infinitely polished bourgeois, Clamence was nothing if not loquacious, and, ever the lawyer, he sought to dominate through the intricate web of words that he weaved, while the renegade quite literally cannot speak, for his tongue has been cut out by the Saharan tribe that he had tried to convert to Christianity. The basic difference between Clamence and the renegade is, in fact, the difference between bourgeois and working-class *ressentiment*. Thus, from the start of the story, we see that the renegade has been drawn to Christian missionary work for the wrong reasons: the son of a "boorish mother" and "a pig of a father" who provided little, he tells us that he "dreamed of absolute power, the kind that makes people kneel down, that forces the adversary to capitulate, converts him in short, and [thus] . . . establishes the royalty of whoever brought about his collapse." As these words suggest, despite the renegade's more humble origins, his project is much like Clamence's, and, like Clamence, he thinks that the road to such power is through utter self-abnegation, because "to be noticed" one must go "out of [one's] way for punishments," and otherwise "heap accusations on [one]self" (EK, pp. 37–9).

The story itself starts with the renegade waiting on a trail for the missionary that is to take his place. The tongueless renegade, who can barely mumble *gra gra*, (somehow) tells us that he had abruptly fled his seminary in Algiers (but not before robbing its treasury) for the most barren part of the Sahara, the home of the most brutal of tribes. Taken captive by the tribe, he is turned into their slave. Badly beaten, horribly degraded, and stripped of his tongue, he lives in a "cell of salt" that houses the tribe's Fetish, a double ax-head that he must serve. In a rather short period of time, the renegade comes to genuinely worship the Fetish, revering in it "the evil principle of the world," and he comes to genuinely admire his imperious "lords and masters," who, in ruling over "their sterile homes [and] black slaves," are ignorant of pity, and, "like masters, they want to be left alone, to progress alone, to rule alone" (EK, pp. 43–4). Ultimately, however, Europeans show up and impose conditions on the tribe, to which the tribe accedes, and the renegade escapes to kill the missionary that the tribe is forced to accept, for the "faith" that he now seeks to defend is the tribe's. Feckless as ever, the renegade cannot pull this off, and he is subdued before he can kill the missionary. Then, after wailing "O Fetish, why hast thou forsaken me," he considers the possibility that he might have been wrong, and that perhaps he should aim to "rebuild the city of mercy," which concludes the story. As an epitaph, however, a final remark is offered by Camus: "A handful of salt fills the mouth of the garrulous slave" (EK, p. 61). Camus is rejecting here the worship of power, whether it manifests itself in the form of Nietzsche's masterly blond beast or a slavish Christian, for in modernity both reflect, albeit in different ways, a disfigured, resentment-driven will to power.

The middle-aged characters in "The Adulterous Woman" and "The Silent Men," who are straightforwardly confronted with the problem of what to make of "the remains of the day," are much more sympathetic, and, while both are relegated to silence (as is the renegade, for obvious reasons), their silence is particularly telling. Although the renegade is literally silent, his interior life is characterized (as Camus puts it) by a certain "garrulousness," an incessant monologue that evidences his own misguided project of redemption and, ultimately, his inability to recognize the need for a thoughtful, nuanced response to the complexities (social and existential) that confront him. Conversely, the housewife and the worker in these stories maintain a genuine silence out of a deeper recognition of the disconnect between their own needs and "the ways of the world," and how their respective silences differ is highly instructive.

In "The Adulterous Woman," the major character, Janine, is married to a bore of a man. A small-time merchant whose only real interest is business, Marcel has dragged Janine into the desert so that he can have her company while he attempts to sell his merchandise. During the trip, Janine and Marcel come into contact with many Arabs, whom Marcel generally takes to be either sullen, inscrutable, or impudent, and one gets a strong feeling of how out of place these *pieds-noirs* are. Self-conscious with respect to the Arabs that surround her, Janine becomes self-conscious with respect to herself, as her desert experience serves as the occasion for her to ruminate on how she has sold herself short, and how, in the time that she has been married to Marcel, she had gotten heavy. As a result, she begins to feel out of place in her own body. And, finally, as the trip takes place during the winter, she is numbed by an unexpected desert cold, which only exacerbates her physical and emotional discontents. The trip thus turns into a thoroughly depressing experience for Janine until she and Marcel climb the stairs of the local fort to look at the desert from its terrace. For Janine, the image of the limitless desert before her triggers the recognition that her life could be much more, and she feels duty and habit begin to lose their grip on her. At the sight of nomads freely moving about in the distance, however, she is overcome by a "sweet, vast melancholy": "She knew that this kingdom had been eternally promised her and yet that it would never be hers" (EK, p. 24). Oblivious to his wife's experience, Marcel drags her from the terrace, but late that night, as Marcel sleeps, Janine leaves the hotel room, races back to the terrace, and, surveying the desert, has an epiphanic experience. On returning to her hotel room, however, the "adulterous" Janine, weeping profusely, responds "it's nothing" to Marcel's semi-conscious questioning, and thus the story ends.

"The Silent Men" is set in the context of a failed strike, and the workers, *pieds-noirs* and Arabs alike, must return to work. The major character, Yvars, is one of the senior workers, and, although barely 40, he already feels the ravages of age, which are significantly exacerbated by the physical hardships of his craft, cooperage. Among his few pleasures is sitting on his terrace at the end of the day with a glass of anisette in his hand and his wife and son beside him, and "at those times he didn't know whether he was happy or felt like crying, for at least he felt harmony in such moments, [when] he had nothing to do but wait quietly, without quite knowing for what" (EK, p. 64). Like his fellow workers, Yvars is barely making ends meet, but the problem is that cooperage is fast disappearing, other shops have not gone on strike (presumably for this reason), the union was not in a reasonable position to support the walkout, and the boss is really a decent sort who has promised that when business gets better he will raise his workers' pay. Dispirited, the workers return to work, but they refuse to speak to the boss, silently following his orders.

On the first day back, however, an ambulance is summoned for the boss's daughter, who is quite ill, and Yvars (as well as many of his fellow workers) is torn by his desire to maintain his silence in solidarity with his fellow workers and his desire to offer words of hope and concern to his boss. Ultimately, neither Yvars nor his fellow workers break ranks by offering such words, and with a heavy heart Yvars heads home, where he tells his wife everything, takes the blame for his current condition, and laments the fact that he and his wife are no longer young enough to go "across the sea" in search of a better life.

The major characters in "The Adulterous Woman" and "The Silent Men" share a number of traits. Both are *pieds-noirs*, and, as such, are neither at home with Arabs, who only see them as colonialists, nor with the *colons* that employ them, who only see them as laborers. What's more, coming out of the lower-middle and working classes, respectively, both stoically see themselves as responsible for their failures, which are, in no small part, engendered by a larger sociopolitical context whose influence they only dimly perceive. Finally, and most of all, both are relegated to silence in the face of what are at least potentially transformative experiences. Along these lines, however, they differ with respect to what, exactly, they take to be ineffable. Although economic and cultural considerations surely impinge on her, the experience that engenders silence in Janine is essentially existential, as it arises from the recognition of her unlived freedom, and her silence evidences the fact that this experience will remain utterly unmediated. In a certain sense, it must be noticed, this makes good the attack on Camus's concept of nature as potentially liberating, as Janine sees no basis for incorporating the insights that this experience provokes into her life with Marcel, on whom she has come to emotionally depend. Still, by decentering Janine, it could be argued, this experience does open up possibilities for her, possibilities that neither can nor should be disavowed so cleanly. Conversely, the experience that engenders silence in Yvars (which he later discusses with his wife) is less about his own life choices than about two different and, for the moment, incompatible notions of solidarity that are whipsawing him. As an initial matter, therefore, Yvars's silence is less existential than social, as it is a direct manifestation of the social circumstances in which he finds himself. Yet, existential considerations lurk beneath the surface, as Yvars implicitly blames himself for his prior choices, which have put him in this situation. As a result, he retreats into a stoicism that nevertheless permits a final "if only he were young again" to break through.

In "The Guest," the major character, Daru, is much more at home with himself than either Janine or Yvars, and the lesson of the story is that although one might distance oneself from bad sociopolitical circumstances, they will eventually catch up with one. Daru, a teacher, lives alone on a high, remote plateau in a small room next to a classroom, where he teaches less than 20 students from tiny villages in the area. The high, remote plateau is akin to Janine's desert – "the region was cruel to live in [but] *everywhere else* he felt exiled" (EK, p. 88) – and he likes his job. Alone for days because of a recent snowstorm, Daru is visited by a local policeman, Balducci, who is bringing with him a prisoner at the end of a rope. Balducci informs Daru that the Arab had killed another Arab in a fight, and that Daru must escort the Arab to the province's police headquarters, roughly 12 miles away. Daru refuses, inadvertently insulting the good-natured Balducci, but he is told in no uncertain terms that he must carry out this task. Affronted, Balducci leaves, and the next day, after listlessly guarding the Arab (in the hope he might escape), Daru starts off with his captive. One hour into their trip, Daru gives the Arab food and money and then points in two directions: in one direction is the police headquarters, while, in the other, are pasturelands, where the Arab can be sheltered by nomads. On his way back to the schoolhouse, Daru turns and sees the Arab heading on the road to the police station, and, on returning to the classroom, he finds a message on the blackboard: "You handed over our brother. You will pay for this" (EK, p. 109). The ambiguous nature of not simply the *pied-noir* but also Camus himself is evidenced in this story. As an initial matter, the very status of the relationship between Daru and his Arab prisoner is called into question by the story's French title, *L'Hôte*, which can be translated as either "host" or "guest." The implication here is that it is not clear who is "the host" and who is "the guest," a question not answered by the fact that Daru hails from Algeria. Moreover, given Daru's disgust with respect to Balducci's demands (i.e., the colonial administration of "justice") and the Arab's murder (i.e., terrorism), he finds himself in the disagreeable position of alienating *pieds-noirs* and Arabs alike, unable to convey the solidarity that, in principle, he feels for both. Thus, as Camus indicates in the last line of the story, "in this vast landscape he had loved so much, he was alone" (EK, p. 109), which is surely how Camus saw himself in terms of the Algerian crisis.

In "The Artist at Work," which is largely autobiographical, Camus returns to the tension between the individual's objectives and those of the larger society. Gilbert Jonas, Camus tell us, "believed in his star," and with the "trusting modesty" of one who believes that his star will not let him down, he becomes an eminent painter, as well as a husband and father of three. Yet, with artistic success (which breeds disciples and critics who aim to prop themselves up at his expense) and his growing family, the kindhearted but naïve Jonas starts to feel hemmed in on all sides. As he produces fewer and fewer paintings, his artistic career and family life increasingly suffer, and as his reputation plummets, he avoids people, seeking consolation in both liquor and extramarital affairs. Eventually, Jonas builds a loft in his apartment, which, over time, he never leaves, but he can no longer find his star, and therefore, while secluded, he creates nothing. One day, however, Jonas feels inspired, and on completing his work he shows it to his wife and close friend. On an otherwise empty canvas a small word appears in the center, but it is not clear whether the word is "solitary" or "solidary." This story, whose main theme appears in Camus's Nobel Prize Address, points to the conflicting but intertwined relationship between an individual's hopes and society's expectations, but what it actually portends for Jonas, Camus, or the reconciliation of this tension is far from clear.

The last story in *Exile and the Kingdom*, "The Growing Stone," is the most optimistic, as the major character, D'Arrest, is able to move through an act of kindness toward a solidarity that does not compromise the solitary. An engineer, D'Arrest has agreed to build (without charge) a dam in Iguape, a remote Brazilian village on the outskirts of the Amazon jungle, and he is taken there by Socrates, his good-natured chauffeur. D'Arrest is struck by the disparity between rich and poor, favoring the company of the poor to that of the leading citizens, who are as haughty to the poor as they are solicitous of D'Arrest. While at the village's Feast of Good Jesus, D'Arrest meets a poor ship's cook, who will play the lead role at the festival's concluding procession the following day. The cook tells D'Arrest that out of gratitude for the fact that he had miraculously survived a shipwreck years earlier, he had made a solemn promise: every year he would assume the task of carrying a 100-pound stone on his head to the village church during the final day of the festival. He also informs D'Arrest that there will be a party late that night, and he asks D'Arrest to attend. D'Arrest is painfully out of place at the party, in which the orgiastic partyers "danced to die," and thus he is asked to leave. The reveling cook chooses to stay, however, and, consequently, the next day he does not have the strength to carry the stone. When he collapses in front of the entire village, D'Arrest jumps in to take his place, but instead of carrying the stone to the church, he carries it to the poor cook's hut and throws it into the center of its one spare room. Then, "with eyes closed, he joyfully acclaimed his own strength [and] a fresh beginning in life," at which point the cook's family declares "Sit down with us" (EK, pp. 212–13).

"The Growing Stone" is rich in symbolism. At one level, the ugliness of colonialism is to be found in the dealings between the village's leading citizens, who are of Spanish or Portuguese descent, and the poorer natives. Moreover, as the last line attests, D'Arrest has gone to Iguape in search of a rebirth of sorts, and, indeed, prior to the events of the concluding day, we are told that he had been eagerly awaiting his trip, "as if the work he had come to do here were only a pretext for a surprise or for an encounter he did not even imagine but which had been waiting patiently for him at the end of the world" (EK, pp. 180–81). Thus, D'Arrest is not going to Iguape to do "charity work," or at least not in the self-righteous way that Nietzsche so reviled, but, instead, he is on a spiritual quest. When the poor cook calls D'Arrest "Captain," he quickly rejects the title, and he is sympathetic to the cook's disdain for market-based societies: "Buying and Selling, eh! What filth! And with the police, dogs command" (EK, p. 182). Finally, the cook's agony while carrying the stone obviously calls to mind Jesus's trials at Golgotha, and D'Arrest's final actions have a universal spiritual significance. Although D'Arrest is not able to experience the sacred on the locals' terms – at the party he says to Socrates "I do not dance," to which Socrates replies "in your country there's only the Mass and no one dances (EK, p. 199) – he can still commune with the cook and his family with his concluding act of fraternity. Nevertheless, despite the imagery, D'Arrest should not be viewed as a Christ-figure, if by this we mean in Christian terms, just as Nietzsche's Zarathustra should not be viewed as a Christ-figure despite the Christian imagery Nietzsche uses in *Thus Spake Zarathustra*. D'Arrest reflects, rather, the best of secular humanism, which, as Nietzsche would claim, still operates in the shadow of the Judeo-Christian God, as did such figures as Marx.

Despite the upbeat ending to "The Growing Stone," which reflects Camus's belief that radically different existential sensibilities could still experience a meeting of the minds in regard to certain universal human themes, there is still the question of where things would go from here. D'Arrest is not that society's *pied-noir*: he is unencumbered by its history, and it is not likely that he will remain in Iguape, which means that he is unencumbered by the requirement of reshaping its future in the face of this experience (which, in terms of the society's elite, remains a solitary one). He would, accordingly, have the same problem as Janine and Yvars, namely, working this transformative experience into the fabric of his daily existence. In the end, as the stories in *Exile and the Kingdom* suggest, we might all be *pieds-noirs*, which reflects the modern predicament, a deep feeling of "homelessness," and the question still remains as to how to negotiate between a profane past and the seeming impossibility of redemption.

Rebirth

One *thing is needful* – To "give style" to one's character – a great and rare art! It is practiced by those who survey all the strengths and weaknesses of their nature and then fit them into an artistic plan until every one of them appears as art and reason and even weaknesses delight the eye. . . . In the end, when the work is finished, it becomes evident how the constraint of a single taste governed and formed everything large and small.

Friedrich Nietzsche, *The Gay Science*[3]

This feeling of "homelessness" figures prominently in Camus's final novel, *The First Man*. The unfinished manuscript, recovered from the scene of the automobile wreck that took Camus's life on January 4, 1960, was not published until 1994, when Camus's children deemed that the time was appropriate. As his daughter, Catherine Camus, explains it in her preface to the novel, given the antipathy toward Camus from the right and left at the time of his death, "to have published an unfinished manuscript . . . might well have given ammunition to those who were saying Camus was through as a writer," but "between 1980 and 1985 voices began to be heard saying that perhaps Camus had not been so wrong" (FM, pp. vi–vii). Given the condition of the unfinished manuscript – it is highly personal and unpolished – Catherine Camus's previous concerns were justified, and when the novel was finally published in 1994, it was widely praised.

Although it assumes the form of a novel, *The First Man* is more or less straightforwardly autobiographical. The book begins with the difficult circumstances surrounding Camus's birth, during which we get only a vague sense of his father. (Camus takes the name Jacques Cormery, the surname of his father's grandmother.) Then, in the second chapter, the 40-year-old Camus, at the behest of his mother, visits the grave of his father, who had died at the Battle of the Marne less than a year after Camus's birth. Lethargically approaching the task of visiting the grave of a man that he did not know, Camus looks at his father's headstone and begins to reel at the concept that the man buried beneath it is much younger than he: for Camus, time slips "out of joint," and "in the strange dizziness of that moment, the statue every man eventually erects and . . . into which he then creeps and there awaits its final crumbling – that statue was rapidly cracking, it was already collapsing" (FM, p. 26). The balance of the book constitutes Camus's search for himself, which will entail going back through his own life to his father's life, and, beyond that, the history of the French Algerians. In the final analysis, Camus's search will prove fruitless – the last chapter is titled "A Mystery to Himself" – but it is still an extraordinary one. Replete with stories about the Algerian landscape, but now from a personal perspective that includes detailed descriptions of his family members (a semi-deaf mother, a stone deaf uncle, and a severe grandmother, all of whom are illiterate), childhood experiences, and social context (including the relationships between *pieds-noirs* and Arabs), the book offers an unsentimental account of his family's struggle simply to get by and of Camus's own dawning awareness that there is a "something more" whose contours he can scarcely imagine.

Although Camus learns relatively little about his father (and, perhaps, least of all from his inexpressive mother), what he does learn reveals the hopelessness of his search. Camus's father, who spoke only when absolutely necessary, had been a hard and bitter man: he "had worked all his life, had killed on command, had submitted to everything that could not be avoided, but had preserved some part of himself where he allowed no one to trespass. A poor man, after all. For poverty is not a choice one makes, but a poor person can protect himself" (FM, p. 66). Along the same lines, Camus's mother, a kind, submissive woman who worked long days as a "domestic," would frequently retreat into her own world, silently staring for hours from the tiny apartment's balcony onto the street below. (Camus's mother, whom Camus takes to be a Christ-like figure, is the hero of the story, and the book is dedicated to her: "To you who will never be able to read this book.") Despite the economic and cultural poverty of Camus's early life, his existence was marked by the bountiful sensations of Algerian life, in which he was "triumphant in his kingdom of poverty" (FM, p. 47), and it was only when he attended the *lycée* (high school) after winning a scholarship under the tutelage of his beloved primary school teacher that he first began to realize the extent of his family's impoverishment. On the first day of school, Camus is informed by his friend that under "Parents' Occupation" he ought to write "domestic," and "all at once he knew shame and . . . the shame of having been ashamed" (FM, p. 204). More generally, he sees his life as irreparably split between his 12 hours at the *lycée*, where his imagination could run wild, and his 12 hours at the apartment, and he could speak in neither place about the other.

Camus's ruminations on the effects of poverty, and, in particular, its effects with respect to personal and moral development, are remarkable. He emphasizes that even if his mother had been put in a standard household, in which objects are plentiful, "she would only have made use of what was strictly necessary," and that all objects in his apartment were "named with common nouns" instead of the "proper nouns" attributed to the objects of those who are better off (FM, p. 60). He points out that memory (which is so integral to self-identity) is much less developed in the poor than in the rich, as "poor people's memory . . . has fewer landmarks in space because they seldom leave the place where they live, and fewer reference points in time throughout lives that are gray and featureless": Proust's "remembrance of things past is just for the rich" (FM, p. 80). And, finally, this man who would come to be called the moral conscience of his generation tells us that, in the world in which he grew up, morality itself was not even a part of his vocabulary:

No one had actually taught the child what was right and what was wrong. Some things were forbidden and any infraction was severely punished. Others were not. Only his teachers would sometimes talk about morality, when the curriculum left them the time, but there again the prohibitions were more explicit than the reasons for them. All that [he] had been able to see and experience concerning morality was daily life in a working-class family, where it was evident no one had ever thought there was any way other than the hardest kind of labor to acquire the money necessary to their survival. But that was a lesson in courage, not morals. (FM, p. 88)

For Camus, in short, there was "no past, no family home, no attic full of letters and photos," only "a most elementary morality," distinguished by little more than some unquestioned prohibitions (FM, p. 209), and the rituals of a religion that played "no part in their lives" (FM, p. 164). In this way, Camus was "the first man" in his fatherless family, and for reasons that transcended the fact that he was fatherless.

Indeed, for Camus, the title "the first man" refers to the experience of the *pieds-noirs*, more generally. He relates the story of how poverty-stricken French laborers began to settle Algeria in 1848 in the hopes of a better life, and how most of them had died early on. These people, as well as their descendants, had "found themselves on this land as he himself had, with no past, without ethics, without guidance, without religion, but glad to be so and to be in the light, fearful in the face of night and death" (FM, p. 193). Despite the tenor of his analysis of the *pieds-noirs*, Camus never claims that their rights supersede the rights of the Arabs whose land they settled, and when he defends them it is almost always against the attacks of what he views as a complacent French bourgeois class dabbling in radical politics from their armchairs. For example, lamenting the xenophobic tendencies of the *pieds-noirs* on labor issues, he sarcastically remarks that it is an "attitude that is certainly disconcerting to those intellectuals who theorize about the proletariat, and yet very human and surely excusable" (FM, p. 257). Much like Sisyphus, "proletarian of the gods, powerless and rebellious, [who] knows the whole extent of his wretched condition" (MS, p. 121), it is Camus, powerless and rebellious, who knows the whole extent of the economic and cultural conditions that have put his contemporaries and ancestors in an untenable situation, and he is intent on pointing out that it is all too easy for bourgeois intellectuals to place the blame on certain victims for the conditions in which their victimization has put them. Crucially, however, his attack does not extend to the Arabs themselves, whom he also views as unmitigated victims, and whose rights he never fails to uphold. He indicates how the sons and daughters of Arab and French Algerians had died for France during World War I (FM, p. 70), and he offers many examples of how the Arab population has been wantonly victimized. In the concluding pages of the novel, moreover, Camus acknowledges his own limitations as a *pied-noir*, intimating that the dark colonial underside of his Algerian experience "was like a second life, truer perhaps than the everyday surface of his outward life" (FM, p. 281). And, finally, in his notes for what was to be the remainder of his novel, which included his experiences during the Resistance, he examines the issue of terrorism, and not cavalierly, even as he disagrees with it.

The final words of *The First Man* (in the abbreviated published version, and, presumably, what would have been the complete version) express Camus's hope that he will be able to "grow old and die without rebellion" (FM, p. 284), but it is doubtful that this would have been the case. As one of Camus's favorite authors, Leo Tolstoy, famously declared, "tranquility is a dishonesty of the soul," and Camus's "soul" was much too honest to have ever been tranquil. As Nietzsche maintains in the passage that begins this section, it is less a question of one's personal strengths and weaknesses than how one weaves them into an "artistic plan" so as "to 'give style' to one's character," and there were very few figures in the twentieth century that had Camus's style. Yet, beyond style, and, for that matter, lucidity, Camus had what many "great minds" do not possess, decency and courage, and while he often manifested Nietzsche's "human all too human," he was undoubtedly one of the best among us.

notes

1   David Sprintzen, *Camus: A Critical Examination* (Philadelphia: Temple University Press, 1988), p. vii.
2   Franz Kafka, *The Castle*, trans. Willa Muir and Edwin Muir (New York: Schocken Books, 1982), p. 3.
3   Friedrich Nietzsche, *The Gay Science*, trans. Walter Kaufmann (New York: Random House, 1974), p. 232.

further reading

Showalter, England, Jr., *Exiles and Strangers: A Reading of Camus's Exile and the Kingdom* (Columbus: Ohio University Press, 1984).
Tarrow, Susan, *Exile from the Kingdom: A Political Rereading of Albert Camus* (Tuscaloosa: University of Alabama Press, 1985).

chapter 9

epilogue

> [Camus] represented in this century, and against History, the present heir of that long line of moralists whose works perhaps constitute what is most original in French letters. His stubborn humanism, narrow and pure, austere and sensual, waged a dubious battle against events of these times. But, inversely, through the obstinacy of his refusals, he reaffirmed the existence of moral fact within the heart of our era and against the Machiavellians, against the golden calf of realism.
>
> Jean-Paul Sartre, "Albert Camus"[1]

Sartre's eulogy, which appeared days after Camus's untimely death, is usually the starting point for retrospectives on Camus, and not without good reason, as Sartre's characterization captures something fundamental about him. When interpreted from a contemporary standpoint, however, Sartre's eulogy has a tendency to distort no less than to illuminate. Although Camus rejected the notion that ethico-political imperatives ought to be determined by the movement of History, he would not have denied that our concepts and, especially, our ethico-political concepts, do change with the passage of time. Moreover, as Camus himself pointed out in *The Rebel* when examining such historical personages as Hegel and Marx, the same can also be said of the reputations of the dead, which can be infelicitously appropriated by the living so as to serve their own interests. It is, therefore, necessary to qualify Sartre's words.

To begin with, Camus's reputation has waxed and waned since his death. In the English-speaking world, he was one of the most influential writers during the 1960s and early 1970s, as his ethico-political commitments, aesthetic sensibilities, and personal style were seen by the New Left as a compelling alternative to orthodox Marxism. When the New Left waned, however, so did Camus's reputation, and from the late 1970s through the 1980s he was *persona non grata*: politically, there was a hard turn to the right, as evidenced by Thatcherism and Reaganism, and, philosophically, there was a hard turn toward poststructuralism, which had little use for Camus's humanism. (In France, the ebb and flow of Camus's reputation was rather different: when he died he was already largely *persona non grata*, and by the 1960s even Sartre was eclipsed, first by structuralism and then by poststructuralism.) In the 1990s, Camus's fortunes changed again: with the collapse of communism and a putative end to "ideology" (whether of the left or right), there was, ostensibly, a renewed commitment to such cosmopolitan ethico-political concerns as dialogue and human rights, the precise things that Camus had championed in the late 1940s and 1950s. (And, indeed, this was the case in Mitterand's France no less than in Clinton's America and Blair's Britain.) In some sense, therefore, Camus's daughter was right to assert in her 1995 foreword to *The First Man* that "voices began to be heard saying that perhaps Camus had not been so wrong." Both politically and philosophically, then, it would appear that Camus is a man for our times. Appearances can be deceiving, however.

Insofar as it was authentic, it is true that, politically speaking, the international emphasis on dialogue and human rights in the 1990s was in accord with Camus's strongest commitments, but it must also be remembered that he was committed to a thoroughgoing republicanism, which is wholly at odds with the period's burgeoning neo-liberal politico-economic policies (in which, for example, international trade agreements that supersede democratic determinations at the local and national levels were hammered out). These neo-liberal policies, which find direct expression in the neo-conservative program of the Bush administration – indeed, the Bush administration's neo-conservatism might well be their logical upshot – would be an anathema to Camus. Camus was certainly no fan of the so-called free market: he never deviated from his anarcho-syndicalist inclinations and, more generally, his commitment to some variant of libertarian socialism. It was always from *this* standpoint that he attacked communism, and thus, while such neo-conservative ideologues as Norman Podhoretz extol *The Rebel* precisely because of its attack on communism, they stand for a politics that Camus himself would have taken to be morally repugnant. So, too, whatever his ambivalences may have been with respect to the Algerian War, Camus would have had no use for the "clash of civilizations" thesis that has held sway among the American political classes.[2] And, lastly, needless to say, Camus's "humanism, narrow and pure" (as Sartre puts it), has almost nothing to do with the way in which many currently make sense of morality. His unrepentant sensuality, his emphasis on human nature as the fount of human happiness, more generally, and his core existential commitment to the right of the individual to freely fashion his or her own life, is wholly at odds with the "family values" crowd (religious and secular), which has politicized morality in ways that would have reminded Camus of the Vichy government.

Philosophically speaking, Camus anticipates a number of trends, although it would be a mistake to push this contention too hard. With his liberal commitment to dialogue, grounded in the concept of communicative rationality, as well as his commitment to at least some variant on republicanism (which is ostensibly made good when the preconditions of what he calls an "ideal speech community" are operationalized), Jürgen Habermas seems to share a number of Camus's most important commitments. Yet, Habermas's anti-subjectivistic and overly formal philosophy is hard to reconcile with Camus's quite distinct substantive commitments. Moreover, in various respects, Camus also anticipates another *pied-noir*, Jacques Derrida. In a practical sense, Sartre might be right to say that Camus's humanism is "narrow and pure," but it must not be forgotten that Camus was also "the philosopher of the Absurd," and that the concept of the Absurd opens the door to the anti-humanism that is implicit in Derrida's deconstruction and poststructuralism, more generally. Indeed, Camus's belief in the ungroundedness of human affairs, as well as his conviction that language tends to falsify (which is one of the reasons that, however mistakenly, he saw Meursault as a "hero for the truth"), is on all fours with Derridean deconstruction. And, like Derrida, Camus believed that this counsels a certain degree of modesty in all human affairs. Yet, unlike Derrida (who, like Habermas, was also anti-subjectivistic), Camus never got caught up in the paradoxes inherent in deconstruction's "endless death of metaphysics" problematic, and his moves in the ethical realm were marked by a humanism that sharply contrasts with Derrida, whose own belated move toward ethics was marked by strong theological overtones.

Ultimately, Camus attempted to cover a lot of ground, and, no doubt, much more ground than he could ever possibly justify. He attempted to negotiate the differences between liberalism and republicanism, between aestheticism and moralism, and, perhaps most elementally, between humanism and anti-humanism. As all professional philosophers know, however, these dualities cannot be navigated so easily, if at all, and perhaps this is why Camus eschewed the title. When Camus prefaces his collection of political essays, *Resistance Rebellion, and Death*, with Pascal's famous line about greatness – "A man does not show his greatness by being at one extremity, but rather by touching both at once" – he is conveying something essential about his own intellectual proclivities, and even if he (necessarily) fell short of this definition of greatness, perhaps his own greatness is to be found in the fact that he did not give up trying. In an age in which philosophy tends toward the imitative, and thus, wittingly or not, a mere recapitulation of the status quo, this Sisyphean endeavor is surely not for nothing. However "dubious" Camus's battle "against the golden calf of realism" might have been, it is, perhaps, in this very sense that he is a philosopher for our own times after all.

notes

1 Jean-Paul Sartre, "Albert Camus," in *Situations*, trans. Benita Eisler (New York: Fawcett Publications, 1965), pp. 79–80.
2 Norman Podhoretz, "Camus and his Critics," in *The Bloody Crossroads: Where Literature and Politics Meet* (New York: Simon and Schuster, 1986). See also Podhoretz's *World War IV: The Long Struggle Against Islamofascism* (New York: Doubleday, 2007).

index